Legal Reference for Librarians

Legal Reference for Librarians

HOW AND WHERE TO FIND THE ANSWERS

PAUL D. HEALEY

American Library Association
Chicago   2014

Paul D. Healey is both an attorney and a librarian and is currently senior instructional services librarian and associate professor of library administration at the Albert E. Jenner, Jr. Law Library, University of Illinois at Urbana-Champaign. He is the author of *Professional Liability Issues for Librarians and Information Professionals*, as well as a number of scholarly and professional articles on a variety of librarianship-related topics, most notably librarian liability and librarian ethics. He was the editorial director of *AALL Spectrum,* the official monthly magazine of the American Association of Law Libraries, from 2001 to 2007, and worked closely with authors on content for the magazine. He has an extensive background in professional speaking and has been a featured speaker at conferences and seminars across the United States and Canada.

© 2014 by the American Library Association.

Printed in the United States of America

18 17 16 15 14   5 4 3 2 1

ISBNs: 978-0-8389-1117-4 (paper); 978-0-8389-9693-5 (PDF); 978-0-8389-9694-2 (ePub); 978-0-8389-9695-9 (Kindle). For more information on digital formats, visit the ALA Store at alastore.ala.org and select eEditions.

Library of Congress Cataloging-in-Publication Data

Healey, Paul D.
    Legal reference for librarians : how and where to find the answers / Paul D. Healey.
      pages   cm
    Includes bibliographical references and index.
    ISBN 978-0-8389-1117-4
    1. Legal research—United States. 2. Pro se representation—Services for—United States. 3. Librarians—United States—Handbooks, manuals, etc. I. Title.
    KF240.H38 2014
    025.5'2—dc23   2013020182

Book design by Karen Sheets de Gracia. Cover image (c) Shutterstock, Inc.
Text composition in the Gotham and Charis typefaces by Dianne M. Rooney.

CONTENTS

Preface   *vii*

Acknowledgments   *ix*

PART 1 : LEGAL AND ETHICAL ISSUES

1   Who Is Asking Legal Reference Questions,
and Why Does It Matter?   *3*

2   Parameters of Legal Reference Service   *13*

3   Tips and Tools for Serving the Pro Se Library User   *21*

PART 2 : LEGAL RESEARCH BASICS

4   The Structure of Law and the Legal Research Process   *31*

5   Secondary Legal Resources   *43*

6   Statutes and Constitutions   *53*

7 Case Law *65*

8 Regulations and Administrative Law *77*

Appendix: Online Legal Resources 83

Index 203

PREFACE

REFERENCE QUESTIONS ABOUT LEGAL TOPICS OCCUPY A special niche in the universe of topics handled by reference librarians. On the one hand, law is a popular topic. It affects every aspect of our lives, and it only makes sense that library users would have questions about it. On the other hand, law is a complicated technical discipline, and legal materials are generally not user friendly, especially for the untrained layperson. This can put the reference librarian in the middle between users and the information they seek.

If that weren't enough, there is another issue that complicates legal reference interactions: the possibility of legal liability for the librarian if the question is not handled properly. The result can be a conundrum for a librarian who sees herself trapped between an enquiring user, difficult-to-use materials, and the threat of liability.

This book will try to help you unravel this conundrum, so that you can handle legal reference questions without fear. In part 1, we will look at the legal and ethical issues that are present in reference interactions. We will start, in chapter 1, by looking at the users who are asking for legal information. We will explore their status and look at how that status affects the kinds of information they are seeking and the potential for liability they present.

In chapter 2 we will look at the parameters of legal reference service, including where the threat of liability comes from and how it can be handled properly while still providing services to users. Chapter 3 will provide tips and tools for successfully assisting users with legal questions, covering everything from policies and training to handouts and public notices. By the end of part 1 you should understand the issues and have a solid plan for how to deal with them.

Part 2 of this book will increase your understanding of law and legal materials so that you can better assist users. We will look at law from a bibliographic perspective, exploring where law is published, its bibliographic structure, how it is navigated, and how legal tools work. We will start, in chapter 4, by examining the structure of the legal system in America and how legal publications flow from that structure. Chapter 4 also includes an overview of the legal research process and how it applies to questions from library users. Then, in succeeding chapters, we will explore how to work with legal materials. Chapter 5 will discuss what are known as secondary legal materials—materials that help you find out about the law but are not themselves law. In chapters 6, 7, and 8, we will look at law itself, in the form of statutes, case law, and regulations, respectively.

Last but not least, the appendix to this book will provide you with a vast array of web-based legal resources—most available for free. You will have at your fingertips a guide to finding online sources of law for every state and the federal government, as well as aggregate and self-help sites. The hope is that you will end up not only with a better understanding of the issues present in legal reference interactions and a greater ability to guide users in using legal materials, but also that you will have the resources at your disposal to help answer their questions.

HOW TO USE THIS BOOK

Most readers will benefit from reading part 1 in its entirety. Doing so will provide you with an understanding of the issues involved in answering legal reference questions and provide you with some tools for handling them properly. If you will be helping users with legal questions on a regular basis, you will also want to read part 2. This will give you some background and an understanding of how legal materials work, which will in turn allow you to be more efficient in handling legal questions. If necessary or desirable, part 2 can also be used as a reference source, providing information on legal materials on an as needed basis. Finally, the appendix of online resources is purely a reference tool listing legal resources. That said, if you have the time and inclination, you might want to explore the listed resources for your state and for the federal government, as well as the aggregate and self-help sites listed in the first section. Again, familiarity with these resources can increase your efficiency in assisting users.

Answering legal reference questions need not be stressful or confusing. With a little knowledge, any librarian can competently answer such questions, or know when to refer them to experts. The goal of this book is to help you reach that level.

■ ■ ■

In writing about legal reference it is only natural to mention specific publishers, publications, and websites. The author has no relationship with, and receives no compensation from, any publisher or website mentioned in this book. The opinions and comments about publishers and publications are strictly those of the author.

ACKNOWLEDGMENTS

AS IS SO OFTEN THE CASE, MANY PEOPLE HELPED TO MAKE this book a reality. First and foremost I'd like to thank Xiaolu (Renee) Zhang, who, while a student employee in our library, researched and verified almost all of the resources that appear in the appendix of this book. Renee is one of the finest people I have ever worked with, and I wish her every success.

Christopher Rhodes of ALA Editions proposed this project to me, talked me into it, and then gave me room to write. I appreciate his faith in me and his vision for this project.

I am thankful to the Board of Trustees of the University of Illinois for granting me a nine-month sabbatical in order to write. I am further grateful to the faculty of the Albert E. Jenner, Jr. Law Library at the University of Illinois, who picked up the slack during my absence, and particularly to the library's director, Janis L. Johnston.

Russell Harper took on the herculean task of editing my manuscript. He has been a joy to work with, as has everyone at ALA Editions. Any errors in this book are absolutely mine and mine alone.

Finally, eternal gratitude to the "gang of four" who keep me going: my son Cory Healey, and my friends Peggy Berg, Mary Rumsey, and Dr. Timothy P. Hogan.

PART ONE

LEGAL AND ETHICAL ISSUES

1

WHO IS ASKING LEGAL REFERENCE QUESTIONS, AND WHY DOES IT MATTER?

I T MAY SEEM STRANGE TO SPEND AN ENTIRE CHAPTER DISCUSS-ing who is asking legal questions at the reference desk. Rest assured, this actually is a very important issue, and understanding who is asking legal questions, and why, can have a big effect on how you go about assisting them.

You may be aware of the fact that nonlawyers who ask questions at the reference desk of a dedicated law library cause much anxiety and even fear among law librarians. You may have heard the term *pro se* being applied to such users and wondered what, exactly, that meant. A fear of such users may be one that you share, or it may be shared by your colleagues.

In fact, there are three broad reasons why pro se library users engender such a negative reaction. The first is that answering legal reference questions is thought to create potential legal liability for the librarian and the library. The second is that many librarians fear that users who are trying to handle their own legal matters without the help of an attorney are doing something that might end up being danger-ous or damaging to the user's own interests. Quite reasonably, many librarians are uncomfortable being a party to such activity. Third is that legal questions are often very complex, and may deal with topics and materials that neither the librarian nor the user fully understand.

We will look at the risk of liability, and the ethical issues of potential harm to the user, in chapter 2. We will try to help with the complexity of legal materials in part 2 of this book. In this chapter we will look at who these users really are and why law librarians react to pro se users the way they do.

In fact, the pro se issue is just the beginning. In this chapter you will learn the distinction between three types of library users asking legal questions: the lay, or casual, user; the pro se user; and the self-represented litigant. These three different user groups present very different challenges and provide different possibilities for liability. We will discuss the motivations people have for representing themselves in court and take a look at how big the problem is. By the end of the chapter you should have a much better understanding of who this user group is and why they do what they do.

WHO IS ASKING LEGAL REFERENCE QUESTIONS?

To begin with, let's dispose of one type of person who might be seeking legal materials at the reference desk, a group we might call legal professionals. Under this rubric we find lawyers, paralegals, court personnel, and law students. What they all have in common is that they do not raise issues of liability (why this is will be explained in more detail in chapter 2), and they are familiar with legal research and legal materials. This means that legal professionals generally only want assistance locating library materials that they already know they need. They will not be asking the librarian how to use various resources, how to do research, or for advice on legal issues. As a result, because legal professionals do not present a risk of liability and because the assistance they need from the reference librarian will usually be minimal, we can forgo any further discussion of this user group. Instead, let's turn our attention to people asking legal reference questions who are not legal professionals.

In this book we will draw a distinction between lay users, pro se users, and self-represented litigants. Most librarians, including most law librarians, refer to any nonlawyer library user who is asking legal questions as a pro se, without distinguishing further. In fact, the distinctions are important, as we shall see, and are worth understanding.

All three of these user groups have two important things in common: they are pursuing a legal topic in the library, including asking reference questions, and they have no training in law. Beyond that, the three groups vary widely.

Lay Users

The group we are referring to as lay users, or casual users, are researching a legal topic but are not doing so to pursue or protect their own legal interests. This distinction is crucial. It is the fact that pro se users or self-represented litigants are pursuing their own legal interests that raises the legal and ethical issues we will be discussing in the next chapter. A lay user who is researching a legal topic that is not related to his own immediate legal interests does not raise these issues.

Lay users might be asking legal questions for a variety of benign reasons. They might be working on a school homework assignment, or they might be curious about legal issues in general or about how the law works. They may want information about a recent Supreme Court decision or about a controversial legal topic. They may want information about a legal issue a friend or relative is struggling with. Lay users may be researching the history of law or investigating the nature of other legal systems.

The bottom line is that, so long as lay users are not dealing with their own legal interests, they do not pose any heightened risk of liability. As a result, they can be treated just like any other library user asking questions at the reference desk.

Pro Se Library Users

Pro se library users are those who are not trained in law and who are using the library to pursue their own personal legal issues or interests. The key distinction here is that pro se users have some sort of personal legal interest at stake. Without a personal interest at stake, they are simply lay users of the type described above, but once a personal issue is in play, they present the potential for creating legal and ethical problems for librarians.

The term *pro se* is actually Latin for "in person." In law the phrase is usually translated as "on one's own behalf" and is used to designate someone who is not represented by an attorney while pursuing some legal issue or interest. In some parts of the country, particularly California, you may hear the term *pro per*. *Pro per* is a contraction of the Latin phrase "in propria persona," which means "in one's own proper person." In the usage of the courts and, by extension, librarians, *pro per* means the same thing as *pro se*, and they can be used interchangeably. However, *pro se* is by far the more common term.

When we think of someone who is pro se, we often think of someone who is representing him- or herself in court, but in fact there are a broad variety of pro se activities that don't involve litigation or appearing in court. As such we can draw a distinction between pro se library users and self-represented litigants. A user can be considered pro se whenever he is pursuing his own legal interests and doing something that would normally be done by a lawyer.

A pro se library user may be drafting his own will or trust, negotiating a lease or contract, handling legal issues related to a business, or pursuing a change in government or other advocacy issues. The important point is that, in pursuing their own legal issues, pro se users raise the potential for liability for the librarian and may be harming themselves as well. Sometimes the problems they are creating can be hidden for years. For example, if a pro se library user drafts a defective will, it generally won't pose a problem while that user is alive, but afterwards, it will cause problems for others.

Self-Represented Litigants

Self-represented litigants are, by definition, pro se, but are differentiated by being actively engaged in some sort of litigation or court action. While the legal and ethical challenges presented by self-represented litigants are about the same for librarians as those of other pro se library users, the situation of the self-represented litigant is very different. This can complicate the reference interaction.

To understand why, let me point out here that, as we will see in chapter 4, American law can be divided into two forms: substantive and procedural. Substantive law is what most people

think of when they think of law. It is the rules of society. On the other hand, procedural law is the law that governs how litigation takes place. It covers how a lawsuit is started, what the parties have to do at each stage of the litigation, and how an aggrieved party can appeal a court decision. So, for instance, criminal law is the substantive law of what constitutes a crime and how crime should be punished. Criminal procedure is the process by which a prosecutor can indict someone who is alleged to have committed a crime, what actions the defendant can take to defend him- or herself, and so forth.

Pro se library users are generally interested in substantive law. They may want to know how to exclude someone from their will, or what elements are required for a contract to be legally binding. Pro se library users are rarely interested in procedural matters because procedural law is irrelevant to what they are doing.

Like other pro se library users, self-represented litigants are looking for information about substantive law. However, because of the fact that they are involved in litigation, they will also need information about procedural law. Procedural law is highly technical and complex. It usually involves producing various types of documents—petitions, answers, motions, briefs, and so forth—and requires that these documents be produced under strict deadlines and along complicated timelines.

For example, someone who has just been served with a petition for dissolution of marriage, and who has decided to represent himself, is faced with the need to find the substantive law of divorce—his rights to property, child custody, and many other things—but he also needs to find out about the procedural law of the divorce action, including what documents need to be filed when and so on. In most jurisdictions, there will usually be an immediate need to create a document called an answer, which has specific requirements, and get the answer filed with the court, usually within ten days of being served with the petition.

The result is that self-represented litigants have much greater information needs than other pro se library users, and they are under much more pressure. Add to this the general anger and frustration about whatever dispute they are litigating, and it becomes logical that self-represented litigants might feel overwhelming stress, anxiety, and anger. Unfortunately, these feelings can overflow at the reference desk.

To sum up, lay users, pro se users, and self-represented litigants can be differentiated as follows:

- Lay users include any person without legal training who is doing legal research. This includes users whose research purpose is completely benign.
- Pro se users are lay users who are doing research to pursue their own legal interests. This includes those who are working on a nonlitigation legal matter, such as preparing a will or drafting a contract.
- Self-represented litigants are pro se users who are actively involved in litigation of some kind.

ABOUT THE PRO SE LIBRARY USER

Because of the important issues presented in the library by people who are handling their own legal interests, it is worth our while to explore who these people are, what motivates them, and what kind of experiences they can expect to have. In doing so, let's concentrate for now specifically on self-represented litigants.

The Right to Self-Representation

At the outset, it is important to understand that every American has the right to represent themselves in court in almost any legal proceeding. Although the right to self-representation is not in the U.S. Constitution, it was included in the very first Federal Judiciary Act signed by President Washington in 1789. The provision that allows self-representation survives to this day as Section 1654 of Title 28 of the *United States Code*. The current language reads as follows: "In all courts of the United States the parties may plead and conduct their own cases personally or by counsel as, by the rules of such courts, respectively, are permitted to manage and conduct causes therein." This language directly opens the doors of the federal court system to self-represented litigants.

Many of the states also have provisions in their constitutions that protect the right to self-representation. In addition, in the landmark 1975 case of *Faretta v. California*, the U.S. Supreme Court found that the Sixth Amendment to the U.S. Constitution, which protects a defendant's right to have an attorney, protects by corollary an individual's right to proceed without representation. It is interesting to note that the Sixth Amendment was enacted the day after President Washington signed the Federal Judiciary Act and is therefore actually a younger law. Be that as it may, the holding of *Faretta* extends the right of self-representation to every court in the land.

It is also important to note that while every state has prohibitions against the unauthorized practice of law (more on which in chapter 2), each state also specifically excludes self-representation from its unauthorized practice provisions.

There is no question that every American has the right to represent him- or herself in court. The real question is, should they?

The Perils of Self-Representation

When they make the decision to represent themselves in a legal matter, most people don't really understand the task they are taking on. There are many reasons for this, and we will look at some in the next section. For now, let's look at the nature of this task that the self-represented litigant is taking on. In short, a person who decides to proceed in a legal action without representation is entering into a very serious conflict against a highly trained and experienced adversary. The system in which this conflict takes place, the courts, will attempt to be fair to all parties but cannot assist one party more than another. In addition, this system is very complex, and no one will help the self-represented litigant understand it.

Let's pick this situation apart and look at the various perils that exist for self-represented litigants. First, the legal system in America is adversarial in nature. This means that any legal action consists of two opposing parties, each of which is expected to fight hard, within the rules and the law, with the idea that the truth will emerge from this honestly fought fight. A key part of the adversarial conflict is that the court must remain absolutely neutral toward both parties. The judge in a trial cannot, and will not, reach out to help a self-represented litigant just because he is being outdone by the experienced lawyer on the other side. Nor will the attorney on the other side be asked to help or moderate her attack just because her opponent is untrained in law. The self-represented litigant steps into the ring of litigation alone, without assistance.

Another peril is the complexity of the system in which litigation takes place. The practice of law requires rigorous legal training and often years of experience to become proficient. Many people assume that law school teaches law students the law, as if it were simply a set of rules. While law students will learn the basic concepts of the areas of law they study, the real task in law school is to learn legal analysis and the logical and reasoning skills that actually form the core of legal practice. These skills, often called "thinking like a lawyer," are the real tool that lawyers use to protect their clients' interests.

In addition to thinking skills, law school teaches lawyers to use the complex legal materials that are the tools of the practice of law. Lawyers understand how to parse a statute or analyze a court case and how to link the information in that law or case to the argument they want to make. This is a highly refined process that most people not trained in law simply can't do. These tools help the lawyer deal with both the law and the procedural requirements necessary to win a case. The result is that litigation takes place in an adversarial environment and is itself a highly complex process drawing on complicated legal tools.

Another peril of self-representation is one of judgment. Put simply, self-represented litigants are not in a position to bring to their own problems the sort of dispassionate judgment and advice required to effectively handle a serious legal situation. When they are at their best, lawyers not only aggressively protect their clients' interests but also offer a careful, balanced assessment of each client's situation and provide advice on how to proceed that is grounded in careful analysis of the facts and the law. This, quite frankly, is what really makes legal representation worth the expense. Self-represented litigants have to rely on their own judgment and typically have to do so when they are emotionally upset, under threat, and trying desperately to understand the law and procedure of the case.

Finally, there is the issue of risk. There are often significant interests at stake in litigation, which means that the self-represented litigant has much to lose. Let's look at some of the more common interests that can be at stake in litigation.

In criminal matters there is the threat of prison or jail, which means that your very right to liberty can be in peril. Similarly, in competency or mental health proceedings, there is the risk of forced hospitalization or treatment. Other constitutional rights can be at risk as well. For example, if you are convicted of a felony, whether or not you go to jail or prison, you can lose your right to vote, or to own or possess firearms.

Litigation can threaten your ability to live in your home. For instance, landlord-tenant conflicts can result in eviction, and mortgage foreclosure or condemnation actions can result in loss of a home. Other property can be at risk as well. Both civil and criminal litigation can result in large fines, damage awards, or sanctions, as well as court costs and the obligation to pay legal fees for the opposing party. Contract disputes can involve significant money or property, and zoning issues can affect how realty can be used or decrease its value.

Perhaps most fundamentally, litigation can affect rights and duties relating to your family and children. Divorce affects rights to property, where you can live, and the nature of your relationship with your children. Custody proceedings can fundamentally affect both relationships and monetary interests. Paternity actions can lead to the creation, or loss, of rights related to children, as well as significant financial obligations. Finally, juvenile court actions can affect your right to live with and have custody of a child and even lead to permanent loss of parental rights.

There are very few legal actions that are so trivial in nature that they don't affect significant interests for those involved. So the question becomes, why do they do it?

Motivations for Self-Representation

Given the perils of self-representation, why would anyone do it? There are probably as many reasons for deciding to handle a legal matter without representation as there are pro se litigants. The decision to self-represent is a highly personal one and indeed may in some cases be more emotional than rational. We can, however, describe some common motivations.

The most prominent, of course, is money. Legal representation is extremely expensive, and getting more so every day. Only criminal defendants whose liberty is at stake—that is, who face a jail or prison term if convicted—have a right to an attorney at state expense if they cannot afford one. Everyone else, including criminal defendants who either do not face incarceration upon conviction or who have the resources to pay for counsel, and all civil litigants, must find and pay for their own attorney or go without.

This means that a significant number of people who represent themselves do so because they have no choice, no matter how serious the matter is. They can't afford an attorney, and no one is going to provide one for them. On the other hand, some self-represented litigants do have the money to afford an attorney but choose not to. This might be because they feel attorneys overcharge for their services, or because they think the matter can be handled easily and that it would be better to save the money. This can be an expensive mistake.

Another reason for self-representation is a distrust of attorneys. As a former practicing attor-

ney myself, I wish I could claim that this fear is completely unjustified. To be fair, most lawyers are both honest and competent and can be trusted, but there are enough members of the bar who are incompetent or dishonest to warrant this fear in some limited cases. However, this fear is also partly based not on actual incompetence or venality but arises as a result of the often-unpleasant experiences people almost always have being involved in litigation. Attorneys deal with some very difficult and frustrating aspects of people's lives, and it is not surprising that they become a target for their clients' negative emotions.

In almost every legal matter, people have unpleasant experiences with the procedure or the outcome of the case. To take a typical divorce as an example, the process will often take much longer than anticipated, and both parties will end up losing, or giving up, things that are important to them. Under the circumstances, even if their attorney did the best job possible, the parties may begin to believe that their losses were because of their attorney's incompetence or deceit and not an inevitable part of the process. The next time one of the parties is confronted with a legal matter, they may decide they are better off going it alone.

On the other hand, some people represent themselves because they believe the system will protect them. As we have seen, this is a fundamental misunderstanding of how the adversarial justice system works, but some people believe it nonetheless. In this case, the self-represented litigant might believe that the court is obligated to do justice, and because of that, the court will protect them, no matter how bad a job they do at representing themselves. Of course, nothing could be further from reality.

A variation of this idea is the belief that proceeding pro se might confer a tactical advantage in litigation. They hope that, by not having an attorney, they will be seen as the weaker party, and therefore be given breaks and advantages by the court. Once again, this kind of treatment is explicitly against the rules and generally does not occur.

Some self-represented litigants have a blind belief in their own innocence, or in the righteousness of their cause, and believe that the court will see this and act to protect them. This reasoning is based on the idea that a court is bound to do justice and that if they are truly in the right, the court will take care to make sure that they win. Unfortunately, the adversarial nature of our court system means that even the truly innocent or righteous need to protect their interests vigilantly.

Another pernicious idea is the belief that law is simple and that an attorney is therefore simply unnecessary. Much of the practice of law looks simple to the naked eye. Lawyers look things up in books, write documents, and go to court and argue. Anyone can do that, right? Portrayals of the practice of law in movies and on television have exacerbated this idea by emphasizing exciting courtroom clashes and witty office conversations while hiding the hard work of legal analysis.

This particular belief, that law is simple, can have a big effect on library reference interactions. It is very common for people untrained in law to approach the reference desk with the idea that the answer to every legal question, and the procedural directions for every legal action, are simply written in a book somewhere, if they can only find it. They assume that the reference librarians will know where that book is. In fact, as we will see later in this book, legal research is much more complicated than that. There are very few simple answers, and very few legal materials that simply guide someone through a legal process.

Another factor is mental illness. It is an unfortunate fact that a certain portion of self-represented litigants are mentally ill. As such, the desire to represent themselves arises from impaired judgment about their situation, their skills, the nature of the other parties, their interests, or the risks involved.

There is a final motivation for self-representation that is worth mentioning briefly, that of actual competence. Some litigants will proceed pro se because they have the benefit of previous experience and can actually represent themselves competently. For instance, a landlord who has extensive experience with landlord-tenant legal issues may well know enough to handle an eviction or debt collection matter properly. Similarly,

a person with an extensive criminal background may actually know more about criminal defense than an inexperienced attorney.

Who Are These People?

There is very little hard demographic data on who proceeds in court pro se. A 1990 survey conducted for the American Bar Association looked at 1,900 domestic relations cases that took place in the Superior Court of Maricopa County, Arizona. It found the following:

- Lower-income people were more likely to represent themselves.
- Younger persons were more likely to self-represent than older persons.
- The most common level of formal education for self-represented litigants was one to three years of college.
- People with no children were much more likely to self-represent than people with children.
- People who did not own real estate or significant personal property were significantly more likely to self-represent than people who did own such assets.

How Big an Issue Is Self-Representation?

It would be nice to have solid figures about how common it is for pro se library users to present themselves at the average reference desk looking for help. We don't have any such figures. The one place that there has been some study of the issue is in academic law libraries.

Most law librarians in institutions open to the public believe that a significant portion of their users are members of the lay public. Statistics on pro se use of law libraries are hard to come by, but at least one study from the 1970s confirmed that pro se law library users were a significant percentage of the users of university law libraries. This study concentrated on law school libraries but found that in tax-supported law school libraries in particular, an average of 20 percent of users were laypeople or pro se litigants, and that at some institutions this number was as high as 48 percent. More recent figures, admittedly based on a very informal survey, indicate that members of the public generate between 30 and 70 percent of reference questions at public law libraries in major metropolitan areas.

If we can't find figures from libraries, we can take a different approach. Although it is necessarily imprecise, if we can determine how common self-represented litigants are in the courts, we can extrapolate that a certain percentage of them are going to come to the library in search of legal information.

Unfortunately, while pro se representation is a national issue, statistics from the courts are frustratingly hard to come by, although there is no question that the high number of people proceeding pro se in legal actions is very real. In the past decade or so, the National Center for State Courts (NCSC) and committees or task forces in several states have collected statistics on pro se representation, but the offerings are far from complete. Some of the figures for individual states are as follows:

California: In 2004, over 4.3 million court users were self-represented in California courts. For family law cases, 67 percent of petitioners at filing (72 percent in the largest counties) were self-represented, and 80 percent of petitioners at disposition hearings for dissolution cases were self-represented.

Florida: At a family court in Osceola County in 2001, 73 percent of court hearings involved at least one pro se participant, up from 66 percent in 1999.

Iowa: In 2004, a random survey of a week of district court schedules in one county showed that 58 percent of cases set for trial that week involved at least one pro se party.

New Hampshire: In 2004, 85 percent of all civil cases in the district court and 48 percent of all civil cases in the superior court involved a pro se party.

Utah: In divorce cases filed in 2005, 49 percent of petitioners and 81 percent of respondents were self-represented. For small-claims cases, 99 percent of petitioners and 99 percent of respondents were self-represented. Seven percent of pro se litigants reported going to a library for assistance.

Wisconsin: In 2000, as many as 70 percent of family cases involved litigants who represent themselves in court. There was an increase in pro se litigants in family law cases from 1996 to 1999 in both the Tenth Judicial Administrative District and the First Judicial Administrative District, from 43 to 53 percent and from 69 to 72 percent, respectively.

Other publications have provided similar figures for state court litigation. According to an article in *Bench and Bar* (McEnroe, 1996), 88 percent of litigants in Washington, D.C., family court proceeded pro se, as did 60 percent in Santa Monica, California (an increase from 30 percent five years earlier). In Hennepin County, Minnesota (the county containing Minneapolis), more than 30,000 people a year represented themselves in Conciliation Court.

The volume of cases in the federal courts is less than those of the state courts, but at the federal level pro se litigation is also a significant issue. Recent statistical reports from the federal courts on the number of pro se civil filings in the U.S. indicated that of a total of 278,442 district court case filings, 77,703 pro se cases were filed during the twelve-month period ending September 30, 2012, compared to 200,739 non–pro se cases. This means that pro se cases constituted 28 percent of cases filed in the federal courts in 2012. Of the pro se cases filed during that period, 50,844 were filed by prisoners, and 26,859 were filed by nonprisoners. Nonprisoner pro se filings thus constituted about 10 percent of federal court filings.

These statistics only track the pro se status of the person filing the petition and not that of other parties to the action. For this reason, the actual incidence of pro se representation in the federal courts may be higher than the statistics indicate. With such numbers, it is only logical to assume that pro se litigants are coming to law libraries for information and assistance.

The bottom line is that there are many, many self-represented litigants in our court systems. In the course of their legal action they will need information, and it is likely that they will come to the library in search of it.

BACK TO THE BROADER VIEW OF THE PRO SE LIBRARY USER

The section above has dealt specifically with the self-represented litigant. For reasons that were explained, this type of user is in a particularly acute situation and can be both problematic and demanding at the reference desk. Lest we forget, there is another type of pro se library user who, for all we know, may be even more common at the reference desk than the self-represented litigant. This other type of pro se user is the one who is handling some aspect of her legal affairs but is not actively engaged in litigation.

These are the people who are drafting their own will, prenuptial agreement, or contract, or pursuing some other nonlitigation legal matter. They are not as likely to be in crisis as the self-represented litigant, but they present the same issues relating to liability and ethical issues. For that reason, it is best for our purposes to consider the broader body of pro se library users as a single group. Anyone who is doing legal research in order to handle his own legal affairs without the assistance of an attorney falls into this group. The legal and ethical parameters of legal reference service described in the next chapter apply to them all.

CONCLUSION

Reference questions about law and legal resources have an unusual problem attached to them. This problem is the potential for liability for the librarian answering them—that is, if the answer can be seen as giving legal advice or engaging in the unauthorized practice of law. This means that legal reference questions must be approached with a certain amount of caution.

Those who are asking legal reference questions can be divided into four groups. This first are legal professionals. Such people do not pose any risk of liability, as information provided to them will not be construed as legal advice. In the second group are people asking legal questions but who are not pursuing their own legal interests. Examples include someone doing legal research to write a school paper or asking for information out of interest in law as a subject. Since they are not pursuing their own legal interests, such people also do not present any danger of liability, and their questions can be handled just like any other reference request.

The final two groups of users do pose risks. These are people who are pursuing their own legal interests in some way, and they break down into those who are actively engaged in litigation (self-represented litigants) and those who are not. While their situations are very different, both of these groups present the same risk for liability, and both can be referred to as pro se library users.

Having established who these user groups are, and that they are present in the library, we can now to turn to how to deal with them as users, in chapter 2.

2

PARAMETERS OF LEGAL REFERENCE SERVICE

WE HAVE SEEN IN CHAPTER 1 THAT PRO SE LIBRARY USERS are present in increasing numbers, and it has been alleged that such users present potential liability and other issues in the library. In this chapter we will explain fully what those issues are. Whenever a library of any kind undertakes to answer legal reference questions for the public, there are certain parameters that come into play. These are issues, or realities, that should be considered and accounted for. The point of this chapter is to fully explain those issues. In the next chapter we will go on to suggest how reference services to pro se library users can be structured and provided so as to limit the possibility for liability while providing the maximum amount of service to users.

This chapter includes four main sections. The first discusses the topic of liability. Although it has never happened in practice, the possibility of a librarian being accused of giving legal advice when answering reference questions is real, and if it were to happen, the librarian could be liable for damages. This section will help you understand how and why that is.

The second section is about the unauthorized practice of law. Again, the fact that being accused of unauthorized practice of law is a remote but real possibility makes it necessary to fully explore how this could work. The third section discusses ethical and professional issues that arise when assisting pro se library users.

The final section of the chapter covers institutional considerations concerning serving pro se library users. We will look at how such users affect the institution and what aspects of serving them might be of concern to the mission of the library.

Some of the material in this chapter is a bit technical, but it can be understood if read carefully. Understanding these issues will not only help you protect yourself and your institution but also increase your knowledge of at least one area of the law.

LIABILITY

An extensive discussion of professional liability for librarians is beyond our scope. In order to understand what you need to for our purposes, some basic concepts about librarian liability should suffice.

Liability occurs when someone fails to uphold a recognized legal duty to another person, and the other person is harmed by that failure. Legally, this is referred to as negligence. In order for this to happen, there must be a recognized legal duty. For example, every person who drives a car has a duty to follow traffic rules and drive with care. A driver who fails to stop at a stop sign, and in doing so causes an accident, will be liable for the damages because he failed in his duty to follow traffic rules.

On the other hand, if there is no recognized duty, then there can be no liability. As an example, if someone falls into a river and is drowning, and another person sees this happen but does nothing to help, the onlooker will not be liable when the victim drowns. This is because he has no duty to assist a stranger and also has no duty to put himself at risk to help someone else. The situation is unfortunate, but the onlooker did not cause the incident and had no duty. Therefore there is no negligence, and the onlooker cannot be liable.

Professional liability is a form of negligence that occurs when a professional fails to adhere to the standards of her profession and because of that failure someone is harmed. Thus if a doctor fails to exercise appropriate skill in diagnosing and treating disease, and because of that failure one of her patients dies, she could be professionally liable. Keep in mind, though, that the fact that harm occurs does not automatically mean the professional is liable. It is entirely possible that a doctor could have correctly diagnosed a patient's illness and treated it appropriately, and the patient died nonetheless. As long as the doctor's actions were consistent with the standards of her profession, she will not be liable for the patient's harm because she will not be considered negligent.

Professional liability is based on the idea that professionals have a duty to their clients, and when this duty is violated, liability should follow. While such a scenario is possible for many professions, librarianship has not, so far, been one of them. Although librarians strive to provide excellent service to library users, there is nothing about what takes place at the reference desk that creates a duty. This is partly because other professionals, such as doctors and lawyers, take full responsibility for a client's problem and seek to solve the problem itself. Librarians, in providing library users with information, are assisting individuals who remain fully responsible for assessing and using the information that they seek. As such, there is no duty created that, if violated, would reasonably mean that the librarian bears responsibility for the user's harm. (For an extended discussion of this issue, see chapter 4 of Healey, *Professional Liability Issues for Librarians and Information Professionals* [Neal-Schuman, 2008].)

The crucial distinction is this: library users expect librarians to be experts at locating the information that they are seeking; they do not, however, expect the librarian to be an expert on the topic itself. A librarian may know good sources for information on law, or medicine, or engineering, or history, without knowing much at all about the topics themselves. As part of this librarians cannot, and do not, provide guarantees to the user that they are providing exactly what the user needs. Users must evaluate that for themselves. As long as that responsibility remains with the user, there is no duty created that would make the librarian liable for harm suffered by the user.

There is, however, one potential exception to this rule. That would be if the librarian presented himself as not just a librarian but as a subject expert on the topic of the reference request, such that the user reasonably could assume that she was not just getting information but was in fact getting professional advice on the topic at hand. For the most part, such a situation seems unlikely. Remember that in order for the user to rely on the librarian, the user's reliance must be seen as reasonable. In most cases, that is hard to imagine. A user may expect the reference librarian in a public library to help her find law on a given subject, but it would hardly be reasonable for the user to rely on the librarian as an expert on law.

If, however, the librarian were to affirmatively assert himself as a subject expert, then it could become reasonable for a user to rely on his advice. Where this is especially possible is in a specialized library such as a law library or medical library. In such an environment, if the librarian asserts himself as an expert on the library's subject matter, reliance could be seen as reasonable and therefore lead to liability. Even in regular academic and public libraries, such a situation could be created if the librarian were to assert himself as an expert. If a public librarian implied to a user that he was trained in law, reliance might be seen as reasonable. In that case, liability for the user's harm is possible.

The key to controlling liability in the library is both simple and straightforward. Librarians should restrict themselves to their role as experts at finding information rather than as experts on the information they find. That distinction should provide complete protection from the risk of liability. This means allowing the user to evaluate and decide which materials to use, and it also means refraining from speculation about the topic or from offering personal opinions about the user's situation.

One form of professional liability that is mentioned often is malpractice. Malpractice is like other forms of negligence, except that the specific duty owed by the professional is determined by the standards of the profession. Thus, whether or not a doctor or lawyer is negligent would be determined by comparing her actions with the standards of practice for medicine or law. Because librarians do not engage in activities that can lead to liability, a discussion of malpractice is moot, but it is worth noting that even if librarians did have some duty to users, standards of practice for librarians are notoriously vague and would be unlikely to provide sufficient guidance for determining liability. So malpractice is not an issue for librarians.

If a librarian were to hold himself out as a subject expert, such that a user reasonably relied

on his advice and was harmed, then the malpractice standards that would be applied would not be those of librarianship but rather those of the profession he claimed expertise in. For example, any librarian who claimed an expertise in law, on which a user reasonably relied, would be held to the standards of legal malpractice. The same would be true of a librarian who claimed to be an expert in medicine, or architecture, or whatever. If the user's harm arose from reasonable reliance on the librarian as a subject expert, the profession related to that subject of expertise would supply the malpractice standards for determining liability.

Once again, the key point is this: so long as librarians hold themselves out as experts on finding information for users, and not as experts on the information itself, liability can be avoided.

UNAUTHORIZED PRACTICE OF LAW

The possibility of engaging in the unauthorized practice of law when answering legal reference questions needs its own discussion. While such a charge, if successful, would lead to liability, it is a different kind of liability, with different ramifications. We need to discuss it because being accused of unauthorized practice of law is a theoretical possibility when answering legal reference questions.

As with professional liability, no librarian has ever been accused of unauthorized practice of law for answering a legal reference question. While the likelihood of it ever happening seems very remote, librarians who will be answering legal reference questions would do well to at least understand some basic concepts about unauthorized practice of law.

In America, the practice of law is governed at the state level. Each state has a system for licensing lawyers based on education and performance on the bar exam. These functions are usually administered by the state supreme court, often in conjunction with the state bar association. In addition to admitting lawyers to the bar, the state supreme court will supervise attorney discipline and set standards for ethical practice. Just as it can license attorneys, the court has the power to discipline lawyers and to suspend or revoke their license to practice law.

Because the practice of law is a licensed profession, all fifty states have prohibitions against practicing law without a license. Someone who claims to be a lawyer when she is not can, depending on each state's laws, be subject civil injunctions, fines, and even criminal charges. The purpose of these sanctions is to protect the integrity of the legal profession while at the same time protecting the public from fraudsters as well as unscrupulous, untrained, or incompetent people claiming to be lawyers. To be brutally honest, over the years much of the litigation over unauthorized practice of law has been protectionist in nature. Most commonly, complaints have been made about other professionals, such as accountants, real estate agents, and bankers, who are doing things that lawyers also do and would like to control. However, there have been plenty of cases in every state where dishonest people have held themselves out as lawyers in order to defraud innocent people, and these people have been the targets of enforcement actions as well.

A key difference between the professional liability discussed in the previous section and the unauthorized practice of law is that professional liability would result from being sued by a user who had been harmed by your professional actions. As such, the legal action is between you and the other person, as a private person. Being prosecuted for unauthorized practice of law is an action by the state, and you would answer to the state either in a civil or criminal action.

It is possible that an especially wayward librarian could be the defendant in both kinds of actions. Should a librarian hold herself out as a lawyer or legal expert, and not only provide a pro se user with legal information but also offer advice on how to proceed, and should the user rely on that advice to his detriment, it is entirely possible that the librarian could be sued by the user for legal malpractice on the basis of the faulty legal advice at the same time that she was being prosecuted by the state supreme court for unauthorized practice of law.

This would probably all be of only academic interest if it weren't for one very troubling fact. Nobody has ever actually defined the practice of law. It seems incredible, but it is true. While many states have definitions that talk about the functions of a lawyer, each of those functions is vague and at some point shades into an activity that is not the practice of law. The problem is that no one knows where the line is between the form of a lawyerly function that is practicing law and the form that is not.

Let's take, as an example, the concept of legal advice. Giving legal advice is a lawyerly function that appears in almost every state's definition of the practice of law. And indeed, legal advice is clearly at the heart of the lawyer-client relationship. There is no question that legal advice is a lawyerly function, but what is legal advice exactly? If I tell my son that he shouldn't exceed the speed limit when he drives, that is, by definition, legal advice, but surely I am not acting as a lawyer at that point. This is the fundamental conundrum that creates the risk of unauthorized practice of law at the reference desk.

The problem is deceptively simple: At what point does helping someone find and use legal information become offering them legal advice? The short answer is, nobody knows. Since giving legal advice can be seen as the unauthorized practice of law, and answering a legal reference question could conceivably be giving legal advice, the risk of being accused of unauthorized practice of law at the reference desk is real.

Keep in mind, this question comes into play only when, as we discussed in the first chapter, we are assisting people who are not legal professionals and who are pursuing their own legal interests. In other words, the risk is only present when assisting pro se library users. As was explained in chapter 1, legal professionals remain responsible for their use of legal information, and giving information to those who are doing legal research that is not about their own legal interests is, by definition, not legal advice.

Fortunately, while the risk is real, the chance of a librarian being prosecuted for unauthorized practice of law seems very remote. In addition, the basic advice for avoiding unauthorized practice is the same as that for avoiding liability: librarians should stick to being experts on finding information and not on the information itself. By restricting ourselves to trying to find information requested by users, and refraining from advising on or discussing the subject matter of the request, librarians should be able to steer clear of any danger of being accused of unauthorized practice of law.

This may seem obvious, but I have found that many nonlawyers feel that they know a lot about law and like to share their knowledge with others. One common example of this is divorce. Many people in our society have been divorced and feel that they have learned something about the law of divorce in the process. These people tend to have lots of advice when they are talking to someone else who is going through a divorce.

In most situations that is fine. But at the reference desk, if the user has a reasonable belief that the librarian is a subject expert in law, such advice could constitute the unauthorized practice of law. The better practice on the part of librarians is to keep silent about the topic and restrict your activities to finding the information the user seeks.

ETHICAL AND PROFESSIONAL ISSUES

In addition to potential legal issues, assisting pro se library users raises a number of ethical and professional issues for librarians. And whereas the legal issues of professional liability and unauthorized practice of law have thus far not come up in real life and therefore remain speculative in nature, the ethical and professional issues presented by pro se library users are real. If you assist pro se users, you will deal with these ethical and professional issues in just about every reference interaction.

Ethical Issues

Let's begin with a discussion of library ethics as it relates to pro se library users. If you have been thinking about the implications raised by the discussion of liability and unauthorized practice of law, you probably have already sensed a conflict between those implications and the librarian's ethics concerning reference service. To put it simply, the ethics of librarianship dictate that librarians provide zealous reference service for users, including conducting a full reference interview. The possibility of liability or unauthorized practice of law dictates the opposite—that librarians avoid a full reference interview and provide only minimal service to pro se library users. This is a problem.

For background, let's look at some of the relevant ethical statements. The Code of Ethics of the American Library Association (ALA) contains the following language that addresses reference service: "We provide the highest level of service to all library users through appropriate and usefully organized resources; equitable service policies; equitable access; and accurate, unbiased, and courteous responses to all requests" (www.ala.org/advocacy/proethics/codeofethics/codeethics). The implications of this exhortation would be that limiting service to library users because of their pro se status would be unethical.

I think it is fair to say that this stance on the part of ALA reflects a global view of reference services and does not take into account the unique realities of answering legal reference questions.

The American Association of Law Libraries (AALL) also has a set of ethical principles. As you might expect, these are more attuned to the realities of providing legal reference services. The AALL Ethical Principles (www.aallnet.org/about/policy_ethics.asp) contain the following text under the rubric of service:

> We promote open and effective access to legal and related information.
> We uphold a duty to our clientele to develop service policies that respect confidentiality and privacy.

We provide zealous service using the most appropriate resources and implementing programs consistent with our institution's mission and goals.

We acknowledge the limits on service imposed by our institutions and by the duty to avoid the unauthorized practice of law.

The ethics of our profession demand that we provide the most complete reference services possible. However, to do so in a way that risks professional liability or the unauthorized practice of law surely is not recommended. As a result, a balancing of interests is required. In essence, we should provide the most comprehensive reference services possible so long as we don't enter into activities that would constitute the practice of law.

Professional Issues

Our discussion so far may have given you the impression that the issue is a simple conflict of ethics between the need to provide service and the need for personal protection. In fact there are other professional issues at work as well. These are issues like confidentiality, conflict of interest, and reliance or harm. Although we will discuss them separately, these issues don't separate cleanly and tend to all be part and parcel of the dilemma of providing appropriate reference services for pro se library users.

CONFIDENTIALITY

There is no law that protects confidentiality at the reference desk. This is in direct contrast to the situation with circulation records, which are protected by law. A reference librarian who fails to maintain the confidentiality of reference requests is not risking prosecution. However, the ethical imperative to protect confidentiality is clear. Both the ALA Code of Ethics and the AALL Ethical Principles, cited above, demand that librarians protect confidentiality in reference interactions.

The fact that confidentiality should be sought but cannot be guaranteed leads to several implications for practice. On the one hand, reference librarians should do all that they can to protect the confidentiality of reference requests and should never discuss reference requests with other users or persons not on the library staff. On the other hand, users should be made to understand that confidentiality cannot be guaranteed at the reference desk. Pro se library users should be encouraged to omit unnecessary personal details or extended descriptions of their situation from their reference requests as a way of preserving their confidentiality.

CONFLICT OF INTEREST

The concept of conflict of interest can play a special role when dealing with pro se library users. A conflict of interest occurs when a librarian acts in a manner that hurts the interests of a user, either to favor her own interests or to favor the interests of some other party. In most reference desk situations, it is hard to imagine how this might occur. But there are several aspects of providing legal reference that can raise conflict of interest issues.

As an example, if a library user were to ask for assistance with filing a divorce, it is entirely possible that the user's spouse could also seek reference help on the matter. In such a situation, the librarian must provide equal service to both parties and refrain from taking sides.

There are two basic practice points for dealing with conflict of interest. The first is that librarians should treat all users consistently and in accordance with library policy. The second is that a librarian should never become involved or take sides in a legal dispute or come between pro se library users.

RELIANCE AND HARM

Reliance and harm are not topics that come up often for librarians. This is because, as has been discussed, the activities that take place at the reference desk are not of the type that any reliance is justified, at least in the legal sense, and therefore being responsible for harm is not possible. But apart from such strictly legal analysis, I think we can look at the concepts of reliance and harm from the point of view of ethics and broaden our analysis a bit.

The difficult question is this: To what extent should a librarian limit her services to users because the users might end up being harmed by their own activities? In most cases, the question is really beyond the scope of what we do as librarians and further requires an unacceptably patriarchal view toward our users. But for someone who is handling his own legal affairs, the potential harm is much more knowable, and much more immediate, and the question of withholding services becomes an active ethical question. Let's look at the main factors at work here.

The most basic form of reliance, and the most legally dangerous, occurs when a librarian gives a pro se user the impression that she has provided accurate, complete legal advice, as opposed to simply providing information. Librarians should always make it clear that they are providing requested legal information, not advice.

Another issue at work is the fact the proceeding pro se in a legal matter is inherently dangerous. It is highly likely that pro se library users will end up being harmed legally in some way by their attempts to represent themselves. It's not the place for librarians or libraries to prevent this, but we can, and should, do what we can to not add to the problem. There are several ways to do this.

In the first place, librarians should make it clear to users not only that they are simply providing requested information and not legal advice but also that the information that the users receive may not be all that they need. Librarians should also carefully restrict their involvement with the pro se library user to that of a normal reference interaction. This would mean, for example, not offering advice based on personal experience or knowledge.

In offering to help pro se library users in ways that are beyond the bounds of normal reference service, a librarian runs the risk of creating unrealistic expectations in pro se library users. Users might come to believe that they have received full and complete legal advice, that the librarian has given them everything that they need for their situation, or that they have received the advice of an expert and do not need to do further research or analysis. The result of such over-involvement by a librarian can be that the pro se library user ends up more harmed by his self-representation than he would have been otherwise.

Another ethical reason to take a minimalist approach to assisting pro se library users is that allowing them to encounter the complexity and difficulty of legal materials and legal research can motivate them to seek legal advice or representation. With this in mind, librarians should neither overstate nor minimize the complexity of legal materials, and they should never give legal advice.

Looking at the larger picture painted by these ethical issues, along with their legal implications, several themes appear:

Liability for answering legal reference questions is theoretically possible but highly unlikely, *provided that librarians restrict themselves to legitimate reference activities.*

Ethical considerations indicate that doing anything other than providing normal reference services to a pro se library user could inadvertently lead to greater harm for the user.

Taken together, the ethical and legal considerations indicate that librarians should

- give fair, balanced, and complete reference service to those with legal reference questions;
- avoid becoming involved in a user's legal research or issue;
- avoid presenting themselves as an expert on law or legal matters; and
- avoid advising users on legal topics.

INSTITUTIONAL CONSIDERATIONS

Your library's approach to serving pro se library users will depend very much on its priorities and mandates and will also have a direct impact on library resources. On the one hand, some libraries are restricted to serving particular user groups, such as members or faculty and students. In such cases pro se users may be effectively excluded from the user group. In a similar way, some specialized libraries do not collect or hold any kind of legal materials. In this case, whether or not any of the library's users are pro se becomes irrelevant because the library is not designed to serve them on that subject.

Some libraries are open to the general public and serve as a general library. In such cases, pro se users can usually be expected to be some part of the mix of library users. Still other libraries may be specifically geared toward legal topics or even toward pro se library users. Depending on such a library's mission, it may take a more aggressive or proactive stance on assisting pro se library users.

Where your library fits on this continuum will determine both how commonly you will deal with pro se library users and what sorts of legal resources you will have available as part of your formal collection. Serving pro se users will have a variety of effects on library resources, including the collection, personnel, and facilities.

Although, as we will see, the Internet has opened up a whole new world of free or low-cost legal resources, the fact remains that collecting legal materials is a difficult and expensive task. In the world of traditional legal publishing, most resources are published by companies owned and operated by just two conglomerates, currently Thomson Reuters, which owns West Publishing and Westlaw, and Reed Elsevier, which owns a number of legal imprints, most notably Lexis-Nexis. These two companies dominate the legal information market, and their prices are geared to professionals.

Legal materials, by their very nature, tend to be published as serials. This is because the law is always changing, and so legal materials must be regularly updated. Statutes and administrative codes must be updated at least yearly to reflect new legislation and rules, and case reporters must issue new volumes as new decisions are published. This means that deciding to buy your state's statutes or case reporters is not simply a matter of purchasing the set once but of committing to purchase updates or even new sets on a yearly basis. Thus legal materials often involve an ongoing expense in the same way that a journal or other serial does.

A library that wishes to serve pro se users will almost certainly need to acquire some basic legal materials, such as statutes and case reporters, and the ongoing costs of such materials must be accounted for.

Personnel are also affected by the decision to serve pro se users. For their own good, and for the good of the library, library workers who will be interacting with pro se library users should be trained on the basic issues that pro se library users create and on library policies about these issues. A decision to assist pro se users may involve an increase in library traffic, which could, in turn, require additional staff to serve them.

In a similar manner, an increase in users could require additional seating areas or additional computers and other equipment for user needs.

CONCLUSION

There are important parameters to consider when it comes to providing legal reference service. Unlike most other areas of reference service, legal reference includes the risk of personal liability for the librarian, in the form of either a legal malpractice claim or a charge of engaging in the unauthorized practice of law. Fortunately, both risks can be minimized by restricting librarian activities to finding information and by avoiding any attempt to cast the librarian as an expert on the information itself. Legal reference also raises ethical issues. These can be minimized by taking a minimalist approach to legal reference interactions. In this case, reference librarians should respond to requests by supplying appropriate information but avoid becoming involved or giving advice.

Providing legal reference services can also have an effect on the operation of the institution, including staff training and the expense of legal materials. These issues will be discussed more completely in the next chapter.

3

TIPS AND TOOLS FOR SERVING THE PRO SE LIBRARY USER

NOW THAT WE HAVE AN UNDERSTANDING OF WHO PRO SE library users are (chapter 1) and the basic issues that they raise for librarians and libraries (chapter 2), let's take a look at some basic practical suggestions for serving the pro se library user. Most of these tips involve forms of preparation for serving the pro se population and include areas such as staff training, pathfinders and handouts, public notices, and referrals. We will look at each of these in turn, but let's start by looking at the most important tip of all: collaboration.

COLLABORATION

Ideally, a general academic or public library will be able to provide pro se library users with a continuum of service, by providing some information on the spot and by consulting with or providing appropriate referrals to specialist libraries as needed. Enter the American Association of Law Libraries (AALL) and its chapters and special interest sections. AALL is, of course, the main professional organization for law librarianship in America. Its members come from all kinds of specialist law libraries: academic law libraries, state and county law libraries, court libraries, law firm libraries, and corporate law libraries. Most state, county, and court libraries, and many academic law libraries, have a mandate to serve the public. As part of this mandate, law librarians from such libraries participate in efforts to support and assist general academic and public libraries as they try to serve pro se library users.

Efforts to reach out to public and general academic libraries are taking place within AALL, both at the local chapter level and as part of the work of several of the special interest sections within the organization. Of particular note is the effort being made by AALL's Legal Information Services to the Public Special Interest Section (LISP-SIS), which has assembled a Public Library Toolkit, available on its website (see below). This toolkit has information on basic research, finding a citation, and other legal requests, and also offers state-specific toolkits for about thirty states. In addition, the site offers a downloadable document titled "How to Research a Legal Problem: A Guide for Non-Lawyers." These resources are specifically aimed at public libraries as well as general academic libraries.

In addition to the efforts of LISP, many of the local chapters of AALL are making outreach efforts within their geographic areas. AALL has thirty-one local or regional chapters around the country. These chapters vary in the nature and amount of effort they are making at outreach, but many are doing interesting and useful things.

Some things are happening at an even more local level. As an example, the University of South Carolina School of Law has designed an excellent program for public and community college libraries in the state called the Circuit Riders Outreach Program (www.law.sc.edu/library/circuit_riders). Law librarians hold training sessions around the state for public librarians to teach them about doing legal research and to set up referral and collaboration channels. This is an excellent example of what can be done, but it's not the only one.

If you want to start collaborating with law librarians, your first step would be to contact someone in your area who might be able to help. If there is a law school library or large public or court library nearby, you might want to contact the director to discuss possible collaboration. Depending on the situation, such libraries may be willing to accept referrals or respond to questions from librarians and in some cases even provide some training for your staff.

Another approach would be to contact the head of the AALL chapter that covers your geographic area. AALL chapters, for their part, have been initiating efforts to reach out to public and academic libraries in various ways. Once again,

you could inquire about referrals, questions, and possible training.

The following AALL resources can be used as potential contact points to get you started with your collaboration efforts:

AALL: www.aallnet.org
AALL Legal Information Services to the Public, Special Interest Section (LISP-SIS): www.aallnet.org/sections/lisp
LISP-SIS Public Library Toolkit: www.aallnet.org/sections/lisp/Public -Library-Toolkit
AALL Chapters (including list of websites): www.aallnet.org/main-menu/ Member-Communities/chapters

STAFF TRAINING

Staff training is an essential component of serving pro se library users. All staff should be trained on the library's policies and procedures and should be made aware of the serious nature of legal reference. Staff who do not work at the reference desk should be trained to refer legal reference questions to the reference desk and to refrain from trying to answer such questions themselves.

Reference librarians should be trained to answer legal reference questions to the extent that library policies and mandates require them to do so. In any event, reference staff should be made aware of all collaboration and referral resources that are available to the library and be encouraged to use them liberally.

A reference librarian's basic judgment when answering a legal question should err on the side of caution. If you can be absolutely sure the question does not involve the user's own legal interests, such as the example of a student doing research for a paper, then you can do whatever your training or reference style dictates. But once someone steps into the pro se category, caution should be your watchword.

Some basic guidelines for handling reference questions include finding information without expressing an opinion or judgment about the information itself, avoiding expressing a legal opinion or suggesting a solution to a legal problem, and acknowledging the point where doing legal research requires expertise or resources that you do not have at hand.

Here are suggestions for handling reference questions that may be presented at a reference desk:

Ready-reference requests. Questions that ask for a particular item or source should be handled as such. This would include requests for a particular source, such as the state code, or for help finding something like a particular case or code section when requested by citation. Theoretically, such requests raise no potential liability or other problems, so long as they are handled as information requests.

Research requests. Any request that asks that the reference librarian make any kind of judgment about an issue should be declined, and the user should be referred to sources instead. This would include questions like "What is the law on . . . ?" "Is it legal to . . . ?" or "What form should I use to . . . ?" All such questions are asking for a legal opinion and should not be answered on those terms.

Instruction on using sources. Sometimes it may be necessary to show users how a source works—for example, by showing them the index to a code set or how to search in a legal database. In doing so, the reference librarian should restrict herself to bibliographic instruction and not be drawn into participating in answering the question.

Determining sources. Unfortunately, even helping a user determine what source to use can involve rendering a legal opinion. For example, deciding whether the question a user had would best be answered by researching case law or statutes can potentially involve a legal opinion. It is important to avoid making such decisions for a user.

More generally, interactions at the reference desk should involve clear parameters, and librarians should know when and how to refer users elsewhere:

Maintain boundaries. The reference librarian should be firm about determining what she can and cannot do for a user. At the reference desk of my law library, it is common for users to want to debate whether their question requires a legal opinion, in the hope of getting assistance. Librarians should remain firm about the amount of help they are willing to give, and it is essential that management support this stance.

Avoid extended discussions. Many pro se users will want to tell their story, hoping that it will engender sympathy and spur the librarian to action. This is time consuming and usually pointless. Although it may feel a bit rude, it is best to cut users off from telling their stories and ask specifically what kind of information they are looking for. If they don't know, then the best solution is to provide them with a source that might help them figure it out, such as a self-help legal website.

Resort to handy phrases. While every interaction has to be improvised, there are some good phrases that can be used in many situations. Some suggestions:

- "I can help you find information, but I can't tell you what that information means."
- "I am forbidden by law from giving you a legal opinion, even if I wanted to."
- "I am not a lawyer, and I don't know about law. My training is in helping people find information."
- "I am not allowed to express an opinion about your situation."
- "Nothing that you tell me here at the reference desk is confidential. It would be best if you could just ask for whatever information you think you need."

Maintain a good attitude. Pro se user requests can be tense and even adversarial. In spite of this, I find that such interactions go best when I approach them from a friendly, helpful, and sympathetic viewpoint. While I am firm about maintaining boundaries and not giving advice, I try to make it clear that I sympathize with the user's plight and that I wish I could be of more help. Feel free to blame rules and policies for the limitations on your service.

Refer, refer, refer. As has been made clear in other places in this book, most pro se users are not doing themselves any favors by trying to handle their own legal problems. Although this state of affairs may be inevitable in some cases, reference librarians can do users a big service by suggesting they seek formal legal help and by making sure they know about resources that may be available to them. Here are some guidelines:

- Suggest consulting an attorney. It is perfectly acceptable to tell a user that his question would be best handled by an attorney. You can do this in several ways, such as "If I had this problem I'd speak to an attorney" or "This kind of question probably requires legal training to answer properly" or "This involves legal research using professional tools that lawyers have, and we don't have anything like that in this library." Users can be referred to lawyer directories or state bar referral services if they need help finding an attorney.

- Refer users to legal aid services or free legal clinics. Make use of referrals to whatever resources your community or locality has for low-cost or free legal assistance. Your local legal aid office is probably restricted as to what cases they can take, but their attorneys will often meet with someone to give small amounts of advice. In addition, many communities have regular events where attorneys will evaluate cases or give advice on a one-time, low-cost or free basis. This is where your referral materials come in handy.

- Refer users to law libraries. If a public law library is in your area, you can feel free to refer users with legal questions to such an institution. You can explain that such libraries have better resources for their questions. However, please do not imply that library staff in such a library can or will render greater assistance than you can. Law libraries have better tools for legal questions, but law librarians are just as restricted in how they must approach pro se questions.

- Steer clear of courthouses. Please do NOT refer users with legal questions to the local clerk of court or other court personnel. No one will help them, and both the users and the courthouse personnel will end up angry about the referral. Clerk's office personnel are forbidden from giving legal advice (their situation is very similar to librarians on this issue), and judges will not review someone's case or give advice. Please don't make such a referral, even if you are desperate to get a pro se user to leave. That said, it is possible that your local courthouse has a self-help legal center or pro se assistance booth. If such a facility exists, a referral would be both appropriate and useful.

PATHFINDERS AND HANDOUTS

Many libraries find handouts and pathfinders to be very useful. Handouts can describe library policies and also explain the scope of the resources that the library has. Handouts can also contain referral information, both for dedicated law libraries and for legal service providers.

Pathfinders can help users conduct legal research. Pathfinders can be created for the tools the library has in its collection and also for online resources. Pathfinders can be useful for taking pressure off reference librarians because users can be more self-directed in their research. Pathfinders do not run the risk of unauthorized practice of law because they do not respond directly to a user's question and therefore cannot be construed as offering legal advice.

Many law school and public law libraries have pathfinders on their websites. You should explore what legal research resources are available from such institutions in your state.

PUBLIC NOTICES

Publicly posted notices of library policies on legal reference questions can help pro se library users understand the parameters and limitations of library services before they ask a librarian for help. Such notices can also bolster the librarian's authority in limiting services. Because the limitations are posted, users cannot claim that the librarian is acting arbitrarily or with malice in refusing to provide legal research services. Such notices can also provide a more detailed list of what the librarian will and will not do, helping to forestall arguments over those issues as well.

Here are some examples of language that could be included in public notices concerning assistance with legal topics. Such language could be posted on signs in the library and at the reference desk and could also be posted on the library's website.

If you have a question on a legal topic, we would like to help you, but there are limitations to what services and information we can provide:

- *We have only limited legal sources available in our collection. We do not have any legal forms.*
- *Our librarians are not legal experts and cannot provide legal advice or explain legal procedures.*
- *We do have a limited amount of legal referral information. This information can help you find a lawyer or an institution with a larger legal information collection.*

Our librarians are required by law and library policy to limit the assistance they provide to patrons researching legal topics. These service limitations are intended to protect both patrons and librarians from potential liability and other legal problems.

REFERRALS

Often, the most appropriate way to help library users with a legal question is to refer them to another library that is better equipped to help them, assuming such a library is available within a reasonable distance. Such referrals would most usually be to nearby academic law libraries or law libraries open to the public, such as county or court law libraries.

MORE INFORMATION

Web Resources

The NCSC has an excellent website. Some pages of interest concerning pro se litigants include the following:

Self-Representation Resource Guide. www
.ncsc.org/Topics/Access-and-Fairness/Self-
Representation/Resource-Guide.aspx.
Self-Representation State Links. www.ncsc
.org/Topics/Access-and-Fairness/Self
-Representation/State-Links.aspx.

Books

Minow, Mary, and Tomas A. Lipinski. *The Library's Legal Answer Book.* Chicago: American Library Association, 2003.
Healey, Paul D. *Professional Liability Issues for Librarians and Information Professionals.* New York: Neal-Schuman, 2008.

Articles

The articles and annotations below are taken from Paul D. Healey, "Pro Se Users, Reference Liability, and the Unauthorized Practice of Law: Twenty-Five Selected Readings," *Law Library Journal* 94, no. 1 (2002): 133–42, available online at www .aallnet.org/main-menu/Publications/llj/LLJ -Archives/Vol-94/pub_llj_v94n01/2002-08.pdf.

Begg, Robert T. "The Reference Librarian and the Pro Se Patron." *Law Library Journal* 69 (1976): 26–32.

This is one of the earliest articles on the topic. Begg lists various possible motivations for becoming a self-represented litigant and also discusses the problems pro se users are perceived to cause for the library. He recommends excluding pro se users from the library entirely if possible. Otherwise he suggests enforcing registration and fees for library users, enforcing service limitations, identifying problem users, making referrals, and using pamphlets and research guides—anything short of giving them "the old run around." Begg's descriptions of why people become self-represented litigants, and the issues they raise, are quite useful.

Brown, Yvette. "From the Reference Desk to the Jail House: Unauthorized Practice of Law and Librarians." *Legal Reference Services Quarterly* 13, no. 4 (1994): 31–45.

This is one of the most widely cited articles on the topic. Brown feels that almost any reference interaction involving legal materials is, in some sense, practicing law. She says that pro se users are "seeking legal advice" and are "unaware of the fundamental differences between the services of an attorney and the services of a librarian." She worries that reference interviews can lead to unintentionally dispensing legal advice. The article proposes a number of measures to be taken, from verbal disclaimers to distributing handouts and other materials. Worth reading for these suggestions.

Condon, Charles J. "How to Avoid the Unauthorized Practice of Law at the Reference Desk." *Legal Reference Services Quarterly* 19, no. 1/2 (2001): 165–79.

This article sums up a fairly reasonable approach to dealing with self-represented litigants at the reference desk. Of particular note is Condon's mention of the potential uses for online resources in assisting pro se users.

Graecen, John M. "'No Legal Advice from Court Personnel': What Does That Mean?" *The Judges Journal* 34, no. 1 (Winter 1995): 10–15.

This oft-cited article relates directly to court personnel but has plenty of implications for law librarians. Graecen points out that the practice of law is undefined, and consequently it is impossible to determine what is legal advice and what isn't. He feels that this ambiguity has negative implications for the court and the public, and that court personnel must sometimes assist people in ways that could be seen as giving legal advice. He concludes with guidelines.

Healey, Paul D. "Chicken Little at the Reference Desk: The Myth of Librarian Liability." *Law Library Journal* 87, no. 3 (1995): 515–33.

This article looks at the general risk of liability for activities at the reference desk. It surveys the literature and then tests the theories presented in other articles against standard legal theory. The conclusion is that there is virtually no risk of liability for reference activities so long as librarians act as experts on finding information rather than experts on the information found.

Healey, Paul D. "In Search of the Delicate Balance: Legal and Ethical Questions in Assisting the Pro Se Patron." *Law Library Journal* 90, no. 1 (1998): 129–47.

This article looks at the attitudes of librarians toward pro se library users and then explores the underlying theories on which those fears are based. The article concludes that the risk of being accused of unauthorized practice of law in the library is slight, but that questions of ethics indicate that librarians should take a hands-off approach to assisting pro se users.

Leone, Gerome. "Malpractice Liability of a Law Librarian?" *Law Library Journal* 73 (1980): 44–65.

Leone feels that law librarians are not overstepping the bounds of unauthorized practice in their normal duties and that authorities concede much greater latitude than librarians realize. He also raises the issue of whether pro se users in fact have an affirmative right to legal assistance from law librarians. Leone says that law librarians are not limited to handing out books but can also suggest topics. He also says that if the assistance provided to a user does not amount to the unauthorized practice of law, then unauthorized practice of law should not be employed as an excuse for not serving a user.

Mills, Robin K. "Reference Service vs. Legal Advice: Is It Possible to Draw the Line?" *Law Library Journal* 72 (1979): 179–93.

By any standard, this is one of the classic articles on the topic of legal advice and reference service. Mills takes the position that almost any reference interaction involving legal materials is, in some sense, practicing law. She fears that there might be an implied attorney-client relationship at the reference desk through the concept of agency, or that an attorney/librarian might be held to an attorney-client relationship with pro se users and liability could result. In spite of this, law libraries are unlikely targets for enforcement even if they are giving advice. In fact, Mills worries that users have little recourse for harm from law librarians.

Mosley, Madison, Jr. "The Authorized Practice of Legal Reference Service." *Law Library Journal* 87 (1995): 203–9.

This article is one of several that takes a more open and proactive approach to pro se users. In contrast to Brown (above), Mosley questions whether pro se users, even when they see law librarians as subject experts in law, actually confuse this with being a lawyer. He contends that pro se users in a law library are seeking reference help, not legal advice, and know the difference between the two. He feels that legal reference can be differentiated from the practice of law by avoiding the performance of legal services for a third party, and that law librarians supplying legal reference services are not performing lawyerly functions. Mosley feels that law librarians should stop focusing on what constitutes the practice of law and begin concentrating on not performing lawyerly functions. He points out that the search for legal materials only brings together the elements which must be analyzed in a legal problem. It is the analysis that constitutes legal advice and that is what law librarians should avoid.

Protti, Maria E. "Dispensing Law at the Front Lines: Ethical Dilemmas in Law Librarianship." *Library Trends* 40 (1991): 234–43.

Protti is another activist on the issue of assisting pro se users. She feels that any difference between legal reference service and legal advice is a fallacy. Law librarians should be proactive, dispensing understandable, timely, relevant, complete, and appropriate information to pro se users. She feels that lawyer librarians may well know more than other lawyers about a given area, and in such a case should advise a pro se user. In contrast to Mills (above), Protti feels that the availability of legal remedies protects the user and therefore should not prevent a librarian from interpreting the law. She also feels that accountability may improve the provision of information.

Schanck, Peter C. "Unauthorized Practice of Law and the Legal Reference Librarian." *Law Library Journal* 72 (1979): 57–64.

This article focuses on practical advice in dealing with pro se users. Schanck says that suggesting a book, index terms, or a source might all be activities that constitute interpretation of the law. He proposes some "don'ts" for avoiding the unauthorized practice of law, including not soliciting a detailed description of the user's situation, not responding to an abstract question with a black-and-white answer, and not telling a pro se user what something means.

PART TWO

LEGAL RESEARCH BASICS

4

THE STRUCTURE OF LAW AND THE LEGAL RESEARCH PROCESS

I N THIS CHAPTER WE WILL TAKE A BROAD LOOK AT LEGAL RE-
search and its components. We will start by looking at the structure of the American legal system, with an eye to how this structure is documented and how the
structure affects documentary access. Then we will look at some basic legal concepts
that need to be understood in order to work with legal information.

Next up is a look at the weird world of legal citation style, followed by the most
common legal topics that library users ask about. For each of those topics we will
point out the underlying forms of law and what legal tools or documents would be
used to answer the question. From there we will move on to a look at the legal research process, at least as it applies to the general reference desk context.

THE STRUCTURE OF THE AMERICAN LEGAL SYSTEM

The American system of government consists of a federal government, fifty state
governments, fourteen territories, and 310 tribally sovereign Native American Indian
reservations. The fifty states contain 3,140 counties or county-equivalent administrative units and approximately 84,500 local government units. Each of these almost
90,000 governmental bodies makes and enforces laws or rules in some form. There's
a lot of law out there.

Doing legal research requires a working knowledge of the structure of the relevant unit of government, the forms of law created by the government, and how and
where that law is published or accessed. If this all sounds overwhelming, don't worry.

There are several factors at work that make this much simpler than it looks.

The most important governmental units for legal research purposes are the federal government and the fifty states. This is because federal and state laws govern the majority of issues that come up in daily life, from basic rights to contracts, marriage relations, and such mundane things as driver's licenses. Fortunately, these fifty-one governmental bodies have basically the same structure and issue law in basically the same forms. This makes learning the basics of legal research fairly simple, because things like statutes, cases, and codes are researched in basically the same way in any jurisdiction.

Local governments vary quite a bit in structure and powers, but as a practical matter, most reference questions will be restricted to local governments in the immediate vicinity of the library, making it much easier to climb the learning curve. As for the more unusual forms of government—territories, Native American Indian reservations, and so forth—these are really specialist topics, although if you live or work in or near one of these, you will want to learn about them. In this book we will restrict our scope to federal and state law and will not cover local law or law of the territories and so forth. That said, this book's appendix of online resources does include some local law resources.

Basic Structure

In the United States, we live under a federal system that is a bit unusual as governments go. In most countries, there is a central government, and regional, or state, governments are simply subdivisions of the central, national government. In America, the fifty states are each separate, sovereign governments. They are gathered together under the yoke of the federal government, but the power of that government is limited, and the states are left to govern themselves on most matters. For this reason, American law is a sometimes confusing pastiche of federal and state law. Part of the task of learning to do legal reference

is learning how the roles of these governments, and their laws, differ.

The American federal government and all fifty state governments consist of three branches: a legislative branch, a judicial branch, and an executive branch. You may be familiar with the old saying that the legislature makes the laws, the executive enforces the laws, and the courts adjudicate disputes under the law. This is all true, but in fact it is a bit too simplistic. For instance, it sometimes surprises people to find out that all three branches of government make law. As such, legal research requires the ability to find the law as promulgated by any of the three branches.

The source of this three-part structure, and of many of the powers of government, is a document called a constitution. The federal government and each of the fifty state governments have a constitution. Constitutions have been referred to as organic law. The word *organic* is used here in the sense that the constitution delineates the form and powers of the government it creates and lists rights and liberties of individual citizens. A constitution is thus the foundation document for our form of democracy and is the vehicle by which the people agree to be governed.

Constitutions will be discussed in more detail in chapter 6. For now, it is enough to understand that constitutions have three broad roles in government. They delineate the form of government, describing the three branches and the details of their makeup and operation; they enumerate the powers of the government; and they enumerate the rights and liberties of citizens.

The Constitution of the United States sets up the federal government, defines areas of federal interest, and enumerates rights enjoyed by all U.S. citizens. A key point to understand about this is that federal law has supremacy in its areas of interest. This means that states cannot legislate in areas of federal interest that are listed in the U.S. Constitution, such as copyright or bankruptcy, and that states cannot pass laws that limit individual rights guaranteed under the U.S. Constitution.

State constitutions address the forms of government for each state and the powers of state constitutional bodies and offices. State constitutions can also list individual rights and liberties and grant citizens of the state broader rights than those provided under the U.S. Constitution. However, as mentioned above, a state constitution cannot limit individual rights in a way that contradicts the U.S. Constitution.

Legislation

When most people think of law they think of legislation, or statutes. There are good reasons for this. The U.S. Congress and state legislatures are the bodies set up within our system of government specifically for the purpose of making law. (I will use the term *legislature* to refer generically to any legislating body, whether the U.S. Congress or a state legislature.) The lawmaking process legislatures use is deliberative in nature and results in an organized body of laws. As we shall see, the judicial and executive branches also make law in our system of government, but the legislature is the most prominent and widely known. Legislatures also have the broadest powers to make law on any subject they choose, provided that law doesn't violate either the federal or any applicable state constitution.

Legislatures in our system of government consist of elected members who represent specific geographical areas of their state, based on population. Most legislatures in America, in fact all but one, consist of two chambers, usually referred to as an upper and lower chamber. (Nebraska has a unicameral, or single chamber, legislature.) The lower chamber is usually called the house of representatives. Its more numerous members represent smaller districts and usually run for reelection every two years. The upper chamber, usually called the senate, is a smaller body whose members represent larger districts, or the entire state, and who serve longer terms, usually four or six years.

Legislatures are empowered to make law on any topic within their purview, unless proscribed by the federal or a state constitution. The purview of the legislature is delineated by our federal system. Thus the limited purview of the U.S.

Congress is to make laws within the sphere of federal interests as described in the U.S. Constitution, provided those laws do not violate any of its provisions. Conversely, state legislatures have a fairly broad mandate to legislate, provided their laws do not violate the terms of either the federal or the applicable state constitution, or intrude on an area reserved to the federal government.

In order for a law to come into being, a bill in the legislature must be considered and approved by both chambers. Once a bill is passed, the executive must sign it. Once this occurs, the bill is law. In order to make legislation easier to find and use, all laws of general application and currently in force are organized into a topical set of laws called a code. There is a federal code, and each state has its own code as well. All this will be explained at length in chapter 6.

Case Law

The federal government and each of the fifty states constitute separate jurisdictions, and each has its own court system. These systems are all fairly similar in structure. Each court system has one or more trial courts and a court of last resort, usually known as a supreme court. Most have an intermediate court of appeals as well.

Under our system, as will be explained at length in chapter 7, appellate courts—that is, the courts of appeal and supreme court of a given jurisdiction—can render decisions that are treated as law and must be followed by courts in that jurisdiction in future disputes. The body of those decisions is called common law, or more generically, case law. It is important to note that the common law is the product of decisions that result because of disputes brought before the court. Thus common law is reactive in nature, in the sense that courts make law in the process of reacting to that which has been brought before them. A judge cannot simply decide to make law on a given subject, the way a legislator can. Judges can only react to disputes.

In sum, case law is reactive in nature, made in response to a dispute and restricted to the boundaries of the dispute. Again, much more on all this in chapter 7.

Administrative Law

Administrative law is the law that is made by and governs governmental administrative agencies. Agencies, in the course of their work, can make rules, adjudicate disputes that arise under those rules, and enforce the regulatory agenda of the agencies.

Agencies make law in the form of rules. Agencies make rules when the legislature directs them to do so as part of a law. Such a law is called enabling legislation. In enabling legislation, the legislature makes law on a topic and then directs the appropriate agency to make the necessary rules to carry out the intent of the law. As such, rules can be seen as directed in nature. An agency can make rules only when directed to do so by the legislature, and those rules must be restricted to the intent of the enabling legislation. A more complete description of administrative law is available in chapter 8.

SOME BASIC LEGAL CONCEPTS

Let's turn now from the structure of government to some basic concepts that are integral to understanding how law functions in our society.

Primary and Secondary Legal Information

Legal information is broadly divided into two types, referred to as primary and secondary. The distinction between primary and secondary legal information is fairly simple. Primary legal information sources are the law, while secondary legal information sources provide information about the law. Primary legal information is made up of constitutions, legislation, case law, and adminis-

trative rules. All other legal information sources are considered secondary.

The key test as to whether a given piece of legal information is primary is whether it, standing alone, constitutes legal authority. Thus a statute or an appellate case is primary, because it constitutes legal authority on the issue that it addresses. An entry in a legal encyclopedia or a treatise on the same topic is not a primary authority, even though each may be authoritative in its own way; thus these are considered secondary legal sources.

Jurisdiction

All law exists within the context, and confines, of a particular jurisdiction. Jurisdiction can be defined as the authority granted to a legal body or political leader to make decisions and effect justice. There are three kinds of jurisdiction. The most common is territorial jurisdiction. This gives a governing body such as a legislature or court the authority to rule in matters that arise within the described territory. The Iowa Supreme Court, for example, has jurisdiction over the entire state of Iowa. Its decisions are law in the state of Iowa but are not law in other states. A county court, on the other hand, would have jurisdiction only over disputes that arise within that county. Similarly, a state legislature can make laws that bind the citizens of that state but not other states.

Subject matter jurisdiction gives a court authority over a particular type of dispute and generally restricts its powers to that subject. Examples of this are tax courts or probate courts. These courts hear disputes relating only to their subject matter. Note that a court's jurisdiction can be limited by both territory and subject matter. For example, a county probate court would hear only probate matters, and only those that arise in its county.

Personal jurisdiction gives a court authority over certain persons, regardless of where they are located. A good example of this is military courts. Military courts deal with all kinds of disputes, from all over the world, but only when they involve military personnel.

We will revisit jurisdiction in more detail in chapter 7.

Public and Private Law

In the American legal system, we make a distinction between public law and private law. Broadly speaking, public law governs relations between individual citizens and the state, whereas private law governs relations between individuals. Public law thus consists of such things as criminal law, constitutional law, and administrative law. Private law includes torts, contracts, and to a certain extent property law.

A functional distinction between public and private law is that public law usually exists in the form of constitutions, legislation, and administrative rules, whereas private law consists mostly of court decisions in the form of case law. Don't rely on this distinction too much, though. As we shall see, some precedential court decisions actually constitute public law, and some legislation is actually private law.

Precedent

Precedent is the concept that appellate court decisions create law that must be followed in future disputes. Precedent is bound by jurisdiction, meaning that the decisions of an appellate court must be followed by the courts below that court but not in other jurisdictions. As an example, the Eighth Circuit Court of Appeals is the federal appellate court whose jurisdiction includes the Dakotas, Nebraska, Minnesota, Iowa, Missouri, and Nebraska. Decisions of the Eighth Circuit are binding precedent for all federal trial courts in the states within the circuit but are not binding in other states in other circuits. Nor do Eighth Circuit decisions bind the U.S. Supreme Court, because the federal Supreme Court is above the Eighth Circuit in the appellate hierarchy. Similarly, the decisions of the Iowa Supreme Court are binding precedent for all of the courts in Iowa but not for courts in other states or in the federal court system.

Precedent can be either mandatory or persuasive. Mandatory, or binding, precedent is that which must be followed as law, generally because it is a decision of a higher court within the same jurisdiction. Persuasive precedent is precedent that is from another jurisdiction, or from a lower court in the same jurisdiction, which need not be followed as law. Persuasive precedent is often used by parties in litigation in hopes of persuading the court to adopt the logic of a particular precedent and thus have it become law in that jurisdiction.

LEGAL CITATION

One very common reference request is for help finding, or even identifying, a legal document based on its citation. This can be a challenge because formal legal documents, including court filings, memoranda, and legal journals, use a specific form of citation to cite documents and authority. This citation system is unique to law and is different from such standard citation formats as those prescribed by *The Chicago Manual of Style*, *MLA Handbook*, or *APA Publication Manual*. Legal citation is governed by the rules laid down in *The Bluebook: A Uniform System of Citation*, published jointly by the editors of the Columbia, Harvard, and University of Pennsylvania *Law Reviews* and the *Yale Law Journal*. *The Bluebook* covers citation for all forms of documents, not just legal documents.

Any law student will tell you that *The Bluebook* is complex, dense, and difficult to use, and unless you are going to be deeply involved with legal documents, there is probably no need to study it. In this section, I'd like to explain a few of the more common citation forms that a librarian may encounter, with some hints on how to decipher them.

Case Citation

A citation to a published appellate decision case will look like this:

Franklin v. United States, 992 F.2d 1492 (10th Cir. 1993)

Someone who knows legal citation could tell you at a glance that this is a 1993 decision from the federal appellate courts, specifically the U.S. Court of Appeals for the Tenth Circuit, and that it can be found on page 1492 in volume 992 of a set of books called the *Federal Reporter*, second series, published by West Publishing. It is a decision in a case that originated somewhere in Oklahoma, Kansas, New Mexico, Colorado, Wyoming, or Utah. Similarly, the citation

Taylor v. Super Discount Market, Inc., 441 S.E.2d
433 (Ga. Ct. App. 1994)

is to a 1994 decision of the Georgia Court of Appeals, and it is published in volume 441 of the *South Eastern Reporter*, second series, also published by West.

Being able to decipher a case citation can help in finding the document in question. Basic case citation consists of the following four elements: party names, case reporter information, jurisdictional statement, and a date. The party names are usually the last names of the two opposing parties, listed as plaintiff versus defendant. The reporter information is the volume and starting page number of the case in whatever case reporter it is published in. The jurisdictional statement indicates what court rendered the decision, and the date is the year that the decision was handed down.

The result looks like this:

Party Names
[plaintiff] v. [defendant],
Reporter Information
[vol.] [reporter] [page number],
Jurisdiction, Date
([court] [year])

It is worth noting here that in spite of the fact that many cases are now published primarily online, the reporter volume and page system remains the most common way of citing to a case, and this information will find a case even in an online environment.

Here are some more examples of actual case citations:

Bonbrest v. Kotz, 65 F. Supp. 138 (D.D.C. 1946)

This case involves a plaintiff named Bonbrest, who sued someone named Kotz. The abbreviation "F. Supp" indicates that the case is published in a West reporter called the *Federal Supplement*, in volume 65, starting on page 138. The jurisdictional statement "D.D.C." indicates that this is a case from the federal district court of the District of Columbia, which is the trial court for Washington, D.C. The fact that this is a federal district court case is reinforced by the fact that the *Federal Supplement* reporter series only publishes federal district court cases. Finally, the decision was handed down in 1946.

Here's another example:

Fowler v. Roberts, 556 So. 2d 1 (La. 1989)

This tells us that this was a case in which the plaintiff, Fowler, sued the defendant, Roberts. The case is published in volume 556 of the West regional reporter called *Southern Reporter*, second series, beginning on page 1. The abbreviation "La." tells us it is a decision of the Louisiana Supreme Court, handed down in 1989.

We will discuss the case citation system in more depth in chapter 7.

Statute Citation

As will be discussed in chapter 6, statutes are published in sets called codes. Statute citation varies from state to state, but it usually involves the following elements: a major code division (often title or chapter), an abbreviation of the name of the set of statutes, a section number or designation, and the year (in parentheses). Again, there is much variability from jurisdiction to jurisdiction.

Let's take the example of the crime of arson. Here is the citation for a statute concerning arson in the *United States Code*:

Title	Code	Section	Year
18	U.S.C.	§ 844	(2006)

And here are some code citations for state laws against arson, showing some of the variations in citation style. State codes often dispense with a title or chapter number, so that the citation consists of an abbreviation for the code name, a section number, and a year:

Code	Section	Year
Iowa Code	§ 712.1	(2008)
Wyo. Stat. Ann.	§ 6-3-101	(1977)
Conn. Gen. Stat.	§ 53a-111	(2008)
Tenn. Code Ann.	§ 39-14-301	(2008)

You will generally see citations abbreviated as above. In addition to abbreviated state names, which are usually easy to figure out, common code citation abbreviations include "Ann." for "Annotated," "Gen." for "General," and "Stat." for "Statutes." These terms will be explained fully in chapter 6.

Some states have more complicated statute citation schemes. Here is the citation to the Illinois statute defining arson:

720 ILCS 5/20-1.1

When working with such a citation, the citation should be parsed from left to right. In other words, the first division in the citation above to look for will be 720, then within 720 look for section 5. Within section 5 will be a subsection 20-1.1.

Several states, notably California, New York, and Texas, divide their statutes into separate topical codes. Thus the New York statute on arson is cited as follows:

N.Y. Penal Law § 150.20 (McKinney 2008)

Journal and Book Citation

Citations to journals, magazines, and books all look different in legal citation than they do in the citation styles most librarians are familiar with. For books, citation information includes the author (first name first), title, page number being referenced, and a date in parentheses. If the edition is anything other than first, edition information precedes the date within the parentheses. There is no mention of publisher or location. Here is an example:

Deborah L. Rhode, *Justice and Gender* 56 (1989)

Edited works get a slightly different treatment, in which the title is immediately followed by the page number, and then editor and date information follows in parentheses. Again, no publisher information is included in the citation. Here is an example:

AIDS and the Law 35 (Harlon L. Dalton et. al. eds., 1987)

Books that have section or paragraph numbers are referenced by section or paragraph, not page. Books that are numbered volumes in a series include volume information at the beginning of the citation. Here is an example that uses these two concepts:

21 Charles Alan Wright & Arthur R. Miller, *Federal Practice and Procedure* §1006 (3d. ed. 1996)

Magazines and journals get a different citation treatment depending on their pagination scheme. Consecutively paginated journals, which start page numbering in each successive issue in a volume with the next page number after the last page in the previous issue, are cited like this:

Paul D. Healey, *Chicken Little at the Reference Desk: The Myth of Librarian Liability*, 87 Law Library Journal 515 (1995)

The information in the citation includes author, article title, journal volume number, journal name (often abbreviated: e.g., Law Libr. J.), beginning page number, and year. Page ranges, issue numbers, or date of issue, other than year, are not included.

Nonconsecutively paginated journals, which start each new issue on page 1, are cited as follows:

Paul D. Healey, *Perspectives: The Lighter Side of Dealing with Difficult Users*, AALL Spectrum, Apr. 2002, at 4

The information in the citation includes author, article title, journal name, issue date, and beginning page number preceded by "at." Again, page ranges and volume or issue numbers are not included.

SPECIFIC LEGAL TOPICS

It would be impossible to predict with any accuracy the specific legal topics that get asked about in library reference questions. Even if it were possible, it would be well beyond the scope of this book to provide you with extensive background information on each of those topics. That said, there are some legal topics that are fairly common.

The purpose of this section is to highlight these common topics of legal reference questions and describe briefly some of the basic concepts involved and the sources of law that would address such issues. The operative words here are "briefly" and "basic." At best, the information here will orient you toward answering a question and get you started on the task.

Criminal, Civil, and Regulatory Actions

Legal disputes in America arise under one of three legal rubrics: criminal, civil, or regulatory. Understanding where a dispute falls under this scheme is key to researching the relevant law.

Criminal law, as you probably already know, covers crimes. A criminal action is always an action by the government against an individual, alleging the violation of a criminal statute. This means, first of all, that the parties are always the government as plaintiff and an individual as defendant. It also means that the underlying law is statutory in nature. As we will see in the chapter on statutes, there may be court decisions that interpret the statute that will need to be researched, but any criminal prosecution will arise under a particular statute.

Criminal prosecutions can arise under federal or state law, but state prosecution is far more common. Federal crimes are limited to areas of federal interest, which means the crime must involve some area of federal law or, in some cases, criminal activity across state lines. Common federal crimes include those arising under federally regulated activities, including banking, the mails, and federal income taxes, crimes perpetrated against federal officials, Internet distribution of illegal pornography, transporting illegal drugs, and kidnapping across state lines.

All other crimes are prosecuted at the state level and will arise under the criminal statutes of your state. This can include everything from drunken driving to assault, theft, or murder. Again, the majority of criminal prosecutions take place at the state level.

Civil actions are by far the broadest category of legal disputes. Civil actions involve one party pursuing a legal remedy against another party. The parties involved can be individuals, corporations, or the government, or any combination thereof, depending on the situation. Many civil disputes arise under what is called private law. Private law is the law that governs interactions between individuals. The three most common areas of civil private law disputes are torts, contracts, and property.

Tort law establishes civil liability based on relationships in society. Under tort law, we all have duties to others in society. When a civil duty is violated, and the violation results in harm, the person harmed can seek damages from the person who failed to uphold his duty. The most common and perhaps most overused example of this involves car accidents. When you drive, you assume a duty to follow the rules of the road and to try to avoid accidents. If you fail in that duty, say by going through a red light at an intersection, and because of that an accident occurs, you will be liable for the harm that results. That harm can include expenses for repairing or replacing damaged vehicles and property, medical expenses, and even amounts for lost future earnings, present or future pain and suffering, and loss of life.

Another common source of liability arises from injuries that occur when someone is a guest on another's property. This is where so-called slip-and-fall cases arise. For example, if someone slips and falls in a library because a tear in the carpet was not repaired, that could constitute the failure of a duty to maintain safe premises, and liability could result.

Contract law governs legally enforceable private agreements and allows a party to seek damages if another party to the contract failed to follow through on their part of the agreement. Property law governs the ownership and use rights related to real and personal property. This can cover everything from the purchase or sale of buildings or land to gifts of personal property to wills and estates.

As a general rule, most civil law is case law. This is especially true for tort law. It is also true for contract and property law, but with exceptions. Most states have a commercial code, which is a set of statutes that governs commercial contracts. Similarly in property law, wills and estates are generally covered by a state's probate code, as are some aspects of real estate transactions.

Regulatory actions are, technically, civil in nature. That said, they differ from other civil actions in that, like criminal actions, regulatory matters always have the government as the plaintiff. In addition, regulatory actions will be based on regulations, either on their own or along with an enabling statute. The first stages of a regulatory action will be tried within an agency by an administrative law judge rather than in a court of law. If the administrative law judge's decision is appealed, it will eventually end up in a regular court. Regulatory actions can occur at the federal or state level, depending on the area of law and the agency involved.

The above is all necessarily vague and incomplete. A thorough discussion of each of these areas of law is, unfortunately, far beyond the scope of this book. That said, the table on the following page is an attempt to delineate common legal topics that arise at the reference desk, along with a rough indication of the type of law that is involved and where it can be found.

THE LEGAL RESEARCH PROCESS

Legal professionals are taught a process for conducting legal research. This process may share elements and practices used by researchers in other fields, but it is tailored to the needs of the legal world. The legal research process used by legal professionals is intended to be targeted, comprehensive, and solution oriented, while pursuing maximum efficiency and being sensitive to time and cost.

Librarians working at a public reference desk do not have the time or the specialized resources at their disposal that would be required to follow a formal legal research process. Instead, they must handle legal question in much the same way as other questions.

This is a good place to pause and mention, once again, that legal research is a highly specialized skill, and people who have legal questions, particularly when dealing with their own legal interests, are often not prepared to handle such questions on their own.

One particular issue along these lines is forms. Many people have the idea that litigation filings are basically forms that can be filled out, in the same way a blank income tax form can be filled out and filed. In most jurisdictions such forms do not exist. There are specialized legal resources that provide forms, but such forms are typically made up of many versions of possible language for a motion or filing and are intended to be used by trained professionals.

When dealing with a library user who has a complicated legal question, it is always acceptable to suggest that she talk to an attorney instead. If she won't do that, it is also perfectly acceptable to refer her to a dedicated public law

Legal topic	Federal or state?	Type of law involved	Notes
Litigation (in general)	Either	Court rules of procedure and evidence; also jury instructions, local court rules	Litigation rules are an entire set of procedures that must be followed, in addition to the subject matter of the suit.
Bankruptcy	Federal	Statute, with case law interpretation	Personal exemptions are sometimes covered by state statute.
Contract issues	State	Case law	Commercial disputes may be covered by the Uniform Commercial Code, which is part of the state's statutes.
Criminal charge	State (most commonly) or federal	Statute, with case law interpretation	
Debts, collections, foreclosure, credit	Federal or state, possibly a combination	Statutes and regulations	
Divorce and custody	State	Statute, with case law interpretation	Very common legal question topic.
Employment discrimination	Federal (most commonly) or state	Statute, with case law interpretation	
Employment	State	Statute, with case law interpretation	
Housing	Federal (most commonly) or state	Regulations (mostly) and statutes	
Intellectual property (copyright and patent)	Federal	Statute, with case law interpretation	
Landlord-tenant	State	Statute	Most states have a specific landlord-tenant statute; however, case law might be relevant.
Malpractice (a form of tort)	State	Case law	
Torts (including accidents)	State	Case law	
Wills, estate planning, probate	State	Statute	Many states have a separate probate code. And if a matter goes to court, there may be special probate court procedural rules.

library, where she will at least have access to a better array of legal research tools and more expert assistance.

The rest of this discussion assumes that you have decided to try to help someone with a legal reference question.

As part of your basic reference interview, it is a good practice to try to determine whether the library user is doing research for reasons other than her own personal legal interests (a school paper, basic curiosity, etc.) or whether she is handling her own legal affairs. In the case of the former, the user's question can be treated like any other reference question. In the latter case, all of the warnings from chapter 2 should be heeded.

It would be a good idea to familiarize yourself with any websites in your state that do provide access to forms or discussions on how to proceed with an action such as a divorce. Such sites are often hosted by legal services organizations or law school clinics. Most of these should be listed in the appendix to this book, but you may want to check for yourself. It is also a good idea to have handy access to the website of your local district court, along with the state court system site. This will provide access to court rules and, sometimes, to various forms.

Finally, you may want to refer users to some prominent national websites that provide information on various forms of actions. These are listed at the beginning of the appendix.

Primary legal resources, specifically constitutions, statutes, case law, and regulations, are now abundantly available online. Local primary sources may also be available in your collection (although you should be careful about how up-to-date any paper resources may be). The appendix can point you to websites that should have the primary law that you are looking for.

Although a user looking for a specific statute or case can often be helped with ease, many legal reference questions are actually much more complicated. A key point to remember about legal research is that there are few sources available that simply give a clear, complete answer to a legal question. Sources that do provide such an-

swers are most commonly the expensive, specialized materials that are found only in law offices or specialized law libraries. More often than not, the answer to a legal question must be assembled, piecemeal, by consulting legal sources.

Because of this, the most important part of the search process is preparation. Preparation usually involves listing individual questions to be answered, generating search terms, and selecting sources to be consulted. There are more aspects to a legal research question than you might think.

For example, a person involved in a court action will actually need to find and use two separate bodies of law: the substantive law of the action and the procedural law of the court involved. Take a person whose spouse has sued for divorce and who has decided to represent himself in the action. He will need to figure out the various options available to him under his state's divorce laws. These would have to do with questions of custody, property, debt division, name changes, and many other things. Entirely in addition, he will need to figure out the procedural rules of a divorce action in the court in which the action is taking place. This will include such things as filing an answer, engaging in a process called discovery, making requests of the court through various motions, setting a trial date, and much, much more.

Even those who are trying to do some nonlitigation legal task, such as drafting their own will or writing a contract, should not expect to find straightforward answers to their questions.

Often, the best the reference librarian can do, apart from suggesting that users consult with legal counsel, is to help them find sources that they can peruse on their own. Your state's statutes and case law, either online or on paper, can be useful for this.

Users will often need help understanding what exactly they need to find, and they may have trouble generating appropriate search terms. If you want to help users formulate the questions they need to answer about their situation, provided you do so without offering an opinion on it, you could use questions from the list below. The following items are categories of questions that can be used to generate search terms and search strategies:

Legal theory. The legal theory is the legal basis for the action. What is it? What is the law that makes this claim possible?

Parties and relationships. Who is involved in the case? What are their roles? What relationships, both formal and informal, do they have to each other and to the events in question?

Places and things. Where (and when) did the events happen? What objects were involved? These could be such things as vehicles, tools, ladders, products, and so forth.

Events. What events are relevant to the case?

Claims and defenses. What claims are being made in the case? What defenses are available? Are there possible counterclaims?

Relief sought. What does each party to the action want? What would be a good outcome? A satisfactory one? What is the worst possible outcome for each party?

CONCLUSION

This chapter has provided a lot of information about the legal system, legal citation, and how to approach legal reference questions. What is still missing is a more detailed understanding of the major forms of legal information. We will fill that out in the chapters that follow.

5

SECONDARY LEGAL RESOURCES

FOR LEGAL PRACTITIONERS, SECONDARY LEGAL RESOURCES are key research tools. Some lawyers use secondary materials almost exclusively, looking to primary sources only for final authority. There are a number of good reasons for this. While primary legal sources provide the final legal authority needed to make a case, they can be difficult to work with (as we shall see in later chapters) and often don't provide much context or explanation. Secondary sources step into that gap, providing fuller, more contextual information about the law.

This makes it sound like secondary sources are the ideal solution for non–law libraries. The problem is that the world of secondary legal resources is dominated by very technical, extremely expensive tools that are designed for the use of trained legal professionals. Such resources are not readily usable by those not trained in law, and they are rarely found outside of law offices and specialized law libraries. We will discuss such resources at the end of this chapter, but most of our time will be spent focusing on more general and affordable secondary resources that might be useful in a public or academic library.

SPECIFIC SECONDARY RESOURCES

In spite of the name, secondary legal resources are a very important set of resources for legal research. Indeed, standard legal research doctrine dictates that any legal research project should begin with secondary sources, which should be consulted before proceeding to primary resources.

As we discussed earlier in this book, secondary legal sources are so called because they are resources that talk about the law. Primary legal sources, on the other hand, *are* the law. Primary legal sources include statutes, cases, regulations, constitutions, ordinances, and so forth. Secondary sources include a wide range of publications, from specialized legal dictionaries and encyclopedias to legal treatises and journals to highly specialized research tools designed for expert and practitioner use.

Taken as a group, secondary legal resources are intended to provide general information about the law as well as an overview of legal topics. They also often provide analysis and synthesis, helping the user understand the interactions between different facets of the law and to devise tactical approaches to legal problems. Secondary legal sources are usually created and edited by legal experts, who can provide editorial and scholarly analysis along with criticism and advice. For practitioners, this makes secondary sources very useful indeed.

For people not trained in law, there are some secondary legal resources that can be useful. Others require a large amount of legal knowledge and training to be used successfully and can overwhelm unprepared users with technical details and complex terminology. The most common secondary legal sources, and the most easily understood and used, are specialized versions of reference tools that we all use every day. Here I am referring primarily to legal dictionaries, encyclopedias, journals, and treatises. Let's talk a bit about each of them in turn.

Legal Dictionaries

If there is one legal source that a library of almost any size could benefit from owning, it is a law dictionary. Legal terminology can be confounding and complex, and for the layperson, the danger of not understanding or misunderstanding legal terms is high. This is because the language of the law is a combination of technical terms, terms derived from other languages, and ordinary English words used in unique ways (see text box). Since a good law dictionary can be had for well under $100, having a legal dictionary in the library is highly recommended.

There are a number of legal dictionaries on the market, and all are good. An extensive review of the competing dictionaries is beyond our scope. That said, by far the most popular is *Black's Law Dictionary*, published by West Publishing, a division of Thomson Reuters. *Black's*, first published in 1891, is still the most widely used. As of this writing it is in its ninth edition, edited by the estimable Bryan Garner.

Legal Encyclopedias

The next most common secondary source in law libraries is the legal encyclopedia. Legal encyclopedias are very similar to general encyclopedias, except that they restrict themselves to legal topics. These are very useful sets that provide a broad overview of legal topics, with easy access and plenty of references to other sources. The two most prominent national legal encyclopedias are *Corpus Juris Secundum* (referred to as *CJS*) and *American Jurisprudence*, second edition (referred to as *Am. Jur.*). Both are published by West, and each set is priced at about $10,000. In addition to the initial purchase price, yearly updates are necessary, constituting an added annual expense. These are useful resources even for a lay audience, but the expense is probably prohibitive for most non–law libraries.

Treatises

Legal treatises are designed to provide a fairly in-depth look at a broad legal topic. As such, treatises usually provide a good reference source for basic legal information on a particular area of law. As legal sources go, treatises are relatively affordable, priced in the same range as other professional texts. However, their specialization generally makes them less useful and therefore less cost-effective for most non–law libraries.

Treatises are published by a variety of legal publishers and are available on any imaginable legal topic. Most treatises are single-volume works, but works of two or three volumes are

THE LANGUAGE OF THE LAW

Legal terms are highly technical, and they are often confused with everyday language. Here are some examples of technical phrases and foreign terms, plus some unique uses of everyday words that are commonly found in legal documents. (All definitions are from *Black's Law Dictionary*, 9th ed.)

Technical Language

PROXIMATE CAUSE: A cause that is legally sufficient to result in liability; an act or omission that is considered in law to result in a consequence, so that liability can be imposed on the actor.

RULE AGAINST PERPETUITIES: The common-law rule prohibiting a grant of an estate unless the interest must vest, if at all, no later than twenty-one years (plus a period of gestation to cover a posthumous birth) after the death of some person alive when the interest was created.

Foreign Terms

RES IPSA LOQUITUR [Latin, "the thing speaks for itself"]: The doctrine providing that, in some circumstances, the mere fact of an accident's occurrence raises an inference of negligence that establishes a prima facie case.

ESCHEAT [Law French]: Reversion of property (especially real property) to the state upon the death of an owner who has neither a will nor any legal heirs.

VOIR DIRE [Law French, "to speak the truth"]: A preliminary examination of a prospective juror by a judge or lawyer to decide whether the prospect is qualified and suitable to serve on a jury.

Common English Terms with Very Technical Legal Meanings

CONSIDERATION: Something (such as an act, a forbearance, or a return promise) bargained for and received by a promisor from a promisee; that which motivates a person to do something, esp. to engage in a legal act. Consideration, or a substitute such as promissory estoppel, is necessary for an agreement to be enforceable.

BASIS: The value assigned to a taxpayer's investment in property and used primarily for computing gain or loss from a transfer of the property.

REMAINDER: A future interest arising in a third person—that is, someone other than the estate's creator, its initial holder, or the heirs of either—who is intended to take after the natural termination of the preceding estate.

---

not uncommon. Like all legal materials, treatises are subject to regular updating. This means new editions are fairly frequent. Alternatively, some publishers will issue a yearly supplement, called a pocket part, that is intended to be slipped into a pocket bound into the back cover of the book. Either way, keeping a treatise up to date generally involves an ongoing expense for the library.

Legal Periodicals

Like all disciplines, and all professions, law has both a broad group of scholarly journals and a variety of professional journals and magazines. It is worthwhile to understand what is out there, but both the availability and the usefulness of these journals for the casual researcher is probably limited.

Scholarly legal journals do have one interesting twist. Most academic disciplines use peer-reviewed journals as the hallmark place to publish new research. These journals are often published by learned societies or private publishers and use the peer-review process to test proposed articles for rigor and soundness. Law has almost no peer-reviewed journals in this sense. Instead, scholarly legal journals, referred to generically as law reviews, are published by law schools and edited entirely by students. Though this may be a surprising state of affairs, there is no real concern about the rigor or soundness of legal scholarship. This is partly because the competition to publish in law reviews is very intense, ensuring that the journals have plenty of high-quality research to choose from.

Every accredited law school in America publishes at least one law review. These journals are almost always quarterly and devoted solely to legal scholarship. Most law reviews are general in nature, meaning they will publish scholarly articles on any legal topic, and most issues of a journal will contain articles on a wide variety of topics. Many law schools have more than one journal, and the additional journals are often subject specific. For instance, at the University of Illinois College of Law, where I work, the law school publishes six journals. There is a general law review, the *University of Illinois Law Review*, and five specialized journals: the *Elder Law Journal*; the *Journal of Law, Technology, and Policy*; *Comparative Labor Law & Policy Journal*; the *Illinois Business Law Journal*; and the *Illinois Law Update*. Many law schools publish a similar array of journals.

Some professional legal organizations also publish scholarly journals. These journals are generally restricted in topic to the particular area of legal interest of the professional organization.

These journals sometimes bridge the gap between purely scholarly research and more practice-oriented materials.

Most of America's national and state bar associations publish a monthly magazine referred to generically as a bar journal. Special interest sections of those bar associations and even local bar groups sometimes have journals as well. These publications tend to be very practice oriented, combining news about the profession and the organization with practice-oriented articles about changes in the law and other legal topics.

Professional Secondary Resources

The elephant in the room in our discussion of secondary resources is a large group of such materials that might be referred to as professional secondary resources. These materials have traditionally been referred to as loose-leafs because of the method commonly used to bind them. Since many of these sources have migrated online, that term seems less and less appropriate.

Professional secondary materials are designed for use by legal practitioners. They offer information relating to an area of legal practice and provide a variety of information, including background material, tactical and strategic considerations, practice tips, and much more, along with extensive citations to relevant primary authority. In areas where there are many forms of primary authority to be found and considered, professional legal materials will provide synthesis and analysis of the materials in a way that is a great help to practitioners.

In paper form, such secondary legal resources are often published as huge sets of binders, often in twenty or more volumes. They generally contain tens of thousands of pages and offer a variety of access points and finding aids. The loose-leaf binding allows for regular updates of the material with new pages added on a regular basis to be interfiled in the existing set (see text box).

Increasingly, however, these tools are offered as online resources. When properly implemented, this yields such advantages as the ability to offer

OTHER ALTERNATIVES FOR SECONDARY LEGAL INFORMATION

With many of the tools used by legal professionals out of reach for most libraries because of cost, it might be useful to think creatively about how you can find basic secondary information for your users. While not perfect, here are some suggestions that might help:

ONLINE SELF-HELP LEGAL CENTERS. Self-help legal centers are becoming increasingly common on the web. These are websites set up by legal services offices, court systems, and law school legal clinics that provide basic legal information about their jurisdiction. Some have forms, while others provide step-by-step directions for handling particular matters such as divorce and custody actions. You should check to see if any local or state organization in your vicinity has set up such a center.

ON-SITE SELF-HELP LEGAL CENTERS. These are self-help centers that are usually set up by local courts to assist people who are representing themselves. While they require users to go to the courthouse to use them, they often have a variety of high-quality resources, and often paper forms. Sometimes there will be a volunteer attorney on duty to provide basic advice. In towns where there is a law school, the center may be staffed by law students.

LAW LIBRARIES. If there is a law library that is open to the public near you, you should feel free to refer users there. Academic law libraries and large public law libraries will have all the resources a user can desire, along with trained staff. Keep in mind, though, that some law libraries restrict who can use the library, or restrict how much staff assistance they will provide. Academic and large public law libraries are usually only to be found in fairly large metropolitan areas, but there may be a law library in your vicinity that you have never heard about. In many states, each county has a law library, or each courthouse has a small library collection. These collections are often not staffed by a professional librarian, so assistance may be lacking. However, they may have some useful tools, like treatises and legal encyclopedias, that are at least accessible to your users. You will have to check with your local courthouse to see if such a collection exists and, if so, how one can use it.

ONLINE RESOURCES. The appendix to this book starts out with some very good general legal information sites that are available online. More and more of this type of information is becoming available all the time. See the appendix for details. One particular site worth mentioning here is Nolo.com. Nolo is a commercial publisher of self-help legal books. In addition to showcasing their products, their website provides free legal information that is of very high quality. The biggest drawback to the site, and to the Nolo books, is that they generally are not state specific. On the other hand, the information they do provide is very well done. You may even wish to assess some of their books for your own collection. The books are priced for consumers, in spite of their generally high quality. And no, I have no relationship, business or otherwise, with Nolo.

access for more than one user at a time, as well as full-text searching and other online advantages. Obviously, online reference tools also offer cost advantages in publishing and distribution.

It would not be an exaggeration to say that, in some areas of legal practice, professional secondary sources are the resource most used by attorneys and sometimes the only resource they use. As such, these are very valuable tools for the practice of law.

As far as non–law libraries are concerned, there are two drawbacks to professional legal materials that make them generally inadvisable purchases. The first is obviously the cost. Loose-leafs and their online equivalents are priced for the professional market and generally cost thousands of dollars a year for a single set. Furthermore, the topics these sets cover are fairly narrow, meaning their cost only begins to make sense if there is a high volume of usage in that particular topic.

Perhaps an even more formidable obstacle is that professional secondary materials are simply not designed for casual use. They assume that users have extensive legal knowledge about the topic they are researching before they consult the set. It is assumed that technical terms will need no explanation and that basic legal concepts are understood. There is no introductory material or explanation of the basics that would bring along someone with no knowledge of the subject. Because of this, casual library users will often find professional secondary materials absolutely opaque as a source of information.

OTHER SECONDARY RESOURCES

Before we leave this discussion of secondary materials, we should look briefly at some common secondary legal tools that you will most likely not have in your library but which are commonly used in law libraries and therefore often referenced in other legal works. We will look first at two tools, ALR and restatements, and then take a look at the burgeoning online world created by the two major online legal research tools, Lexis and Westlaw.

ALR and Restatements

One of the great challenges in legal research has always been collecting useful, comprehensive information about a given point of law. Gathering such information requires finding all of the relevant points of precedent and analyzing and

LOOSE-LEAF EXAMPLE:
THE *STANDARD FEDERAL TAX REPORTER*

Federal income tax law is one of the most complex legal topics in U.S. law. Primary authority on taxation can come from the tax code itself, which is part of the *United States Code,* as well as from regulations drafted by the Internal Revenue Service; court decisions by various courts, including specialized tax courts; the rulings of administrative tribunals within the IRS; and IRS internal rules, guidelines, and opinions. This means that both tax planning and tax disputes require that the practitioner have access to, and master, an incredible maze of information.

The legal publisher Commerce Clearing House (CCH) publishes the *Standard Federal Tax Reporter* as an all-inclusive research solution for federal tax law. In paper it is a 25-volume loose-leaf set that must be purchased annually. It comes with weekly updates, which are sent by mail and need to be interfiled in the set. The annual purchase price is about $2,000.00.

The *Standard Federal Tax Reporter* is organized around the provisions of the U.S. tax code. For each code section it provides editorial analysis, code language, and references to relevant regulations, court decisions, and administrative materials. The idea is that practitioners can find the relevant section of the tax code for the their research question and then find along with it all of the materials they need to conduct a proper analysis.

arranging them so that they can be understood by the reader.

American Law Reports, referred to as ALR, began its life as a reporter of U.S. Supreme Court decisions. It originally included the text of major decisions, followed by a report, called an annotation, that gave an extensive analysis of the law of the particular point or subject of the reported

AN EXAMPLE OF RESTATEMENTS IN ACTION: INVASION OF PRIVACY IN MINNESOTA

The various restatements have been used by courts as a rationale to change and evolve the common law in their jurisdiction. The case of *Lake v. Wal-Mart Stores, Inc.*, 582 N.W.2d 231 (Minn. 1998), is one such instance.

In the *Lake* case, two young women from Detroit Lakes, Minnesota, took a vacation to Mexico and, while there, took pictures. On their return home, they took five rolls of film from their vacation to the local Wal-Mart store for processing. When they picked up the photos, they were informed that several of the pictures were not printed because they violated store policy.

At the time, it was the policy of Wal-Mart stores not to print photos that involved nudity. One of the photos in particular, of the two young women together in the shower, violated this policy. While the women were told the photos "were not printed," in fact a copy of the photo had been printed and retained by a Wal-Mart employee. A few weeks later, the two young women began to hear rumors in their small town about the photos, and questions were raised about their activities.

The women sued Wal-Mart for the tort of invasion of privacy. This tort existed as a cause of action in many jurisdictions, but it had never been adopted as common law in Minnesota. (At the time, Minnesota, North Dakota, and Wyoming were the only states that had not adopted invasion of privacy as part of their common law.) At trial, the defense requested dismissal of the case because there was no tort of invasion of privacy in Minnesota. The trial court agreed and dismissed the case. On appeal, the Minnesota Court of Appeals sided with the trial court and upheld the dismissal. The case was then appealed to the Minnesota Supreme Court.

In its decision, the Minnesota Supreme Court reversed the trial and appellate courts and, in the process, adopted invasion of privacy as a tort, and as part of the common law, in Minnesota. In doing so, it explicitly cited the Restatement of Torts. Here is part of what the court said:

> Whether Minnesota should recognize any or all of the invasion of privacy causes of action is a question of first impression in Minnesota. The Restatement (Second) of Torts outlines the four causes of action that comprise the tort generally referred to as invasion of privacy.
>
> . . . Today we join the majority of jurisdictions and recognize the tort of invasion of privacy. The right to privacy is an integral part of our humanity; one has a public persona, exposed and active, and a private persona, guarded and preserved. The heart of our liberty is choosing which parts of our lives shall become public and which parts we shall hold close.

As you can see from this example, the restatements can be a powerful tool used to understand and often change the common law.

case. Gradually, these annotations became the tail that wags the ALR dog. The reporting of cases became vestigial and then was dropped entirely, but the annotations were prized for their close and comprehensive analysis of very specific points of law. Today, ALR exists as over 15,000 of these annotations. Each annotation is very specific in the topic it covers and lists almost all relevant precedent in every jurisdiction. While finding the law on a very specific legal topic can be a daunting task, when an ALR annotation is available it can simplify things immensely. As such, ALR is a popular tool with attorneys.

Restatements are a research tool unique to law, because they were created to solve an information problem also unique to law. We have already had some discussion about the concepts of common law and precedent. One of the functional problems created by having a body of law that consists of case law is that it is very hard to find and organize precedent. Because of that, legal publishers have evolved various methods and tools to do so. This problem is exacerbated by the fact that each of the fifty states has a body of common law on the same topics, but the gist of that law can vary from jurisdiction to jurisdiction. As an example, all fifty states have common law that covers the tort of invasion of privacy, but the details of that law vary from state to state. As a result, it can be very hard to get a sense of what the most common legal position is on a given topic across the country.

Restatements are an attempt to solve this problem. Restatements are written by a group of legal experts called together by the American Law Institute, a professional society of eminent legal scholars, practitioners, and judges. In creating a restatement on a given legal topic, the group of experts distills what is the most common legal position on a given topic from jurisdictions across the country and expresses that distillation as a rule. This rule, along with relevant commentary, is grouped with all other distilled rules for that topic into a restatement. Thus the tool gets its name from the fact that it restates the law. There are restatements on all major common-law topics, including torts, contracts, agency, and so forth. Historically, restatements have been most useful to judges who are considering adopting a new common-law precedent for their jurisdiction, and to lawyers who are arguing for or against such a change. See text box on p. 49.

A Bit about Lexis, Westlaw, and Their Competitors

Westlaw and Lexis are the two largest and most comprehensive online legal databases for legal professionals. Not surprisingly, they are owned by the two biggest legal publishers, respectively. Westlaw is owned by Thomson Reuters, and LexisNexis by Reed Elsevier. It is hard to state how large and comprehensive these databases are. They compete closely, and so, except for proprietary material and systems, they have very similar content.

Both Lexis and Westlaw contain all of the primary law from all American and many foreign jurisdictions. They have every appellate case, every statute, and every regulation from every American jurisdiction. In addition to all this primary law, each service has finding and organizing tools for legal information, as well as online versions of all of the secondary legal resources published by that publisher. Most large law firms, and indeed most lawyers in smaller practices as well, arrange to have a subscription to either Westlaw or Lexis. Such subscriptions are generally very expensive—a large firm will pay several million dollars a year for access—but the sophisticated research tools and broad access they provide make them cost-effective.

One of the key attributes of Lexis and Westlaw are their extremely capable and flexible searching options. In addition to highly developed full-text searching options, both services offer concept-based searches (also known as natural-language searching), as well as online versions of previously print-based research tools like citators and digests.

Westlaw and Lexis started life as dedicated online services in the days before the widespread use of the Internet or the World Wide Web. Users were given a terminal, which was connected via a dedicated phone line to the service's mainframe. As desktop computers and office networks evolved, the services began to distribute software that allowed personal computers to interface with them directly. Finally, in the mid to late 1990s, both services migrated to the web, becoming accessible to anyone who had a web browser and an account. In addition, both services have expanded well beyond simple legal information. They now offer news databases as well as business research resources and much more.

In the process, both services have developed or purchased allied websites that provide services for other markets. These markets include lawyers who do not buy regular subscriptions, colleges and universities, and in some cases, access by the general public.

Reed Elsevier has developed a number of such products. The most prominent of these is LexisNexis Academic, which provides the academic market access to parts of the Lexis and

LIBRARY ACCESS TO WESTLAW
OR LEXIS WITHOUT A SUBSCRIPTION

If you have a steady stream of legal questions at your reference desk, there may be a time when access to Westlaw or Lexis would be the best way to answer a user's question. While having a subscription to one of the services in the library will probably not be cost-effective, there may be ways that you can get some access on a case-by-case basis.

Here are some possibilities, provided you know that some or all of these may not be workable for your library. All of these solutions revolve around the idea that there might be a nearby institution that does have access and could help you on an occasional basis.

Please note, however, that any entity with a subscription to one of these services is bound by the terms of its subscription, which could very well preclude it from providing information from the service to another library. In such a case, you will be out of luck. Alternatively, the subscribing institution may be able to provide information, but on the condition that you reimburse the costs incurred in fulfilling your request.

For these reasons, exploring what is available in advance is highly recommended. Possible arrangements include having the institution provide the information your user is seeking or setting up a referral to send the user to that institution.

LAW LIBRARIES. You should explore what services the law libraries in your area, and state, can offer, particularly in terms of access to Westlaw or Lexis. These would include any academic law library in your state, your state or court law libraries, and any county or city law libraries in your area. Private law libraries or law firms would almost certainly not be able to provide such assistance.

COURTHOUSES. Even if your local courthouse does not have a formal law library, it might still be able to provide occasional access to Westlaw or Lexis. Contact your local court administrator or clerk of court to inquire.

LEXISNEXIS ACADEMIC. You should also check to see if any college or university in your area, particularly publicly funded institutions, have access to the LexisNexis Academic database. As mentioned in the text, this product provides access to case law, statutes, and regulations, along with the Shepard's citator tool. A large public library might also subscribe to this service.

Nexis databases, including legal and business information. One the legal side, it provides access to case law, federal and state statutes, and a limited version of the Shepard's citator tool (which is explained in the chapter on case law). Many colleges and universities have found this to be a cost-effective and useful product.

Both Thomson and Reed Elsevier have moved some free information onto the web as well. The sites they have created have tended to be aimed at both legal practitioners and the general public. Westlaw purchased FindLaw (www.findlaw.com), which had started out as a general legal directory. Westlaw has enhanced FindLaw in several ways, including adding some basic encyclopedia-style legal information, but the site does not provide access to case law or other primary law. It does, however, provide access to an interesting array of legal forms.

Lexis developed a website called LexisOne that offered some free case law and other legal materials. For a while the site offered credit card access to more advanced Lexis features, but that option has since been rescinded. Recently the site has been rechristened as LexisNexis Communities Portal (www.lexisnexis.com/community/portal) and includes a number of new features.

Westlaw and Lexis have a formidable advantage in the online legal research market because they not only possess every American case, statute, and regulation in electronic form, but they also have rich and highly developed finding and analysis tools. Remember, however, that the basic primary law that forms the heart of these databases is information that is in the public domain. Because of this, online competitors have sprung up over the last ten years or so, hoping to compete with Lexis and Westlaw by offering a much cheaper research product, albeit without the bells and whistles (mainly, the sophisticated finding and analysis tools) that the big two offer. A thorough review of these competitors is beyond our scope; however, they all offer a complete run of nationwide case law, along with statutes and, usually, regulations. Here is a brief list of the most popular of these competitors:

LoislawConnect: http://estore.loislaw.com
Bloomberg Law: http://about.bloomberglaw.com
Fastcase: www.fastcase.com
Casemaker: www.casemaker.us
VersusLaw: www.versuslaw.com

6

STATUTES AND CONSTITUTIONS

WHEN MOST PEOPLE THINK OF LAW THEY THINK OF STATUTES. These are the laws that are drafted by our elected legislators and are intended to bring order to society. As we have seen, the world of American law is far more complex than that, but statutes are obviously a very important source of law in our society, and being able to find a statute for a library user is a skill most reference librarians should master.

Before we start discussing statutes themselves, I'd like to take a moment to discuss a very specific form of legislative law—constitutions. Constitutions are seminal legislative documents that set up the form of government and enumerate its powers and the rights of citizens. In America constitutions are drafted and adopted by legislatures, sometimes in conjunction with a constitutional convention or a referendum, both of which can involve private citizens. As such they are a form of legislation, albeit perhaps best described as super-legislation. In any event, the federal government and all fifty states have a constitution, and they are important sources of law. Let's start with a look at the U.S. Constitution.

The U.S. Constitution is the oldest written constitution still in force in the world, and it remains a vital document central to our American democracy. The U.S. Constitution sets up our three-part federal government and enumerates its powers and duties. The Constitution sets up the presidency and the executive branch, along with certain administration officials such as the attorney general. It also requires a court system for federal matters with district courts in each state and a supreme court. But, before it does any of that, it sets up a congress with a house of representatives and senate.

Broadly speaking, the Constitution gives the Congress the power to

- levy taxes;
- raise an army and navy, and declare war;

- regulate foreign and interstate commerce;
- conduct foreign relations;
- make laws relating to immigration, bankruptcy, and intellectual property (copyright and patents);
- establish a post office; and
- preside over the District of Columbia.

A key part of our federal system is that, while state law governs much of our lives, there are certain areas where federal law always prevails. This is called federal supremacy, or federal preemption, and it is most commonly found in two forms. The first is that certain areas of life are governed solely by federal law. This includes things you would expect, like foreign trade and diplomacy, but also such areas as bankruptcy, copyright, and patents. This is important to understand for legal research because, as an example, a library user looking for information on copyright law will be researching federal law, not state law.

The second area where federal supremacy is commonly found is in individual rights. The U.S. Constitution has established certain basic rights that are enjoyed by every citizen, and neither Congress nor any state can deny or limit those rights. Most of these rights are contained in the first ten amendments to the Constitution and include freedom of speech, freedom of religion, freedom of association, the right to trial by jury, and so forth. Although there can be plenty of arguing over the details, by being listed in the Constitution these rights cannot be limited or denied by any government.

State constitutions play the same role, only at the state level. Each state has a constitution, which sets up the form of government, defines

STATE VERSUS FEDERAL: THE CONSTITUTIONALITY OF SAME-SEX MARRIAGE

One of the most salient issues that illustrates the differences between state and federal constitutions is that of marriage equality. The U.S. Constitution does not explicitly address the issue of sexual orientation or same-sex marriage, nor, as of the time of this writing, has it been interpreted as doing so by the Supreme Court. As a result, the U.S. Constitution can be considered to be silent on the issue. (Congress did pass a law, the Defense of Marriage Act of 1996, that defines marriage as being between one man and one woman, but this is legislation and does not rise to the level of constitutional authority. DOMA has since been invalidated by the Supreme Court.)

Meanwhile, several state constitutions have been interpreted or amended in recent years to provide a right for citizens to enter into same-sex marriages, while a number of other state constitutions include specific language that precludes such marriages. Absent a federal constitutional mandate on the issue, states are free to take either stance, meaning that same-sex marriages are currently valid in some states and not others. Should the U.S. Constitution ever address the issue of same-sex marriage, either through amendment or by being interpreted as doing so by the Supreme Court, then state constitutional provisions about same-sex marriages could become void if they contradict the U.S. Constitution.

In other words, if the Supreme Court were to declare that same-sex marriage is a right protected by the U.S. Constitution, or if the Constitution were amended to include this right, then any state's constitutional ban on such marriages would be voided. On the other hand, if the Supreme Court were to interpret the Constitution as not protecting such a right, then state constitutional provisions banning same-sex marriage would remain constitutional, but so would state constitutional provisions that grant same-sex marriage rights. This is because state constitutions can grant personal rights in excess of those in the U.S. Constitution.

the powers of the government, and lists the rights of citizens. The only restriction on a state constitution is that it cannot contradict any part of the U.S. Constitution. This means that it cannot give the state government a power or role that is limited to the federal government, nor can it restrict individual rights or liberties that are protected at the federal level. It can, however, give greater rights than are currently available from the federal constitution.

As an example, a state constitution could not contain a provision that allowed employers to discriminate on the basis of race in employment, because the U.S. Constitution protects citizens from that kind of discrimination, and the state constitution cannot contradict it. On the other hand, the state constitution could extend protection from employment discrimination in ways not covered by the U.S. Constitution—for example, by protecting sexual orientation or obesity—and citizens of that state would have greater protections than they would in other states or under the federal constitution alone.

While the various state constitutions may vary in the rights they protect, they all set up basically the same form of government, and that form matches the form of the federal government. This means that at the federal level, and in each of the fifty states, you will find three branches of government, with a legislature, a judiciary, and an executive. For legal research and library reference purposes, this simplifies things considerably. Even if you've never done legal research involving a given state before, you can take comfort that the law you seek was produced and published in pretty much the same way that it was in your state.

LEGISLATURES AND LEGISLATION

The legislative branch of government is the one most people think of when they think about how the government makes law. This makes sense, because the creation of law is the primary function of the legislature. Legislatures consist of elected representatives, whose job it is to create legislation that will serve the needs of society. At the federal level, and in forty-nine of the fifty states, the legislature consists of two chambers: a senate and a house of representatives. The senate is the smaller body, whose members represent a larger geographic area of the state or, at the federal level, the entire state. The house of representatives has more members, and representatives come from smaller districts. The exception to the two-chamber model, as we saw in chapter 4, is Nebraska, which has a unicameral, or single chamber, legislature.

Since it is the job of the legislature to consider what laws are needed and then craft those laws, we can refer to legislation as prospective in nature. Legislators must restrict their lawmaking to areas of state or federal interest, depending on the legislature, and cannot enact legislation that violates the state or federal constitution. Apart from those restrictions, legislatures have a free hand to craft whatever laws they feel will serve society. This is an enormous power, and it is the reason that representatives must stand for reelection frequently. Shorter terms give the people more frequent opportunities to approve or reject a representative's activities.

The point of having a legislature is that we need someone to anticipate the need for laws in our society and to go about creating those laws in a deliberative and rational fashion. Or that's the idea anyway. As an example, we can anticipate that, over time, certain crimes will occur, like robbery. It is better for society that we have our representatives think about this in advance and create laws that make robbery a crime and specify the appropriate punishment. This puts everyone on notice that robbery is indeed a crime and that is has specific consequences, which will hopefully deter a certain amount of such criminality. When robbery does occur, the law provides a rational way for dealing with it. Legislation related to such areas as commercial affairs, divorce, driving, employment, and many other facets of day-to-day life anticipates similar concerns.

COULD YOUR STATE LEGISLATURE MAKE COFFEE ILLEGAL?

What if a member of your state legislature proposed a bill to make coffee illegal in your state? Can they do that? The short answer is yes. The two main restrictions on the legislative power are that legislation cannot violate the constitution, and it must affect matters within the legislature's sphere of interest. At the state level, this sphere of interest is basically anything not preempted by the federal constitution, or by the state's own constitution.

In the case of coffee, there is no constitutional right involved, and coffee is not a specific matter of federal interest, so your state legislature could indeed make coffee illegal in your state. However, those representatives who voted to make coffee illegal would, within a short time, face reelection. One assumes that their constituents, who without their morning coffee would probably be in an ugly mood, would send them packing and elect someone who would repeal the law. The relatively short terms of representatives are an important check on legislative power.

LEGISLATION, STATUTES, AND CODES

Legislatures create law in the form of legislation. An individual law passed by a legislature is often referred to as an act or a statute. Because legislators are attempting to create a coherent body of law, legislation can be organized topically. This is done through something called a code. Because legislation can change over time, published legislation is time sensitive and must be updated to assure accuracy. Learning to work with codes is the key to understanding how to do research in statutes.

To understand how this works, let's take a closer look at the elements of legislation. The legislative process creates three different types of legal materials:

1. Bills and legislative history, which document the legislature's activity as it considers and passes a law.
2. Session law, which is the initial form of the law after it is passed by the legislature and signed by the executive. It looks just like the bill that was passed, only now it is law.
3. A code, which is a compilation of laws of general effect, currently in force, and arranged by topic.

Let's look at each of these elements separately.

Bills and Legislative History

You probably remember the legislative process from your junior high civics class. If not, there are some good explanations of the process available online from the U.S. House of Representatives at www.house.gov/content/learn/legislative_process. The salient points for our purposes are that bills are introduced into the legislature by members and then considered by a committee. If they are approved by the committee, they are considered again and debated by the originating chamber. If they are passed by that chamber they go to the other chamber, where the entire process repeats itself. If a bill is passed by both chambers, it is sent to the president or governor. If it is signed, it becomes law. Obviously there are many exceptions and details I'm leaving out here, but this is enough for our purposes.

Legislative history consists of draft forms of bills, reports from legislative committees, transcripts of witness testimony before legislative committees, transcripts of floor debates about bills, and so forth. Though a full exploration of legislative history research is beyond the scope of this book, it is important to understand that because legislative history documents only the legislative process, it consists entirely of material that related to the bill before it became law. Such materials can provide information about the legislature's intent when drafting a law, but they are not part of the law itself.

Session Law

Session law consists of the publication of laws presented just as they were passed by the legislature. Its language will be identical to the bills from which it sprang. Session law is published in a set of books (and now, online). In most states and the federal government, an individual session law is given a number. This number is a combination of the number of the legislature and the sequential number of the law as it was passed. For example, a federal session law with the identifier PL110-233 would be the 233rd law that was passed during the session of the 110th Congress. The numbering has nothing to do with the topic of the law, the number of the original bill, or anything else.

When published in book form, session laws are arranged by the sequential order of their passage, as indicated by the session law number. Session law is published in a set of books compiled during each legislative session. At the federal level, this set of books is called the *Statutes at Large*. At the state level the name of the session law set varies but is commonly called the *Laws of X*, where *X* is the name of the state.

Codes

Session law is very important because it is the form of the law that was considered and debated by the legislature and signed by the executive. However, people who want to know what the law says very rarely use session law. This is because the nature of session law is that its language is technical and often fragmented. Also, once a law is enacted, it is often amended by other laws or even repealed later in time. When this happens,

WHAT IS A PRIVATE LAW?

Private laws are pieces of legislation enacted by a congress that affect only one or a few individuals, or a single entity. At the federal level, private laws include laws that would:

Grant citizenship to a given individual, often in recognition of service to this country, as in the armed forces in wartime.

Provide individual veteran's benefits or award medals and decorations.

Name federal facilities. As an example, 144 of the 453 pieces of legislation that became law in the 110th Congress designated the name of a post office or federal facility.

None of these laws are of the type that requires the public notice intended by placing them in the code.

there is nothing in the original publication of the law to indicate that it has been changed. This means that finding the current law in the session law set requires finding the original law and all of its subsequent amendments, and using them to piece together the current language of the law.

The solution to this dilemma is the third form of legislative material: the code. A code is a publication of all of the laws of general effect of a jurisdiction, currently in force, arranged by topic. That's sort of a loaded definition, and each part of it is important. Let's take a closer look.

Keep in mind the following basic, and important, characteristics of a code:

- Codes arrange the law by topic, with amendments and changes presented in context.
- Because of this, codes are time sensitive and subject to change. It is essential that code

language be current. This is particularly an issue for printed codes.

■ Codes are republished on a regular schedule but are usually also updated in the interim.

Each of the fifty states and the federal government have an official code. To repeat, the code publishes the laws of general effect and currently in force, arranged by topic. Laws of general effect, or public laws, are the ones that people need to be aware of. Most laws passed by a legislature would fit this definition. The exceptions include private laws and some laws that change each year and relate to administering the government, such as the budget. Keep in mind that all laws passed by a legislature are included in the session law publication. However, only laws of general effect are then published in the code.

The code is thus a functional document that tells us what the law is now. It does so by containing only those laws currently in force, and by arranging the laws by topic. This means that regardless of when a law was passed, or how often it has been amended, all you will see in the code is the current language. This, in turn, makes the code a time-sensitive document that must be revised often.

Official codes are published by the government and are revised regularly. At the state level, codes are usually republished every two years. At the federal level, the code is revised every six years. In either case, the government will usually issue an annual supplement in years when the code is not due to be republished.

Annotated codes are unofficial versions of the state or federal code that are published by private publishers. For a variety of reasons, official codes are not as useful as they could be for many purposes, and private publishers have stepped in to offer more user-friendly products. These unofficial codes provide value in two main ways. First they publish new language on a timelier basis, in the form of updates. Second, they provide additional material and information that the official codes do not, in the form of annotations.

As we have seen, official codes usually get an annual supplement. This update generally arrives as a separate volume that updates the entire code. Users of a code should be made aware of these supplements, if they exist, and should consult them to see if the language of the code section they are reading has been changed.

In addition to providing better updating than official codes, commercially published annotated codes provide additional material as part of the publication, some of it very important. Remember that in America the courts have the power to interpret legislation, and the court cases that do so in effect become part of the legislation, in that they affect how the law is understood or enforced. An official code will give no indication as to whether a law has been interpreted by an appellate decision. Annotated codes attempt to solve that problem.

The annotations provided by an annotated code provide a number of important things. Most importantly, each section of an annotated code is followed by paragraph-length descriptions of appellate court decisions, if any, that have interpreted that code section. This allows a reader to conveniently check for any case law that needs to be taken into consideration with the code section in question. In addition, annotative material can include the following:

■ The history of a particular code section (that is, a list of amendments and a description of the changes these made to the code section).

■ References to important secondary materials that address the code section. This can include scholarly resources such as law review articles as well as secondary resources such as legal encyclopedias and practice guides.

By not only providing all these supplementary materials but also providing more timely updates, annotated codes have become the tool of choice for lawyers in practice. Such tools are expensive, however, and may not be in the budget for non–law libraries. In that case, an official code will give users the text of the current law, but librarians should be aware that there may be court decisions not listed in the official code that

HOW LEGISLATION IS PUBLISHED

At both the federal and state level, legislation is published in two forms: as session law and as a code. Codes, in turn, are published in either unannotated or annotated form. Let's look at the publication of federal legislation.

Session Law

Federal session law is published in a set called the *Statutes at Large*. It contains all public and
private laws passed during a session of Congress, along with joint resolutions and other
materials. It is an official publication of the federal government.

West Publishing also publishes federal session law in a set called the *United States Code
Congressional and Administrative News,* commonly referred to as *USCCAN* (pronounced
"use-can"). It contains the same materials as *Statutes at Large* but also includes selected
legislative history documents.

Codes

The *United States Code* is the official code for the U.S. government. It is a publication of the federal government and is republished every six years, with annual supplements in intervening
years. It is unannotated, meaning it does not contain materials other than code language.

The *United States Code Annotated (USCA)* is published by West. It is an annotated version
of the *U.S. Code*, meaning that in addition to the language of the code itself, it contains
references to court decisions that have interpreted code sections as well other secondary
materials that can help interpret a code section. The *USCA* is never republished, but it is
updated on a regular basis. It is available both in book form and online, on the Westlaw legal
research system.

The *United States Code Service (USCS)* is published by LexisNexis. It is very similar to the *USCA*
and competes directly with it. Like the *USCA*, it is an annotated version of the *U.S. Code*,
containing references to court decisions that have interpreted code sections as well other
secondary materials. Also like the *USCA,*the *USCS* is updated on a regular basis rather than
being republished. It is available both in book form and online, on the Lexis legal research
system.

State codes follow a similar pattern. Each state has a publication of its session law. (Although state session law is available on both Lexis and Westlaw and is distributed in paper form as part of a state's annotated code, there is no privately published book version of any state's session law.) Each state also publishes an official code and has at least one annotated code published by a private legal publisher. As with the federal code, the official version of each state's code is republished regularly, usually every two years, and the annotated codes are updated regularly but not republished.

could affect how the law is interpreted and understood.

WORKING WITH PRINT CODES

Working with print codes requires some bibliographic acumen. Issues can arise for users with finding code sections, updating them, and finding previous code language.

There are various ways to find a given code section. Very commonly a user will have a code citation in hand. This can come from an official document, a news source, or some other legal publication. It is generally simple to find the citation in the code, so this approach is the easiest to work with. If a user does not have a code citation, other methods are available, particularly in an annotated code.

Both official and annotated codes will provide an index and table of contents. With codes, the index is a particularly powerful tool for finding a relevant code section. Because of the sometimes formal or even obscure language of the law, most codes provide indexes with good cross-referencing, allowing users to look up the term they think describes the section they are looking for and be referred to the term actually used in the code.

In addition, annotated codes, and sometimes official codes, provide other useful finding aids, usually in the form of tables. One such table is the popular names table. This allows users to start their search with the popular name of a law and be referred to the appropriate code section. At the federal level such laws as the Americans with Disabilities Act, the PATRIOT Act (actually the USA PATRIOT Act), or the Civil Rights Act are all examples of laws with popular names. The popular names table of an annotated statute will refer users to the actual code sections for such laws.

Other finding aids in annotated codes include session law tables, which refer users from the original session law citation to the appropriate code section, and references to previous code sections for codes that have been renumbered or rearranged at some point.

Instead of being republished on a regular schedule, an annotated code is updated by supplements provided on an annual or semiannual basis. In book form, supplements take the form of what are called pocket parts. Pocket parts are pamphlets that contain updating material that supplements the printed volume. A pocket part is about the same size as the book it is supplementing and has a stiff card stapled to its back. This card slips into a pocket sewn into the inside back cover of the book (thus the name). Reading a code section in an annotated code involves reading the relevant material in the main volume and then consulting the pocket part for any additional material that has been provided since the volume was printed. Pocket parts contain clear indications of how up to date they are, usually listing both a printing date and a legislative session or session law number through which they include material.

The publishers of annotated codes also provide other updating methods, although these services are unlikely to be found outside of a law library or law firm. One of these services is called a session law service, which will print and distribute pamphlets during the legislative session that contain the language of new laws. Session law updates are often distributed weekly or biweekly. Another updating method is to use a legal citator (discussed in chapter 7). Finally, a solution to all of these updating issues is to use an online code, as discussed below.

PREVIOUS CODE LANGUAGE

There are a variety of reasons why a library user might want to see a previous version of a code. One common reason is that the law has been changed since a legal event of some kind occurred. For instance, if a driver was arrested and charged with driving under the influence of alcohol, and the legal limit for presumed intoxication was changed in the intervening period between the arrest and the trial, the older version of the code would be required, because that was the law in effect at the time of the offense.

Finding previous code language is simplicity itself, if you have access to old versions of the code. However, not many libraries, apart from large law libraries, make a practice of retaining

ONLINE STATUTES—
THE GOOD, THE BAD, AND THE UGLY

Thanks to the Internet, statutes from all over the country are accessible as never before. In fact, all fifty states, the District of Columbia, and the federal government all provide free full-text access to their statutes online. That's the good part.

There are, however, two potential problems with these sites: currency and search capabilities. As we have seen in this chapter, it is essential that you have access to the most current version of the statutes. You might think that a government-run website, the horse's mouth as it were, would have only the most current statutes. Unfortunately, that might not be the case. An article in *AALL Spectrum* by Paul Hellyer called "Research at Your Own Risk" (February 2011, p. 18) pointed out that at that time only a third of government statute sites mentioned the currency of the statutes at all. Of those that did, many had vague statements that statutes are "updated annually" or that the statutes on the site may not include recent laws. He found only one state, Rhode Island, that updated its statute site daily; the others did so at varying intervals. In other words, it can be difficult or impossible to know whether a free online statute site includes all laws currently in effect. This situation is in flux, but it can be assumed that improvement will be slow.

The second problem with government statute sites involved search features. According to Hellyer, all of the states allowed full-text searching, but many had search engines with very limited capabilities—for instance, with the ability to search only for a given word or phrase and not multiple words. Others had very poor relevance ranking. Other basic access points were missing as well. Only sixteen sites had a retrieve-by-citation feature, similarly small numbers offered a browsable subject index, and only four had an online popular names table.

Perhaps most astonishing of all, Hellyer found that none of the government entities certified the authenticity of the content on their statute websites. Indeed, the opposite is often true. Many state statute websites featured disclaimers disavowing any claims of accuracy. As an example, Kentucky is required by law to offer an electronic version of its code online for free, but even in the face of that mandate it includes a disclaimer that says, in part, that no representation is made as to the accuracy or completeness of the online code.

In some ways all this is a reminder that online legal materials are still in their infancy. As online access to such material becomes more expected and accepted, we can hope that these problems will be resolved. In the meantime, librarians should be aware of the limitations of these sites.

old codes. It is important to note that there is a significant difference in this regard between official and annotated codes.

As explained above, official codes are republished regularly, every six years at the federal level and every two years in most states. When this happens, an entire new set of books is published and sent to libraries and others who want them. At this point the old set is completely superseded and can be disposed of or retained,

depending on what your library's policy is. Annotated codes, however, are not republished as a set in the way that official codes are. Instead, as changes to law occur and interpretive decisions accumulate, they are printed in the regularly issued pocket part that goes into the back of the book. When the pocket part for a particular volume gets too large, the most current information is integrated, and the book is reprinted, replacing just that volume. Thus an annotated code set that has been on the shelf for a few years will have a constantly changing mixture of new volumes and older volumes with pocket parts.

The problem this creates is that annotated codes make no attempt to retain older code language. If the language in the printed volume is changed, the original language will remain in the volume until it is reprinted, but then it will be gone. Language in the pocket part can have an even more fleeting existence. As an example, imagine an annotated code volume printed in the year 2000. In 2001 one of the code provisions in the volume is changed, and the new language appears in the subsequent pocket part. If the new language itself is changed in 2004, the 2001 version will disappear completely from subsequent pocket parts and, having never made it into the printed volume, be gone forever. For this reason annotated codes are not useful for finding previous code language.

There is one other method for assembling previous code language, but it involves a fairly tedious and technical methodology. In both official and annotated codes, each section of the code is normally followed by a history section that outlines its provenance in the form of a chronological list of all of the session law that has contributed language to that section of the code. If you have access to session law, either online or in the published set, you can reconstruct the code language that existed at a given point in time by parsing the session law that had been passed up to that point. As I say, this is a tedious and technical process, and it is usually not worth the effort.

As a practical matter, unless your library retains older versions of the code, it would be better to find out if a nearby library does retain older codes, and then refer users who are looking for older code language to that library.

ONLINE STATUTES

Originally, online versions of state and federal statutes were solely the domain of Lexis and Westlaw. In recent years statutes have made their appearance on the World Wide Web and are now easily accessible for free. Unfortunately, the qual-

ity of these online offerings varies (see text box). That said, it is both notable and important that the legislation of the federal government and all fifty states is, in fact, available on the web. In many states, the web version of the statutes may make it unnecessary for a library to purchase a set of statutes. This is certainly true of the *U.S. Code.*

One issue to be careful about with online statutes is search capabilities. As noted in the text box, the ability to search a given state's statutes on the web can vary widely. You may wish to explore how well your state's online statutes will meet the needs of your library users.

UNIFORM LAWS AND MODEL CODES

Librarians may occasionally get asked about two forms of legislation that can be very hard to track down except in a law library. Understanding what these two forms are, and how they work, can lessen the confusion and help you provide an answer for your user. Uniform laws and model codes are two forms of potential or suggested legislation. However, where they come from, how they are created, and how they end up being used are very different.

Uniform Laws

As you know, each of the fifty states has the ability to make its own laws concerning many aspects of life and business. This is fine, until some issue arises in which having different laws in different states causes problems. For example, if certain legal requirements for conducting business vary too much from state to state, it can impede interstate commerce. There are many other areas of society where similar problems can arise. A solution to this problem is uniform laws.

Uniform laws are created by the Uniform Law Commission (ULC) (also known as the National Conference of Commissioners on Uniform

UNIFORM LAWS IN ACTION: DEALING WITH ABSCONDING NONCUSTODIAL PARENTS

Many years ago, I practiced law in Dubuque, Iowa. Dubuque is a lovely city of about 60,000, situated on the Mississippi River, right where the contiguous border of Illinois and Wisconsin meets Iowa's. In fact, Dubuque has two highway bridges over the Mississippi; one goes to Wisconsin, the other to Illinois.

More than once while I was practicing law, I ran into a vexatious problem. There would be a divorce, usually a contentious one, in which the court had given custody of the children to one of the two parents. One day the noncustodial parent would pick up the children for a visit, cross one of the two bridges into Illinois or Wisconsin, and refuse to return, effectively stealing custody from the custodial parent.

This was possible because at the time a court order relating to custody was only enforceable in the state in which it was issued. Once the children left the state, the court had very little power to enforce its orders affecting them.

The National Conference of Commissioners on Uniform State Laws (NCCUSL, now known as the Uniform Law Commission) stepped into this gap in 1997 by drafting the Uniform Child Custody Jurisdiction and Enforcement Act (UCCJEA) and urging each state to adopt it. Under this act, the states that adopted it would agree to work together on matters of child custody and to enforce valid custody orders from other states. Once most of the states had adopted the UCCJEA, the problem of absconding parents became much easier to control because we could count on other states to enforce valid custody orders.

Such an outcome epitomizes the goal of the work of the ULC.

State Laws), a body of legal experts whose commissioners are appointed by each state. The purpose of the ULC is to draft laws with the intention that all of the states will adopt those laws and thus bring uniformity to law across the land.

Once a uniform law is drafted, it must be adopted by each state's legislature before the law can go into effect in that state. It is not uncommon that a uniform law might be amended by one state during the process of adoption, making the law slightly different in that state from others that have adopted the law. In spite of that, the ULC's uniform law system has worked fairly well, in part because its experts try to balance the needs of the various states with the need for uniformity in a given area of law. They hope that the result will be a law palatable to each state.

One of the first uniform laws promulgated by the ULC, and certainly one of the most famous, is the Uniform Commercial Code, which is now the law in all fifty states. As of today, the ULC has drafted more than 200 uniform laws in such areas as commerce, business organization, family law, probate and estates, health law, and conflicts of laws. The wide adoption of all of these laws by the states attests to the success of this cooperative venture.

Model Codes

Model codes, like uniform laws, are an aspirational form of legislation. However, in contrast to a uniform law, a model code can be drafted by anyone. The point of a model code is to create a best version of the law for a given area. This model law might subsequently be adopted by some or all of the states, or it might simply stand as an academic expression of the law as it should be.

While model codes can be drafted by anyone, many have been drafted by experts and have been extremely influential over the years. For example, many states have based all or part of their criminal laws on the Model Penal Code, a model code drafted by the American Law Institute, a group of distinguished legal experts who study American common law.

Model codes such as the model building code and the model fire code are common in regulatory areas, as are codes such as the American Bar Association's Model Code of Professional Responsibility in the professions.

CONCLUSION

Questions about constitutions and legislation are very common at most reference desks, so a good understanding of this form of law is useful. Constitutions set up the form of government, describe a government's powers and areas of concern, and list the rights of citizens. Legislation creates law on those topics within a legislature's area of concern.

Legislation is first published as session law in the order in which it is passed, and then is organized into a code by topic. Codes are the functional form of legislation used for research. Many libraries still have printed copies of the *U.S. Code* and their state code. Otherwise, online versions of codes are available through legislature websites.

7

CASE LAW

C ASE LAW IS AN IMPORTANT FORM OF LAW IN AMERICA, AND
library users often want help finding a case or working with case law. However, case law itself is a complex and difficult area of legal research. This
problem is made worse by the fact that some of the most powerful and useful case
law finding systems are proprietary and will usually not be available outside of a
dedicated law library or law firm.

Case law is a body of law that governs many aspects of our lives. It is made up of
a vast accumulation of appellate court decisions. Each of these decisions contributes
to the body of law in a piecemeal fashion. Because of this, case law is inherently dis-
organized. In addition, the precedent established by any one case can be invalidated
or limited later on by the decision in a subsequent case. Since there is no way when
reading a particular case to know if such an action has taken place, being able to
track subsequent decisions is an important challenge. In this chapter we will explore
what case law is and how it is created and published. Then we will look at various
methods for finding and working with it.

THE JUDICIARY AND CASE LAW

The primary role of the judiciary is to adjudicate disputes. In America, this process
also results in the appellate courts making law through their decisions. The body of
these appellate decisions is referred to as case law. Appellate courts can make law in
two basic ways. The first is to create law in areas where there is no legislation. This
body of case law is called common law, which, as we will see, is very important in

certain areas of legal concern. The second is to interpret statutes when their meaning is unclear or in controversy. Once a court has rendered its decision interpreting a statute, that decision must be taken into account when applying the underlying statute. For these reasons, a person doing legal research will need to research case law.

Before we talk about how courts function and how they make law, let's talk about the structure of court systems in America. Once again, we will restrict our discussion to the outlines of the federal courts and those of the states—the fifty-one court systems that most concern legal researchers. Fortunately, all of those systems are structured in roughly the same way.

Court System Structure

Court systems in America are generally made up of three levels of courts. At the bottom are the trial courts, which can be called by various names, including district court, superior court, and circuit court. The next level is an intermediate court of appeals. At the top is a court of last resort, usually referred to as a supreme court. Although the names for each court level can vary from state to state, the basic function of each level is the same.

The trial court exists to adjudicate disputes. This is where criminal and civil cases are first heard, and the resulting decision of either a judge or a jury binds the parties to the dispute. In state systems, trial courts were often divided up by county, with each county having its own court. While counties in most states today still have a functioning trial court, the courts themselves have often been reorganized into geographic districts of groups of counties, mostly for purposes of administrative efficiency.

At the federal level, trial courts are called district courts, and each state has at least one federal district court. In many states the federal district court is subdivided into more than one district based on geography. A single federal district or subdistrict may have a number of courthouses in different locations.

The intermediate court of appeals has the primary purpose of correcting errors made by the trial courts. In doing so, their decisions can and do become law within their jurisdictions. The makeup and structure of intermediate courts of appeals vary widely from jurisdiction to jurisdiction. Many states, like the federal court system, have a number of separate courts of appeals, each of which covers a specific geographical part of the state. Some states have several courts of appeals that cover the entire state, with each court dedicated to a particular type of dispute, such as criminal or civil cases. A handful of states have no intermediate court of appeals at all. In those states the state court of last resort handles all appeals.

The court of last resort exists to make law as needed under our common-law system (more on that below) and to correct the errors of the appellate courts. In most jurisdictions this court is usually referred to as a supreme court. The supreme court of a jurisdiction has the final word on disputes and case law within that jurisdiction.

Jurisdiction

Common law is precedent only within the jurisdiction of the court that issues it, so jurisdiction is a concept we want to explore. Jurisdiction is a complex topic. Jurisdiction can be defined as the official power to make legal decisions and judgments, and the extent of that power. Jurisdiction is commonly thought of as defining the geographical boundaries of a court's power, but there are commonly other limits as well, as we will see in a moment. That said, every court in America does have a geographical limit to its jurisdiction, whether it is the entire country, as in the case of the U.S. Supreme Court; or a particular state, as with a state supreme court; or a given county, as in a county trial court.

In addition to geography, jurisdiction is limited by sovereign body, level of court, and sometimes additionally by subject matter or type of person. Let's look at those factors. We've already established that every court exists within geographic boundaries. In addition, each court serves a particular sovereign body, most commonly the federal or a state government. This restricts the court's overall jurisdiction to the legal purview of the sovereign body. For instance, a state court cannot hear or rule on a dispute concerning federal law. Technically, there are exceptions to this, with federal courts sometimes hearing disputes involving state law and so forth, but let's not muddy the waters right now with such details. The point is that a court's jurisdiction is restricted to the sovereign body under which it was created.

Level of court is a factor in jurisdiction as well. Trial courts generally hear and adjudicate disputes. As a rule, their decisions bind the parties to the dispute but do not bind others. In essence, trial courts do not create law. Intermediate appellate courts exist to review trial court decisions for errors. In the process of correcting errors, they often make law, but this law applies only to the trial courts within their jurisdiction. The supreme court exists as a final recourse in the case of judicial error and also as the body most responsible for shaping the common law. This is an immense power, and most supreme courts approach it conservatively, refusing to hear a case unless it involves a significant error or an important piece of public policy. Even then they often try to resolve the issue as narrowly as possible.

In the federal court system, trial courts have jurisdiction within the state in which they sit, referred to as its district. Thus you have the United States District Court for the District of Minnesota, or the United States District Court for the District of Nebraska. Some states are divided into two or more federal districts, such as the Northern and Southern Districts of Iowa, or the Eastern or Western District of Wisconsin. The jurisdiction of federal district courts, as trial courts, is restricted by Congress to certain kinds of disputes. These can include civil, admiralty, or criminal actions arising under the laws of the United States (as opposed to the laws of a particular state); disputes involving the U.S. Constitution or U.S. treaties; certain civil actions between citizens of different states; or civil actions where the United States is a party.

Above the trial courts are the federal circuit courts of appeals, which, as the name suggests, are divided into geographical units called circuits. Although most federal appellate circuit courts have jurisdiction over a specific geographic area of the country and hear disputes from trial courts within that area, some have jurisdiction based on subject matter. Thus there are eleven numbered geographic circuits covering the country, with the district courts of Nebraska, Iowa, and Minnesota in the Court of Appeals for the Eighth Circuit, Wisconsin in the Seventh Circuit, and so on. In addition, there is the Court of Appeals for the D.C. Circuit, which hears appeals from the U.S. District Court for the District of Columbia (and has been compared to a state supreme court for Washington, D.C.), and the Court of Appeals for the Federal Circuit, which is a special appellate court restricted to hearing appeals concerning specific federal matters (which can come from anywhere in the United States), such as federal claims, veterans' appeals, trademark and patent appeals, and other designated matters.

The U.S. Supreme Court is the court of last resort for the federal court system and hears cases from all the circuit courts of appeals. It also has original jurisdiction in a small number of cases. Like other supreme courts, the U.S. Supreme Court is very conservative in what cases it will decide. For example, in 2010, there were 9,066 cases appealed to the U.S. Supreme Court. Of those, it heard arguments on just 86 cases and rendered decisions without hearing arguments on another 84 cases. The other 8,896 cases were turned away without being heard or resolved by the court.

In addition to geography and sovereign body, court jurisdiction can be limited by subject matter. Subject matter jurisdiction limitations are common at both the state and federal level. For instance, each federal district court has a bankruptcy court, which is a limited jurisdiction court that handles only bankruptcy matters. Similarly, as mentioned above, the Court of Appeals for the Federal Circuit is limited in its subject matter jurisdiction to certain types of federal law claims.

At the state level, courts with limited subject matter jurisdiction are fairly common. They can include probate courts, juvenile courts, and small claims courts, among others. Each of these specialized courts is restricted in the subject matter of the disputes it can hear.

Finally, there are some courts that are restricted in what persons they have jurisdiction over. For instance, U.S. military courts have jurisdiction only over military personnel and some others who are subject to the Uniform Code of Military Justice, but their jurisdiction over such individuals is worldwide.

COMMON LAW AND PRECEDENT

From a worldwide perspective, the American system is relatively unique in the fact that the courts can make law in the form of case law. In most other court systems in the world, the courts adjudicate disputes, but they do not make law. American appellate courts do make law, and broadly speaking, American case law arises from two types of cases: common-law disputes and the interpretation of statutes.

The common-law tradition is something we inherited from Great Britain. Under this system, an appellate court, when hearing the appeal of a trial court decision, can determine what the law should be concerning the matter at hand in cases where there is no statute that provides the relevant law. In America, common law arises mostly in areas that are referred to as private law. Private law governs the interactions between persons as opposed to interactions between persons and the state. The most well-known topics in common law are torts, property, and contracts.

Tort law is the law governing harm to persons or property. Such issues as liability in car accidents, slips and falls, and defamation are all examples of torts. Property is the law governing the owning and selling of personal and real prop-

erty. Contracts is the body of law covering legally binding agreements between individuals. In each of these cases, the basic law that covers disputes is a body of appellate court decisions.

The concept of precedent is what gives the common law its force. Precedent in case law means that an appellate decision can guide new decisions by compelling the same outcome when the issues and facts are closely similar. This is referred to by the Latin term *stare decisis*, which means "let the decision stand."

It is important to note that only appellate decisions are eligible to be precedent. A trial court decision binds the parties to the dispute but does not function as precedent for future disputes. Only appellate decisions can do that. When an appellate court rules in a way that creates law, and thus creates precedent, the ruling binds the court that issues it and any courts under it in that jurisdiction.

As an example, let's take a ruling from the United States Court of Appeals for the Seventh Circuit. This federal appellate court covers the states of Wisconsin, Illinois, and Indiana. When a Seventh Circuit decision is released, it is precedent in the federal district courts in those three states and for future rulings by the Seventh Circuit itself. It is not precedent in federal district courts in Iowa or Minnesota, for example, because those courts are in the Eighth Circuit. Nor is it precedent for the Eighth Circuit itself.

Once established, precedent does not expire on its own. Legal precedent has an unlimited shelf life. Precedent can change only by being affected by some later appellate court action. Thus precedent can be changed when the original appellate decision is either subsequently reversed within the course of the same action or later overruled or limited in a different case.

Reversal in the same case occurs when an appellate decision is appealed to a higher appellate court. Thus a court of appeals decision can be appealed to the supreme court of the jurisdiction and overruled by that court. As you might expect, supreme court opinions are very rarely reversed, because there is no further avenue for appeals. In rare cases a supreme court might reconsider its own decision, or a case with a federal issue might

STARE DECISIS— AN EXAMPLE OF STABILITY AND CHANGE IN PRECEDENT

A prominent example of how precedent can change is the U.S. Supreme Court decision in *Plessy v. Ferguson.* In the *Plessy* case, decided in 1896, the Supreme Court endorsed the separate but equal doctrine under the U.S. Constitution. The court ruled that it was legal under the Constitution to separate the races in public accommodations, provided those separate accommodations were basically equal. This was the underlying doctrine on which racial segregation was based for the first half of the twentieth century. In 1954 the court revisited the separate but equal doctrine in the case of *Brown v. Board of Education.* At this point the court decided that separating the races did not meet constitutional muster, and it overruled *Plessy v. Ferguson.* The *Plessy* case had been precedent for more than fifty years, but after *Brown* it was no longer considered good law.

In addition to overruling prior precedent, subsequent appellate decisions can serve to limit or change the effect of precedent. This happens when a subsequent decision questions, criticizes, or limits a prior decision. Such actions do not invalidate the precedent outright, but they can affect how and when it is used and what effect it has.

A BIBLIOGRAPHIC LOOK AT CASE LAW

If you think about it, case law presents some real bibliographic challenges. Knowing what the law is on a given common-law topic requires finding and analyzing precedent from a host of cases. This challenge is exacerbated by the fact that case law is not published in a way that provides any topical organization. Cases are published in the order that they are issued, without regard to topic or precedent.

As a result, working with common law requires three basic tools: to find precedent by topic; to access and read the cases that contain relevant precedent; and to update and verify the relevant precedent. The tools that can do this are digests, which organize precedent by topic; case reporters, which provide access to the cases themselves; and legal citators, which allow cases to be updated. Each of these tools is explained below.

Reporters and Case Publication

Let's start with case reporters. Reporters provide access to cases and are the primary method of disseminating case law. Reporters were originally published by the court that issued them. However, over the years that situation has changed dramatically, and today most reporters are published by private companies. In order to fully understand case reporters, we must wrestle with two sets of concepts: published and unpublished cases, and official and unofficial reporters.

be appealed from a state supreme court to the U.S. Supreme Court, but otherwise the supreme court's decision is the last word in a given case.

Far more common is for precedent to change because of subsequent overruling in a later case. This happens when, in evaluating a trial court decision, an appellate court examines the law in question and decides that the law is wrong and needs to be changed. Although the doctrine of *stare decisis* causes courts to be conservative about this, appellate courts can change precedent when, in their judgment, the law is no longer proper for the issue at hand.

PUBLISHED AND UNPUBLISHED CASES

Traditionally, appellate courts have published most, but not all, of their opinions in reporters. Those decisions that were published became precedent, while those that were not published could not be used as precedent. Appellate decisions begin their life as something called a slip opinion. This is the original decision as rendered by the court. One copy of the slip opinion goes into the court file, and other copies are sent to the parties in the case. In addition to filing the decisions, the court will decide whether a particular decision is to be published or not. If it is not to be published, nothing further is done, and the decision simply remains in the court file. If a decision is designated for publication, it is submitted with other published decisions to be printed in the court's reporter series. This process establishes the decision as precedent and makes it publicly available.

In the days of print, before the online world raised its digital head, this was the end of the matter. Unpublished decisions existed only in the court file and the hands of the parties, and it was almost impossible to find any cases other than those that were officially published. Because of this, lawyers could not use unpublished cases as precedent, if they happened to find one, and could not rely on them in court. In other words, paper publication of cases created a clear line between published cases, which were available to the public and functioned as precedent, and unpublished cases, which did not function as precedent and were simply unavailable.

The online world changed all that, however, and, at the time of this writing, the situation is deeply in flux. In the 1970s, unpublished decisions began to find their way into computer databases, thanks to the advent of Westlaw and Lexis, and thus into the hands of more and more lawyers. Inevitably, lawyers began to try to use unpublished decisions as persuasive precedent— that is, not as legal precedent per se but as an example of judicial reasoning that they hoped the present court would adopt.

At present, virtually all decisions by every appellate court in the country, both published and unpublished, are being made available online. At this point most appellate courts are still designating decisions as published or unpublished, and thus as precedent or not precedent, but the ubiquitous availability of unpublished opinions is creating pressure on courts to recognize unpublished decisions as precedent as well.

There is a growing school of thought that claims that it is unconstitutional for a court to designate which cases can function as precedent and which cannot. Under this reasoning, all decisions by an appellate court must have precedential value. Whether or not all courts adopt this idea, the distinction between published and unpublished decisions is beginning to fade, and in the next decade or two may disappear entirely.

OFFICIAL AND UNOFFICIAL REPORTERS

In simple terms, official reporters are those published by the courts themselves, or their official designee, while unofficial reporters are those published by private publishers. As is usually the case with legal publishing, the details are much more complicated.

In the nineteenth century, most jurisdictions had just a set of trial courts and a court of last resort, or supreme court. Intermediate appellate courts were rare. In most cases, the supreme court of a jurisdiction would publish a reporter for its decisions. These were usually printed by the government itself or, less often, by a designated publisher. In any case, these reporters were the official reporter of the court.

There were private publishers that would also reproduce some or all of a particular court's decisions in their own reporters. Because these books were not sanctioned by the courts, they were referred to as unofficial reporters. Unofficial reporters were something of a minor factor in legal publishing until the 1870s, when a Minnesota bookseller named John West decided to publish unofficial reporters and formed the West Publishing Company to do so.

What set West Publishing apart from the beginning was its founder's determination to publish appellate cases from every state in the nation as well as the federal courts. To do this he established reporters first for the U.S. Supreme Court and later for the federal circuit courts of appeals, and then created a set of seven geographically divided regional reporters for state case law, along with sole state reporters for California and New York. The state regional reporters enabled him to sell one set of books covering several states, which significantly lowered his costs. Each of West's regional reporter series carried all of the published decisions of the appellate courts in the geographical area covered by that reporter.

West Publishing quickly became a juggernaut in legal publishing. This was partly because it carried every published case and could supply case law for any jurisdiction in the country. But it was also because it developed a unified topical case-finding system called the West Key Number System, which will be discussed below.

The West National Reporter System, as the West case-publishing system is called, has been spectacularly successful and remains the dominant case-publishing system in America today. In fact, almost half the states have ceased publishing an official reporter of their own and instead designate the appropriate West Regional Reporter as their official reporter. At the federal level, West is the only publisher of cases from the U.S. courts of appeals and the U.S. district courts. These reporters will be discussed below as well.

Case law is also available from other private sources. These can include book publishers and online databases such as the LexisNexis research database, but citation to West's printed reporters is the uniform way of identifying a case. The only exception to this is when a jurisdiction has an official reporter. In that case, citation will often be to the official reporter. However, even then the West reporter cite will often also be included. Citing to a single case in two separate reporters is referred to as parallel citation, which involves listing the location of the case in the official reporter followed by its location in an unofficial reporter.

Digests

One of the problems with case law is that there is no inherent way of organizing it by topic for publication. Appellate cases often deal with a range of legal issues and may contain precedent on a number of topics. As an example, a single appellate case may rule on whether the actions of the defendant truly qualified as a tort, as well as whether the evidence was sufficient at trial to find the defendant liable, whether the trial court erred in its rulings, and whether those errors were properly preserved for appeal. Each of these aspects of the appellate ruling qualifies as a point of precedent and therefore law, and all appear in one case. As this example suggests, there is no practical way of arranging cases by topic within their reporters.

The answer to this conundrum is something called a digest. Digests consist of points of law abstracted from their originating cases and arranged by topic. You might think of a digest as an elaborate index to points of law that appear in a reporter. In other words, digests provide subject access to precedent. Digests consist of small, paragraph-length descriptions of points of law called abstracts. Each abstract consists in turn of a single point of law as found in a particular case, but, as we've seen, each case can provide any number of such abstracts covering any number of legal topics. Digests can be, and are, published by a variety of legal publishers, and they can be general or specific in their coverage. However, once again West dominates this area of legal publishing, with their national, comprehensive digest system, called the Key Number System.

Back in the late nineteenth century, when West began publishing its National Reporter System, it recognized the need for a comprehensive, nationwide digesting scheme. The result was the Key Number System. West provides a digest for every jurisdiction or reporter set that it produces. Every case published in a jurisdiction or reporter set is included in this system. Points of law in the Key Number System are classified under an outline of American law that covers every legal topic and is uniform in every jurisdiction. In sum, the Key Number System provides a uniform topical finding system for case law that covers every jurisdiction in the country. It is the only system of its kind, and it is extremely useful for finding case law.

WEST'S KEY NUMBER SYSTEM

Here's how the system works. Years ago editors at West divided every issue covered by American appellate cases into broad topics. This broad outline has been enlarged and changed as necessary over the years. Each topic has been subdivided into subtopics called Key Numbers, and those subtopics have been further subdivided as needed.

When a new appellate case arrives to be included in a West reporter, a West editor reads the case and looks for those places in the case where the court is determining a point of law. When precedent is found, the editor marks the beginning of the relevant paragraph with a number that indicates the sequential number of that piece of precedent within the case (i.e., number one for the first piece of precedent, number two for the second, and so on). The editor then prepares an abstract of the precedential language and places the abstract at the top of the case, also numbered sequentially. Each abstract at the top of a case is referred to as a headnote. There are as many headnotes at the top of each West published case as there are points of law within the case.

Once a headnote is created, the editor locates where the topic of the headnote should be classed within the topical Key Number System. This topical classification is listed above the headnote. In any West digest that includes the jurisdiction of the case in question, each headnote from the case will appear under the appropriate key number subtopic under which that headnote was classed, along with every other headnote from other cases in the jurisdiction that were classified in the same way. Thus digest users can find all of the case law that covers a particular topic in one place, making finding relevant precedent easy and convenient.

One of the strengths of the Key Number System is its uniform nature. It allows the user to find cases on a given topic for any jurisdiction in the nation, as well as finding every case that has a point of precedent under a given topic. Using the Key Number System, cases that have precedent on a given topic can be found in one of three ways. First, if you have a case that has a headnote that is of interest, you can use the Key Number associated with that headnote to find other cases that address that precedent. Second, if you have access to printed digests, you can use the index of the digest to locate your topic within the Key Number System. Along these lines, if you have access to Westlaw, you can search the key number system directly to find relevant Key Number topics. Finally, you can find the topic you want, and thus cases, by browsing the topic outline of the Key Number system, either on Westlaw or in the printed digests.

Using the Key Number System requires access either to printed West digests or to the Westlaw legal research system. Neither of these are commonly found outside of law libraries or law firms.

CITATION ANALYSIS

So far we have discussed the reporter system of publishing cases and the Key Number System for finding cases on a given topic. The third aspect of the case law management system is citation analysis.

Most scientific and academic fields engage in some form of citation analysis. There are two basic forms of this activity: backward and forward. Backward citation analysis is the most common and involves analyzing the authorities cited for a proposition put forth in scholarly writing. When a scholar writes a paper or an article, she will commonly cite to previously published works, either as part of the flow of the document or in a separate section, often called a literature review. This serves two purposes. The first is to establish the authority for the basic propositions on which the author wishes to build. The second is to place the current writing or scholarship within the larger context of the literature of the discipline. Citation analysis comes into play when readers work to ascertain and explore the nature of the authorities that the scholar is relying on as she builds her argument.

Law follows this tradition and takes it to another level. In both appellate cases and in legal scholarship, citing to an authority for every stated proposition or fact is an absolute necessity. In appellate cases, all decisions must be carefully grounded in the existing law, even when new precedent is being expounded. The advantage to backward citation analysis, which becomes especially apparent in a legal setting, is that it is inherent in the document. Sources cited are listed and can be pursued at will. Indeed, the sources that are listed will include further citations to further sources, and so on, so the process can be pursued ad infinitum.

Forward citation analysis is less common and generally more difficult to perform. It involves taking a particular document and determining what later documents have cited it. Like backward analysis, forward citation analysis is not unique to law. Most librarians will be familiar with such tools as Science Citation Index or Social Science Citation Index, which are both commonly used in forward citation analysis. In any case, forward citation analysis serves a number of purposes. It allows a reader to determine how widely cited a given article has been. It also allows readers to determine how the basic concepts in the original article have been treated by subsequent scholarship. This, in turn, allows readers to determine the current validity of the concepts in the original article.

In law, forward citation analysis is performed by extremely important tools referred to as legal citators. There are two major legal citators; both are proprietary products. The original legal citator was Shepard's Citations, now owned by LexisNexis and available on the Lexis online legal research system. The second legal citator is KeyCite, a product of West Publishing, which

is available on Westlaw. It is important to note these that citators, in addition to being proprietary, are now generally used only online, as part of the Westlaw or LexisNexis legal databases, respectively. The old book form of Shepard's Citations is still available in some places, but it is generally considered inherently out of date when compared to online citators.

Both Shepard's Citations and KeyCite have the primary function of showing which subsequent decisions have cited the decision you have in hand and what the effect has been of those later citing cases. The analysis provided by citators is divided into two types: history and treatment. History is what happens to a case further along in the same litigation. As an example, if an appellate decision is subsequently appealed to the Supreme Court, and a decision is rendered there, that subsequent Supreme Court decision would constitute part of the original appellate decision's history. The key is that both decisions are part of the same line of litigation—that is, the same parties and the same dispute—just at different points in the appellate process.

Treatment is the term for actions taken by other, later cases in relation to the original case. Shepard's and KeyCite will list every subsequent case, anywhere in the country, that cites your original case. They will also indicate whether the subsequent cases merely cite your case or take some action about it, up to and including reversing, criticizing, limiting, or otherwise affecting the precedential value of the case. In other words, you can use a citator to test the validity of the original case.

WORKING WITH CASES—PUTTING IT ALL TOGETHER

For those who do not have access to the proprietary tools, primarily those provided by the Westlaw and LexisNexis legal databases, working with case law can be a challenge. For library users who need to do extensive research involving case law, referring them to a dedicated law library may be the only really viable option. Still, it might be helpful to take a look at the process of finding and using case law as made possible by these proprietary tools, with an eye to understanding how this works as a research system.

As we have seen, working with case law requires three basic tools: to find the relevant case law, to read the cases you need, and to update your case law to see how it has been treated by subsequent cases. The challenge for a non–law library seeking to provide legal information for users is how to find free or low-cost versions of these tools. To a certain extent, the web is providing access to these resources. So far, however, the options are less than perfect.

Of the three required tools, the most accessible are those that allow you to read case law. This is true both for books and online. In book form, case reporters are relatively common, and in many states the official reporters can be had at a low cost. Book reporters can be a challenge because of the shelf space they consume, but apart from that they are at least available. Better yet, and more to the point, appellate cases from all jurisdictions are becoming more and more available on the web. Most state court systems, along with the U.S. courts, are making appellate cases available online through their websites. How far back in time these case databases go can vary, but more and more cases are becoming available for free all the time.

If you wish to provide access to case law for your library's users, but you don't want to deal with book reporters, it would be best to explore what case law is available from your state's official court website. In many cases there will be a fairly good array of case law available for free. The same is true for federal cases. Check the resources listed in the appendix to this book for details. Keep in mind that if your library has a run of case reporters, that set combined with web resources can possibly give your library a complete set of case law, even if the books are no longer being updated.

The other tools, for finding and updating cases, are harder to replicate outside the proprie-

tary systems provided by Westlaw and LexisNexis. Finding is the more accessible of the two. Several free sites that host case law, such as Cornell's Legal Information Institute (www.law.cornell.edu), have made case law searchable and therefore easier to find. Of particular note is Google Scholar (http://scholar.google.com), which now claims to host all state and federal case law. These and other sources listed in the appendix would be worth familiarizing yourself with.

Finding a way to update case law without tools like KeyCite and Shepard's is more difficult. One option is to search a site like Google Scholar for the party names of your case, but crafting a good search is very hard to do.

CASE CITATION

A very common reference question involves having a user approach a librarian with a case citation, hoping to read the case. Given the growing availability of cases online, this is no longer a daunting request, even in a small rural library. The challenge for the librarian can be to parse the citation in order to find the case.

The West Publishing Company's National Reporter System is the only comprehensive source for all published cases from American courts. The system of citation to West Reporters is the dominant method of identifying, and finding, published cases. West publishes the appellate cases of all federal and state appellate courts, along with a smattering of federal trial court decisions.

Here's how a case citation works. Suppose a user approaches the reference desk and presents you with the following:

Franklin v. United States, 992 F.2d 1492 (10th Cir. 1993)

This is a case citation for a federal court of appeals case. In order to understand it, let's look at the basic elements involved and the information that is conveyed.

As we also saw in chapter 4, basic case citation consists of the following elements: party names, reporter information, and then within a set of parentheses a jurisdictional statement and a year. Let's once again take a closer look at each.

The citation begins with the party names followed by a comma, in this form:

[plaintiff] v. [defendant],

Following the party names will be the case reporter information, which is bibliographically the most important. It consists of the volume number of the reporter series, an abbreviation of the title of the reporter series, and then the starting page of the case within that volume. It looks like this:

[vol.] [reporter abbreviation] [starting page number]

Next comes the jurisdictional statement and date, in parentheses:

([court] [year])

Let's look again at our citation example:

Franklin v. United States, 992 F.2d 1492 (10th Cir. 1993)

We can parse this case as follows. It involves the two parties Franklin and the United States. It is published in volume 992 of the *Federal Reporter*, second series, which is published by the West Publishing Company. The *Federal Reporter* publishes cases from the U.S. circuit courts of appeals. Finally, the information in parentheses tells us that this is a case from the U.S. Court of Appeals for the Tenth Circuit, and that it was issued in 1993. For more examples like *Franklin*, see chapter 4.

A complicating factor when reading a case citation is something called a parallel citation. Parallel citation might be used when a case is published in more than one reporter, such as when a case is published in an official reporter published by the state and also in a West Regional Reporter. In such a situation, information for each of the reporters that contain the case might be provided in the cite. Here is an example:

Baltimore & Ohio R.R. v. Goodman, 275 U.S. 66, 48 S. Ct. 24, 72 L. Ed. 167 (1927)

This is a citation to a U.S. Supreme Court case, which is published in three different reporters. Following the party names, each reporter is listed in turn, starting with the official reporter, the *United States Reports*. This is followed by volume and page number information for the West-published *Supreme Court Reports*, and then by *Lawyer's Edition*, published by LexisNexis.

Next is an example of parallel citation involving a state case. In this example, the case is a decision by the Georgia Court of Appeals. The case is published in the official *Georgia Appeals Reports* and in the West-published *South Eastern Reporter*, second series.

Taylor v. Super Discount Market, Inc., 212 Ga. App. 155, 441 S.E.2d 433 (1994)

A final piece of information that might come up in a case citation is something called a pin cite. In this case *pin* is short for *pinpoint*, and a pin citation is an internal citation to a specific place in a case. It is used when the person citing the case doesn't just want to cite the case itself, but wants to cite to specific language within the case. The internal page number is indicated following the starting page number of the case. Here is an example:

TSC Indus., Inc. v. Northway, 426 U.S. 438, 449 (1976)

In this example, the case begins on page 438 of volume 426 of the *U.S. Reports*, but the reader is being referred to language on page 449 within the case.

The biggest problem with parsing case citations is determining what the reporter series abbreviation stands for. The information that follows lists major reporter series and their abbreviations. Unfortunately, there is no way to make these lists completely comprehensive. For more complete information, consult *The Bluebook*.

Federal Courts

The federal court system has three levels—district courts, circuit courts of appeals, and the U.S. Supreme Court—and each level is reported separately.

U.S. Supreme Court

There are three reporters for the U.S. Supreme Court. One is official, and the other two are privately published.

Reporter Name	Publisher	Abbreviation & Series
U.S. Reports	U.S. Supreme Court (official reporter)	U.S.
Supreme Court Reporter	West Publishing	S. Ct.
Lawyer's Edition	LexisNexis	L. Ed., L. Ed. 2d

U.S. Circuit Courts of Appeals

The only publisher of federal courts of appeals cases is West Publishing, which publishes them in the Federal Reporter set. This set is now in its third series. The abbreviations for the first, second, and third series are F., F.2d, and F.3d.

U.S. District Courts

Although their decisions are not precedent, there are a limited number of federal district court decisions published by West Publishing in the Federal Supplement set. The Federal Supplement is now in its second series. The abbreviations are F. Supp. and F. Supp. 2d.

State Court Case Law

The West National Reporter System publishes supreme court and courts of appeals cases from all fifty states and the District of Columbia. The system divides the country into seven regions and has a single reporter set for each region. All of these sets are in their second or third series at this point. This table shows each reporter set, the series abbreviations, and the states included in that set:

Reporter	Abbreviation(s)	States covered
Atlantic Reporter	1st series: A. 2nd series: A.2d 3rd series: A.3d	CT, DE, DC, ME, MD, NH, NJ, PA, RI, VT
North Eastern Reporter	1st series: N.E. 2nd series: N.E.2d	IL, IN, MA, NY, OH
North Western Reporter	1st series: N.W. 2nd series: N.W.2d	IA, MI, MN, NE, ND, SD, WI
South Eastern Reporter	1st series: S.E. 2nd series: S.E.2d	GA, NC, SC, VA, WV
Southern Reporter	1st series: So. 2nd series: So. 2d 3rd series: So. 3d	AL, FL, LA, MS
South Western Reporter	1st series: S.W. 2nd series: S.W.2d 3rd series: S.W.3d	AR, KY, MO, TN, TX
Pacific Reporter	1st series: P. 2nd series: P.2d 3rd series: P.3d	AK, AZ, CA, CO, HI, ID, KS, MT, NV, NM, OK, OR, UT, WA, WY

REGULATIONS
AND
ADMINISTRATIVE LAW

F OR MOST PEOPLE, REGULATIONS ARE THE HIDDEN FORM OF
law. They may be vaguely aware of them, if nothing else from political debates
and the like, but many people don't realize the prevalence and even ubiquity
of regulations as a form of law in our society. Lawyers deal with regulations all the
time, and people with legal questions will run into them far more than they expect to.

Regulations are the third of the three forms of primary law in America. Along
with statutes and case law, they provide precedent on which courts can decide disputes. As we have seen, statutes are created by the legislature and case law by the
courts. Regulations are created by the executive branch of government.

The first thing to understand about regulations as a form of law is their directed
nature. If you remember, legislators can propose legislation on any topic that is not
constitutionally prohibited, making legislation proactive in nature. The courts can
make case law only in response to a specific dispute, making case law reactive in
nature. In turn, the executive branch can make regulations only when directed to do
so by a statute passed by the legislature. This limitation means that regulations are
directed in nature.

The result is that regulations come into existence only when the legislature
passes a law that says, in part, that a given agency should draft regulations in order
to carry out the intentions of the statute. This legislation is referred to as *enabling
legislation*. Regulations cannot exceed the mandate of the enabling legislation. Thus
one of the ways that a regulation can be legally challenged is to contend that it goes
beyond the intent of the enabling statute. This contention, referred to by the Latin
phrase *ultra vires*, or "beyond the bounds," will, if proved true, render the regulation
invalid.

Please note a bit of terminology here. The terms *regulations* and *rules* are both
used in this context. They are entirely interchangeable and mean the same thing.

RULEMAKING AND ADJUDICATION— AGENCIES AT WORK

Suppose your state has a Department of Environmental Quality (DEQ). This state agency's job is to protect the environment by carrying out the environmental laws passed by the legislature. Let's assume the legislature has passed a law outlawing the storage of tires on private property without a permit from the DEQ. The statute, or enabling legislation, directed the DEQ to draft regulations to carry out its intent. The regulations define the qualifications required to get a permit for tire storage, and the penalties and fines for storing tires without a permit. If your neighbor has amassed a huge pile of old tires in the back yard, you or another neighbor can contact the DEQ. It will send out an investigator to check your claim. If the tires meet the definitions of the regulations, and your neighbor has no permit, the DEQ will proceed with a prosecution for violation of the regulations.

This prosecution will take place entirely within the agency. Agency attorneys will prepare a case against your neighbor. If your neighbor chooses to fight the charges, a trial will be held in an administrative court in front of an administrative law judge. These proceedings tend to be less formal than in regular court, but no less serious. The administrative law judge will render a decision and can order your neighbor to clean up his property, to cease and desist from such behavior in the future, and even to pay a fine. For what it's worth, administrative proceedings cannot result in imprisonment. Only criminal charges in a regular court can do that.

The agency will also have an internal appeals process, so if your neighbor doesn't like the outcome, he can appeal within the agency. Eventually, particularly if he is alleging that the regulations themselves are improper or being wrongly enforced, he can appeal to the district court and potentially on up to the state supreme court. As such, the courts are available as a watchdog over agency actions and regulations. In addition, the regulations themselves can be challenged directly in court if they are alleged to be *ultra vires* or otherwise improper.

There might be someone somewhere who can make a slight technical differentiation between rules and regulations, but we don't know what that would be, and it need not concern us.

Agencies not only draft regulations as directed by the legislature, they also enforce them. If there is a dispute about the regulations or the enforcement, the dispute is adjudicated within the agency in a tribunal run by an administrative law judge. This is a judge hired by the agency who only hears cases involving regulations.

Agencies are thus said to have both rulemaking and adjudication powers. These two activities taken together make up the body of what is known as administrative law.

Regulations are a relatively recent innovation in law. Whereas both case law and statutes have histories dating back over thousands of years, regulations really got started, in America at least, around the turn of the twentieth century. Administrative codes are even more recent. At the federal level the first code was developed in the 1930s, and many states still didn't have a formal administrative code as recently as the 1970s or '80s.

In form and function, regulations look and feel a lot like legislation. The drafting and approval process is different, as we'll see, but there is an initial publication of the final regulation, similar to that of session law, after which current regulations are arranged by topic into an administrative code in much the same way that statutes are arranged in codes.

In very simplified form, the drafting, approval, and publication of regulations occurs in roughly the following fashion. Once the agency receives a piece of enabling legislation directing it to create rules, it will begin an internal drafting process. The length of time it takes to draft the regulations can vary widely and can be a point of contention between the agency and the legislature. Assuming the drafting process proceeds smoothly, the agency will make an initial publication of the proposed rules.

This initial publication will take place in a regular, newspaper-like publication of the executive branch of the government called a register. The purpose of the register is to make known the activities of the executive branch, including proposed and final rules, notices of various kinds, and reports of agency activity. At the federal level, the *Federal Register* is published daily. State registers are usually published weekly.

The publication of proposed rules in the register puts the world on notice of the proposed form of the new regulations. Usually, a notice is published along with the proposed rules, giving the public a period of time to comment on them before they are finalized. This comment period is usually several months. At the federal level, and in most states, the agency is required by law to collect comments on proposed rules, consider the comments in good faith, and make changes to the proposed rules as warranted.

Once the comment period has passed and the comments have been considered and any changes made, the rules are published again in the register, this time as final regulations. This publication is the official, final publication of the rule. As such it is the equivalent of session law for statutes or the reporter for cases. From there, as with statutes, the new regulations are added to the administrative code. This is simply a code of regulations for the jurisdiction. Like codes containing statutes, administrative codes contain all rules, currently in force, arranged by topic. New regulations that change or add to existing regulations are interpolated in place by topic.

Also as with statutes, the administrative code is the functional unit for researching regulations. All of the caveats for working with codes apply.

REGULATIONS.GOV

The comment period for proposed regulations is an important part of the rulemaking process. Any citizen or interested party has the right to submit comments on a proposed rule. In order to facilitate this process at the federal level, the federal government has developed a website, Regulations.gov, for the purpose of streamlining the comment process.

The site, which is relatively user friendly and straightforward, allows you to search for proposed regulations, see what's new, and, most importantly, submit comments on any proposed regulation.

Users of your library who are concerned with federal regulation, including anyone involved in business or in political activities or advocacy groups, will most likely be grateful to learn about this site, if they haven't already.

It is essential that your code of regulations be up to date, or that you do research in the register to catch any updates to your regulations. More on this as we look specifically at federal and state regulations.

FEDERAL REGULATIONS

Federal regulations are drafted by agencies of the executive branch when directed to do so by enabling legislation promulgated by Congress. The rules are drafted by the agency and then published as proposed rules in the *Federal Register*. The *Federal Register* is published each day that the government is in operation (which means Monday through Friday except for federal holidays) and serves as the public record and notice of agency actions. Most importantly for our

FEDERAL REGISTER AND *CODE OF FEDERAL REGULATIONS* ONLINE

The *Federal Register and Code of Federal Regulations* are published in paper and received by many depository and law libraries. However, they are usually best accessed online. The Government Printing Office provides both the *Federal Register* and the *Code of Federal Regulations* online and for free. The site is called FDsys, and can be accessed at www.gpo.gov/fdsys. From there, you will find links to those and other important documents.

purposes, the *Federal Register* publishes proposed federal rules, requests for comment on proposed rules, and final rules.

After the comment period, changes are made to the proposed rules as warranted, and then the final rules are published in the *Federal Register*. This is the official publication of the rule and is similar to session law publications by Congress.

New rules are then integrated into the *Code of Federal Regulations*, or CFR. The CFR is the primary research tool for federal regulations. The CFR is updated on an annual basis, with a quarter of its fifty titles, or sections, updated each fiscal quarter. Many depository libraries, as well as law libraries, continue to get the CFR in print. Online, it is available through the Government Printing Office site (see sidebar).

The CFR can be accessed through its index or, online, by full-text searching. Updating the CFR involves checking *Federal Registers* published since the most recent CFR update for indications of changes to the rule in question. The CFR provides a table, called the "List of Sections Affected," or LSA, that provides a cumulative list of CFR sections that have been changed at any time since each CFR title was last updated.

STATE RULES

State administrative rules, for the most part, are similar to the federal rules in how they are promulgated and published. There is usually a register, often published weekly, that contains proposed and final rules and notices of comment periods. In most states this register is available online (see the appendix to this book for information on your state). There is also a state administrative code. Rules themselves can vary widely in format and style, and you would do well to investigate the situation with your state's administrative code.

COURT RULES

Although administrative law refers to the rule-making and enforcement actions of agencies in the executive branch, there are other law-related rules that legal researchers should be aware of. The most important of these are court rules. All court proceedings are run by an elaborate set of rules, which dictate how matters are to proceed and what is to be done when. Anyone hoping to engage in a court-related matter will need to be aware of court rules.

As you would expect, there is set of court rules for the federal court system as well as at least one set of rules for each state court system. Court rules are usually divided up into sections or groups. Some rules are administrative, relating to the actual management and operation of the court, but most are procedural, meaning they lay down rules for a particular kind of court action. The most common bodies of court rules are as follows:

Administrative. Rules that govern the actual operation of the court system.
Civil procedure. Procedural rules that dictate how to pursue a civil action in the courts.

This includes rules on what is required for a civil petition, how discovery will be handled, what kinds of motions will be heard, and how the trial will proceed, among many other things.

Criminal procedure. Rules governing criminal actions. These include rules for indicting someone for a crime, for discovery, and for procedure at trial.

Appellate rules. Rules governing the process for appealing a decision of a lower court, including how to effectuate the appeal, requirements for briefs and other documents, rules for oral arguments, and appellate time lines.

Rules for specialized courts. When there is a specialized court, it will often have its own procedural rules. At the federal level, there are special rules for bankruptcy court. At the state level, there are often separate rules for probate court, juvenile court, and sometimes others.

Local and court-specific rules. Local courts and specific appellate courts will often have rules that govern just that court. Local rules might cover procedures for filing actions or getting orders signed, or for handling group court sessions for criminal sentencing or finalizing divorces. Individual appellate courts may have their own rules covering brief cover colors, oral argument procedures, and so forth.

In today's world, the best place to find court rules, hands down, is on court websites. Courts nationwide have been very good about posting rules. At the federal level, the website for U.S. courts (www.uscourts.gov) has a comprehensive set of rules, and most district and other regional federal courts have a website with local rules. Statewide rules are generally available on your state's supreme court website. In most instances, local trial courts and county courthouses have websites with local rules. See the appendix to this book for more information about your jurisdiction.

APPENDIX

ONLINE LEGAL RESOURCES

THIS APPENDIX PRESENTS A LIST OF ONLINE LEGAL resources that can be used for research on legal questions. It is broken into sections. The first section has nationwide resources; the second section has federal resources (including those for Washington, D.C.); the third section covers each state, from Alabama to Wyoming.

The usual caveats must be mentioned for this sort of list. While we have made every effort to ensure its accuracy as of the time of printing, the volatility of the web makes a certain amount of link rot inevitable. Web addresses change, resources are taken down or merged with other resources, changes occur. These things happen, and some of the links below will almost certainly be invalidated as a result. In addition, although a number of people have reviewed this list looking for errors, it's such a large list of resources that some errors may have crept in. If a link is broken, try some web searching to see if you can find the resource or a similar one. The abbreviation "N/A" (not available) indicates that, at the time of publication, a resource was not publicly available online or could not be found.

Xiaolu (Renee) Zhang did much of the initial searching for and vetting of these resources. I am deeply grateful to Renee for her assistance, and I think the quality of her work is apparent. That said, any errors or problems are fully my responsibility.

SECTION 1: RESOURCES USEFUL FOR MOST STATES AND FOR GENERAL LEGAL RESEARCH

Legal Resource Aggregators/Portals

LawSource Inc., "American Law Sources On-line," www.lawsource.com/also/

Cornell University School of Law, Legal Information Institute, "Law by Source: State," www.law.cornell.edu/states/

AllLaw.com, "State Law Search," www.alllaw.com/State_Resources/

FindLaw, "State Laws," http://statelaws.findlaw.com

Justia.com, "US Law," http://law.justia.com

"Full-Text State Statutes and Legislation on the Internet," www.whpgs.org/f.htm

Washburn University School of Law, WashLaw: Legal Research on the Web, www.washlaw.edu

Fastcase, "The Public Library of Law," www.plol.org

LawResearch Services Inc., "The Internet Law Library," www.lawresearch.com

Resources for Attorneys, "Legal Resources Listed by State," www.resourcesforattorneys.com/statelegalresources.html

General Research Guides

American Association of Law Libraries (AALL), Legal Information Services to the Public (LISP), "Public Library Toolkit," www.aallnet.org/sis/lisp/toolkit.htm

Georgetown University Law Library, "Research Guides," www.law.georgetown.edu/library/research/guides/

Library of Congress, Law Library, "U.S. States & Territories," www.loc.gov/law/help/guide/states.php

Law Librarians' Society of Washington, D.C., "State Legislatures, State Laws, and State Regulations: Website Links and Telephone Numbers," www.llsdc.org/state-leg/

University of Iowa College of Law Library, "Legal Materials by Jurisdiction," http://libguides.law.uiowa.edu/jurisdictions

Yale Law School, Lillian Goldman Law Library, "Research," http://library.law.yale.edu/research/guides/state-law-research-guide

Judicial

Background Information

National Center for State Courts (NCSC), "State Court Web Sites," www.ncsc.org/information-and-resources/browse-by-state/state-court-websites.aspx

Westlaw, "State Court Organization Chart," http://wlwatch.westlaw.com/aca/west/statecrtorg.htm

Knowledge Center, Council of State Governments, *Book of the States 2010*, chapter 5, "State Judicial Branch," http://knowledgecenter.csg.org/kc/content/book-states-2010-chapter-5-state-judicial-branch

Opinions

Hawaii Legislative Reference Bureau, "Library Reference Desk—State Judiciary and Courts," http://hawaii.gov/lrb/desk/st3.html

FindACase, www.findacase.com

Google Scholar legal documents, http://scholar.google.com

Dockets/Court Records

Online Searches LLC, "Court Records Free Reference and Directory," www.courtreference.com

LLRX, "Features—Free and Fee Based Appellate Court Briefs Online," www.llrx.com/features/briefsonline.htm

LLRX, "Court Rules, Forms, and Dockets," www.llrx.com/courtrules/

Court.us, "Court Records, Directory and Case News," http://court.us

NCSC, "Privacy/Public Access to Court Records: State Links," www.ncsc.org/Topics/Access-and-Fairness/Privacy-Public-Access-to-Court-Records/State-Links.aspx

Legislative

Background Information

MultiState Associates Inc., "State Home Page and Legislature Links," www.multistate.com/site.nsf/state

Knowledge Center, Council of State Governments, *Book of the States 2010*, chapter 3, "State Legislative Branch," http://knowledgecenter.csg.org/drupal/content/book-states-2010-chapter-3-state-legislative-branch

Statutes and Session Laws

University of Maine School of Law, "A Compilation of State Materials Available Online," http://mainelaw.usm.maine.edu/library/statematerials.htm

Hawaii Legislative Reference Bureau, "Library Reference Desk—States Legislatures," http://hawaii.gov/lrb/desk/st2.html

FreeAdvice, "State Law and Code Links" [no session laws], http://law.freeadvice.com/resources/statecodes.htm

Legislative History

Research Guides

Indiana University Bloomington, Maurer School of Law, "Legislative History," http://law.indiana.libguides.com/state-legislative-history-guides

Pace Law Library, "Legislative History Research Guide," http://libraryguides.law.pace.edu/legis_history

Bills

National Conference of State Legislatures, "Bill Information | Other Resources," www.ncsl.org/legislative-staff.aspx?tabs=856,34,735

AALL, "Government Relations" [bill chart link], www.aallnet.org/Documents/Government-Relations/

Hawaii Legislative Reference Bureau, "Library Reference Desk—States Legislatures," http://hawaii.gov/lrb/desk/st2.html

Fifty-State Surveys of Laws

Uniform Law Commission (National Conference of Commissioners on Uniform State Laws), www.uniformlaws.org

Bureau of Justice Statistics, "State Court Organization 2004," esp. table 43, "Sentencing Statutes," http://bjs.gov/content/pub/pdf/sco04.pdf

American Bar Association (ABA), "Family Law in the Fifty States," www.americanbar.org/groups/family_law/resources/family_law_in_the_50_states.html

McCullough, Campbell & Lane LLP, "Medical Malpractice Summary Index of States," www.mcandl.com/states.html

Ohio State University, Moritz College of Law, "Research Guides: Same-Sex Laws," http://moritzlaw.osu.edu/librarysamesexmarriagelaws.php

Nolo, "Chart: Statutes of Limitations in All 50 States," www.nolo.com/legal-encyclopedia/statute-of-limitations-state-laws-chart-29941.html

FindLaw, "State Statutes of Limitations," http://law.findlaw.com/state-laws/statute-of-limitations/

Cleveland Law Library Association, "Limited Liability Companies: State Statutes," www.clelaw.lib.oh.us/Public/Misc/REGUIDES/guide24.html#State

FreeAdvice, "Car Accident Laws by State," http://law.freeadvice.com/resources/state-car-accident-laws.htm

Executive

Background Information

State and Local Government on the Net, "State Government Offices, Local US Government, City Government, and Federal Government," www.statelocalgov.net

USLegal, "State Administrative Procedure Acts," http://administrativelaw.uslegal.com/administrative-procedure-acts/

ALA Government Documents Roundtable (GODORT), "State Agency Databases," http://wikis.ala.org/godort/index.php/State_Agency_Databases

Regulations

Administrative Codes and Registers Section of NASS (National Association of Secretaries of State), "Administrative Rules," www.administrativerules.org

Wyoming Secretary of State, "50 States' Information: Rules & Regulations," http://soswy.state.wy.us/Services/Rules50.aspx

University of Maine School of Law, "A Compilation of State Materials Available Online" [no registers], http://mainelaw.usm .maine.edu/library/statematerials.htm

FreeAdvice, "Find Your State's Administrative Law and Code" [no registers], http://law .freeadvice.com/resources/administrativecode.htm

Local Laws

Background Information

National Association of Counties, "Find a County," www.naco.org/Counties/Pages/FindACounty.aspx

National League of Cities, "Member Directory," www.nlc.org/about-nlc/state-league-programs/state -municipal-leagues/state-municipal-league-directory

Ordinances

Municipal Code Corporation, "Code Library," www.municode.com/library/

Coded Systems LLC, "Code Library" [partial coverage], www.codedsystems.com/codelibrary .html

Sterling Codifiers Inc., "Codes Online" [partial coverage], www.sterlingcodifiers.com/codes -online

General Code, "Online eCode360 Library" [partial coverage], www.generalcode.com/ codification/ecode/library

Code Publishing Co. "Municipal Codes" [partial coverage], www.codepublishing.com/elibrary.html

Practice Materials and Self-Help Resources

General Research Guides

LAWCHEK and Lawsonline, "State Court Rules," www.lawsonline.com/directories_info/strules.htm

LLRX, "Court Rules, Forms, and Dockets," www.llrx.com/courtrules/

Legal Research Group, "ILRG Legal Forms Archive," www.ilrg.com/forms/

FindLaw, "State Specific Legal Forms for All States," www.uslegalforms.com/findlaw/

HALT, "Self-Help Center," www.halt.org/self-help -center/self-help-articles

Finding a Lawyer

ABA, Division for Legal Services, "Consumers' Guide to Legal Help," www.abanet.org/ legalservices/findlegalhelp/states.html

FindLaw, "Find a Lawyer," http://lawyers.findlaw.com

HG.org, "Find Lawyers, Law Firms," www.hg.org

Lawyers.com, "State Law and Agencies," http:// research.lawyers.com/State-Law-And-Agencies.html

iLawyer [limited to a few states], www.ilawyer.com

Legal Directories, "Quick Lawyer Search," www.legaldirectories.com

AttorneyPages, "Find and Attorney," http://attorneypages.com

Legal Advocacy and Legal Aid

NCSC, "Legal Aid/Pro Bono: State Links," www.ncsc.org/Topics/Legal-Services/Legal-Aid -Pro-Bono/State-Links.aspx

FindLaw, "State Legal Aid Resources," http://hirealawyer.findlaw.com/do-you-need-a -lawyer/state-legal-aid-resources.html

ABA, Division for Legal Services, "Consumers' Guide to Legal Help," www.abanet.org/ legalservices/findlegalhelp/states.html

Pine Tree Legal Assistance, "Legal Services Links," www.ptla.org/legal-services-links

Pro Bono Net, LawHelp.org, www.lawhelp.org

Legal Services Corporation, "LSC Programs," www.lsc.gov/find-legal-aid

Miscellaneous

LexisWeb [search engine], http://lexisweb.com

ABA, "State and Local Bar Associations," www.americanbar.org/groups/bar_services/ resources/state_local_bar_associations.html

HG.org, "Bar Associations," www.hg.org/bar.html

AALL, "State Summary Updates" [state-by-state reports on authentication of online legal resources], www.aallnet.org/Documents/Government-Relations/authreportupdate.html

FreeAdvice, www.freeadvice.com

Washburn University School of Law, WashLaw, "State, Court, and County Law Libraries," www.washlaw.edu/statecourtcounty/

'Lectric Law Library, www.lectlaw.com

BRBPub.com, "Free Public Records," www.brbpub.com

References

Westlaw, "Glossary for Legal Research Basics," http://lawschool.westlaw.com/shared/marketinfodisplay.asp?code=RE&id=17&mainpage=23&rtid=116&rtcode=re

Cornell University Law School, Legal Information Institute, *Wex* [dictionary and encyclopedia], www.law.cornell.edu/wex/

SECTION 2: FEDERAL GOVERNMENT AND WASHINGTON, D.C.

FEDERAL

Research Guides

General

University of Washington School of Law, Gallagher Law Library, "United States Legal Resources," http://lib.law.washington.edu/research/research.html#fed

New York University School of Law, Hauser Global Law School Program, *UPDATE: A Guide to the U.S. Federal Legal System Web-Based Public Accessible Sources*, by Gretchen Feltes, www.nyulawglobal.org/globalex/United_States1.htm

Topical

University of Washington School of Law, Gallagher Law Library, "U.S. (Federal) Law," http://lib.law.washington.edu/ref/fedlaw.html

Judicial

Court Structure

United States Courts, "Federal Courts' Structure," www.uscourts.gov/FederalCourts/UnderstandingtheFederalCourts/FederalCourtsStructure.aspx

United States Courts, "Structure of the Federal Courts" [diagram], www.uscourts

.gov/EducationalResources/FederalCourtBasics/CourtStructure/StructureOfFederalCourts.aspx

Directories of Federal Courts

Villanova University School of Law, "Federal Court Locator," www.law.villanova.edu/Library/Research%20Guides/Federal%20Court%20Locator.aspx

GovEngine.com, "Federal Courts," www.govengine.com/fedcourts/

Opinions

Research Guide

Supreme Court of the United States, "Where to Obtain Supreme Court Opinions," www.supremecourt.gov/opinions/obtainopinions.aspx

Highest Court—Supreme Court

[last six months]: Supreme Court of the United States, "Slip Opinions, *Per Curiams* (PC), and Original Case Decrees (D)," www.supremecourt.gov/opinions/slipopinions.aspx

[last five years]: Supreme Court of the United States, "Opinions," www.supremecourt.gov/opinions/opinions.aspx

[1990–]: Cornell University, Legal Information Institute, "Supreme Court," www.law.cornell.edu/supct/

[1893–]: FindLaw, "US Supreme Court Opinions," www.findlaw.com/casecode/supreme.html

[1754–]: Public Library of Law, www.plol.org/Pages/Search.aspx

Intermediate Appellate Court—
Circuit Courts of Appeals

[2000–]: FindLaw, "Opinion Summaries Archive," http://caselaw.findlaw.com/summary/

[1950–]: Public Library of Law, www.plol.org/Pages/Search.aspx

Dockets/Court Records

PACER (Public Access to Court Electronic Records) [fee-based], www.pacer.gov

Legislative

Legislative Process

United States House of Representatives, "The Legislative Process," www.house.gov/content/learn/legislative_process/

LexisNexis, "How a Bill Becomes a Law" [diagram], www.lexisnexis.com/help/CU/The_Legislative_Process/How_a_Bill_Becomes_Law.htm

Statutes

Research Guide

University of Washington School of Law, Gallagher Law Library, "Statutory Research Checklist," https://lib.law.washington.edu/content/guides/statrescheck

By Subject (Code)—United States Code

[current]: Cornell University School of Law, Legal Information Institute, "U.S. Code," www.law.cornell.edu/uscode/

[current]: FindLaw, "U.S. Code," www.findlaw.com/casecode/uscodes/

[1994–]: U.S. Government Printing Office, "United States Code," www.gpo.gov/fdsys/browse/collectionUScode.action?collectionCode=USCODE

[1994–]: U.S. House of Representatives, "Download PDF Version of U.S. Code," http://uscode.house.gov/download/downloadPDF.shtml

[1991–]: U.S. House of Representatives, "Search Prior Versions of the U.S. Code," http://uscode.house.gov/search/prevcode.shtml

In Chronological Order (Session Laws)—
United States Statutes at Large

[1995–]: U.S. Government Printing Office, "Public and Private Laws," www.gpo.gov/fdsys/browse/collection.action?collectionCode=PLAW

[1973–]: Library of Congress, "Browse Public Laws," http://thomas.loc.gov/home/LegislativeData.php?&n=PublicLaws&c=93

[1789–1875]: Library of Congress, American Memory, "Statutes at Large, 1789–1875," http://memory.loc.gov/ammem/amlaw/lwsllink.html

Legislative History

Research Guides

Law Librarians' Society of Washington, D.C., "Electronic Sources for Federal Legislative History Documents With Years/Congresses Available," www.llsdc.org/elec-leg-hist-docs/

Pace Law Library, "Legislative History Research Guide," http://libraryguides.law.pace.edu/legis_history

University of Washington School of Law, Gallagher Law Library, "Federal Legislative History," http://lib.law.washington.edu/ref/fedlegishist.html

University of Michigan, "Research Guides," http://guides.lib.umich.edu/congress

Bills

Text

[1993–]: U.S. Government Printing Office, "Congressional Bills," www.gpo.gov/fdsys/browse/collection.action?collectionCode=BILLS

[1989–]: Library of Congress, "Browse Bills & Resolutions," http://thomas.loc.gov/home/LegislativeData.php?&n=Browse&c=101

Tracking

[1973–]: Library of Congress, "Browse Public Laws," http://thomas.loc.gov/home/LegislativeData.php?&n=PublicLaws&c=93

Executive

Directory of Federal Agencies

Washburn University School of Law, Washlaw, "U.S. Federal Resources: Agencies," www.washlaw.edu/doclaw/executive5m.html

Overview of Federal Rulemaking Process

Open CRS, "The Federal Rulemaking Process: An Overview," https://opencrs.com/document/ RL32240/2011-02-22/

Regulations

Research Guide

University of Washington School of Law, Gallagher Law Library, "U.S. Administrative Law Research: General Sources," http://lib.law .washington.edu/content/guides/adminus

By Agency (Code)—
Code of Federal Regulations

[current]: U.S. Government Printing Office, "Electronic Code of Federal Regulations," www.ecfr.gov

[current]: Cornell University Law School, Legal Information Institute, "CFR," www.law.cornell .edu/cfr/

[1996–]: U.S. Government Printing Office, "Advanced Search: Code of Federal Regulations," www.gpo.gov/fdsys/search/ advanced/advsearchpage.action

[1996–]: U.S. Government Printing Office, "Code of Federal Regulations (Annual Edition)," www.gpo.gov/fdsys/browse/collection Cfr.action?collectionCode=CFR

In Chronological Order (Register)—
Federal Register

[1994–]: U.S. Government Printing Office, "Advanced Search: Federal Register," www.gpo.gov/fdsys/search/advanced/ advsearchpage.action

[1994–]: U.S. Government Printing Office, "Federal Register," www.gpo.gov/fdsys/browse/ collection.action?collectionCode=FR

Administrative Rulings

Research Guide

University of Virginia Law Library, "Administrative Decisions," http://guides.lib .virginia.edu/administrative_decisions

Practice Materials and Self-Help Resources

Research Guide

University of California, Hastings College of the Law, "Federal and Multi-Jurisdictional Legal Forms," http://librarysource.uchastings.edu/sp/ subjects/guide.php?subject=fed-legal-forms

Court Rules

Research Guides

Georgetown University Law Library, "Federal Court Rules Research Guide," www.law .georgetown.edu/library/research/guides/federal _court_rules.cfm

Duke University, Duke Law, "Court Rules," www.law.duke.edu/lib/researchguides/courtr

Federal Judiciary Rulemaking Process

United States Courts, "Federal Rules of Practice & Procedure," www.uscourts.gov/rulesandpolicies/ rules.aspx

Text of Rules

Cornell University Law School, Legal Information Institute, "Rules of the Supreme Court of the United States," www.law.cornell .edu/rules/supct

Cornell University Law School, Legal Information Institute, "Federal Rules of Civil Procedure," www.law.cornell.edu/rules/frcp

Cornell University Law School, Legal Information Institute, "Federal Rules of Evidence," www.law.cornell.edu/rules/fre

Forms

LLRX, "Court Rules, Forms, and Dockets," www.llrx.com/courtrules/

Bar Association Public Resources

ABA, Section of Litigation, "Publications,"
www.americanbar.org/groups/litigation/publications
.html

Court Brochures/Self-Help Centers

Federal Judicial Center, www.fjc.gov

Miscellaneous

Federation of American Scientists, Congressional
Research Service, "Publications of
Congressional Committees: A Summary,"
www.fas.org/sgp/crs/misc/98-673.pdf

References

FindLaw, "Legal Dictionary," http://dictionary.
lp.findlaw.com
Nolo, "Free Dictionary of Law Terms and Legal
Definitions," www.nolo.com/dictionary/
United States Senate, "Glossary," www.senate.
gov/pagelayout/reference/b_three_sections_with_
teasers/glossary.htm
Peter W. Martin, "Introduction to Basic Legal
Citation" (online ed. 2012), www.law.cornell.
edu/citation/index.htm

WASHINGTON, D.C.

Washington, D.C., is part of the federal government and is governed by federal law. However,
because Washington is a city, laws have been specifically passed by Congress in order to run it as a
separate city. As a result, it has its own trial court,
city council, and mayor, plus ordinances and
other laws that pertain only to it. The resources
below relate to Washington, D.C., as a city.

Research Guides

General

AALL LISP, "Public Library Toolkit: District of
Columbia," www.aallnet.org/sections/lisp/Public-
Library-Toolkit

Georgetown University Law Library, "District of
Columbia In-Depth," www.law.georgetown.edu/
library/research/guides/dc-in-depth.cfm

Topical

Georgetown University Law Library, "District of
Columbia Voting Rights: A Research Guide,"
www.law.georgetown.edu/library/research/guides/
dcvotingrights.cfm

Judicial

D.C. Court Structure

Georgetown University Law Library, "District of
Columbia In-Depth: Courts and Cases," www.
law.georgetown.edu/library/research/guides/dc-in-
depth.cfm#courts-and-cases
District of Columbia Courts, "Organizational
Structure" [interactive diagram], www.
dccourts.gov/internet/about/orgstructure/main.jsf

Directory of D.C. Courts

District of Columbia Courts, "Addresses and
Phones," www.dccourts.gov/internet/about/
gettinghere/addresses.jsf

Opinions

Research Guide

Georgetown University Law Library, "District
of Columbia In-Depth: Court Opinions,"
www.law.georgetown.edu/library/research/guides/
dc-in-depth.cfm#ii-court-opinions

Highest Court—DC Court of Appeals

[1998–]: District of Columbia Courts, "Search
D.C. Court of Appeals Opinions,"
www.dcappeals.gov/internet/opinionlocator.jsf

Intermediate Appellate Court—None

Dockets/Court Records

Trial Court

District of Columbia Courts, "Court Cases Online,"
www.dccourts.gov/internet/system/apps/CCO.jsf

Legislative

State Legislative Process

Council of the District of Columbia, "How a Bill Becomes a Law," http://dccouncil.us/pages/how-a-bill-becomes-a-law

Statutes

Research Guide

Georgetown University Law Library, "District of Columbia In-Depth: Statutory Law," www.law.georgetown.edu/library/research/guides/dc-in-depth.cfm#statutory-law

By Subject (Code)—District of Columbia Code

LexisNexis, "D.C. Official Code Online," www.lexisnexis.com/hottopics/dccode/

In Chronological Order (Session Laws)—Acts

[1989–]: Council of the District of Columbia, "Legislative Information Management System (LIMS)," http://dcclims1.dccouncil.us/lims/

Legislative History

Research Guide

Georgetown University Law Library, "District of Columbia In-Depth: Legislative History," www.law.georgetown.edu/library/research/guides/dc-in-depth.cfm#v-legislative-history

Executive

Directory of D.C. Departments/Agencies

District of Columbia, "Directory of Agencies and Services," http://directory.dc.gov

Regulations

Research Guide

Georgetown University Law Library, "District of Columbia In-Depth: Regulations," www.law.georgetown.edu/library/research/guides/dc-in-depth.cfm#i-regulations

By Agency (Code)—District of Columbia Municipal Regulations

Secretary of the District of Columbia, Office of Documents and Administrative Issuances, "D.C. Municipal Regulations and D.C. Register," www.dcregs.org

In Chronological Order (Register)—District of Columbia Register

[2003–]: District of Columbia, Office of the Secretary, "DC Register Archive," http://os.dc.gov/service/dc-register-archive

Practice Materials and Self-Help Resources

Research Guides

District of Columbia Bar, "Virtual Library," www.dcbar.org/for_lawyers/resources/virtual_library/

Bar Association of the District of Columbia, "Publications," www.badc.org/i4a/pages/

Court Rules

Court of Appeals

District of Columbia Courts, "Rules of the D.C. Court of Appeals," www.dccourts.gov/internet/appellate/dccarules.jsf

Superior Court

District of Columbia Courts, "Rules and Rule Promulgation Orders," www.dccourts.gov/internet/superior/dcscrules.jsf

State Bar Association Consumer Brochures

District of Columbia Bar, "For the Public," www.dcbar.org/for_the_public/

Court Brochures/Self-Help Centers

District of Columbia Courts, "Public," www.dccourts.gov/internet/public/main.jsf

Looking for an Attorney (for a fee or for free)

Legal Aid/Advocacy Groups/Pro Bono

District of Columbia Bar, "Programs and Services," www.dcbar.org/for_the_public/ programs_and_services/

Pro Bono Net, LawHelp.org, www.lawhelp.org/DC/

Finding an Attorney/Lawyer Referrals

District of Columbia Bar, "Working with Lawyers," www.dcbar.org/for_the_public/working _with_lawyers/

Miscellaneous

Brookings Institution, "Research: Washington, DC Region," www.brookings.edu/research/topics/ washington-dc

References

Westlaw, "Glossary for Legal Research Basics," http://lawschool.westlaw.com/shared/ marketinfodisplayasp?code=RE&id=17& mainpage = 23&rtid=116&rtcode=re

Cornell University Law School, Legal Information Institute, *Wex* [dictionary and encyclopedia], www.law.cornell.edu/wex/

SECTION 3: STATES

ALABAMA

Research Guides

AALL LISP, "Public Library Toolkit: Alabama," www.aallnet.org/sections/lisp/Public-Library-Toolkit

University of Alabama, Bounds Law Library, www.library.law.ua.edu/links/bama.htm

Jones School of Law Library, "Research Cornerstones: Alabama Legal Sources," http:// joneslawlibrary.org/jsllibrary/alabama_res.pdf

Judicial

State Court Structure

Alabama State Bar, "Alabama's Court System," www.alabar.org/brochures/court-system.pdf

Administrative Office of Courts, "Alabama Unified Judicial System Structure" [diagram], www.alacourt.gov/CourtStructure.aspx

Directory of State Courts

NCSC, "State Court Web Sites," www.ncsc.org/ information-and-resources/browse-by-state/state -court-websites.aspx#alabama

Opinions

Highest Court—Supreme Court

[1997–]: FindLaw, "Supreme Court of Alabama Cases," http://caselaw.findlaw.com/court/ al-supreme-court

[1950–]: FindACase, http://findacase.com/research/ advanced-search.aspx

Intermediate Appellate Courts

[1997–]: FindLaw, "Court of Civil Appeals of Alabama Cases," http://caselaw.findlaw.com/ court/al-court-of-civil-appeals/years/

[1997–]: FindLaw, "Court of Criminal Appeals of Alabama Cases," http://caselaw.findlaw.com/ court/al-court-of-criminal-appeals/years/

Dockets/Court Records

Trial Courts

On-Line Information Services Inc. [fee-based], https://v2.alacourt.com

Legislative

State Legislative Process

Alabama State Legislature / Alabama State House, "Alabama's Legislative Process,"

www.legislature.state.al.us/misc/legislativeprocess/
legislativeprocess_ml.html

Statutes

By Subject (Code)—
Code of Alabama 1975

ALISON (Alabama Legislative Information System Online), http://alisondb.legislature.state
.al.us/acas/ACASLoginMac.asp

FindLaw, "Alabama Code," http://codes.lp.findlaw
.com/alcode

Justia.com, "Alabama Code," http://law.justia.com/
codes/alabama/

Law and Legal Research [blog], **"Code of Alabama,"** http://law.onecle.com/alabama/

In Chronological Order (Session Laws)—
Acts of Alabama

[1818–2010]: Public Affairs Research Council of Alabama, "Local Act Database" [fee-based], http://parca.samford.edu/TaxActHome.aspx

[2000–]: ALISON (Alabama Legislative Information System Online), "Session," http://alisondb.legislature.state.al.us/acas/
ACASLoginMac.asp

[2001–2012]: Legislative Reference Service of the State of Alabama [summaries], http://lrs.state.al.us

Legislative History

Research Guide

Alabama Legislature, "Alabama Legislative History: Overview," www.legislature.state.al.us/
misc/history/histoverview.html

Executive

Directory of State Departments/Agencies

Alabama Department of Finance, "The Alabama Directory," http://info.alabama.gov/directory.aspx

State Rulemaking Process

USLegal, "Administrative Procedure Act— Alabama," http://administrativelaw.uslegal.com/
administrative-procedure-acts/alabama/

Regulations

By Agency (Code)—
Alabama Administrative Code

Legislative Reference Service, www.alabamaadministrativecode.state.al.us

In Chronological Order (Register)—
Alabama Administrative Monthly

[2007–]: Legislative Reference Service, www.alabamaadministrativecode.state.al.us/
monthly.html

Local Laws

Directory of State Counties/Municipalities

State and Local Government on the Net, "Alabama State and Local Government," www.statelocalgov.net/state-al.cfm

Ordinances

Municode Code Corporation, "Alabama," www.municode.com/library/AL

Practice Materials and Self-Help Resources

Research Guides

N/A

Court Rules

Alabama Judicial System, Supreme Court and State Law Library, "Alabama Rules of Court," http://judicial.alabama.gov/library/rules
_of_court.cfm

Forms

Alabama Administrative Office of Courts, "E-Forms," http://eforms.alacourt.gov

AllLaw, "State Legal Forms" [fee-based], www.alllaw.com/state_resources/alabama/forms/

State Bar Association Consumer Brochures

Alabama State Bar, "Brochures," www.alabar.org/brochures/

Court Brochures/Self-Help Centers

N/A

*Looking for an Attorney
(for a fee or for free)*

Legal Aid/Advocacy Groups/Pro Bono

Pro Bono Net, AlabamaLegalHelp.org,
    www.alabamalegalhelp.org
American Bar Association, Pro Bono Program
    Listings, http://apps.americanbar.org/legalservices/
    probono/directory/alabama.html

Finding an Attorney/Lawyer Referrals

Alabama State Bar, "ABS Lawyer Referral
    Service," www.alabar.org/lrs/
Mobile Bar Association, "How Can I Find a
    Lawyer?" [under "Public Information"],
    www.mobilebar.com

Miscellaneous

Alabama Appellate Courts, "Appellate Process
    Chart," http://judicial.alabama.gov/chart
    _appellate.cfm
Law Libraries Association of Alabama,
    "Bibliography of Alabama Law Books,"
    www.aallnet.org/chapter/llaa/biblio.html

References

Westlaw, "Glossary for Legal Research
    Basics," http://lawschool.westlaw.com/shared/
    marketinfodisplayasp?code= RE&id=17&
    mainpage=23&rtid =116&rtcode=re
Cornell University Law School, Legal
    Information Institute, *Wex* [dictionary and
    encyclopedia], www.law.cornell.edu/wex/

ALASKA

Research Guides

Alaska Court System, "Legal Research—Alaska
    Resources," www.courts.alaska.gov/aklegal.htm
AALL LISP, "Public Library Toolkit: Alaska,"
    www.aallnet.org/sections/lisp/Public-Library-Toolkit

Judicial

State Court Structure

Alaska Court System, "About the Alaska Court
    System," www.courts.alaska.gov/ctinfo.htm
Court Statistic Project, "Alaska" [diagram],
    www.courtstatistics.org/Other-Pages/State_Court
    _Structure_Charts/Alaska.aspx

Directory of State Courts

Alaska Court System, "Alaska Courts Directory,"
    www.courts.alaska.gov/courtdir.htm

Opinions

Highest Court—Supreme Court

[1960–]: Westlaw, "Alaska Case Law Service,"
    http://government.westlaw.com/akcases/

Intermediate Appellate Court—Court of Appeals

[1960–]: Westlaw, "Alaska Case Law Service,"
    http://government.westlaw.com/akcases/

Dockets/Court Records

Appellate Courts

Alaska Appellate Courts, "Case Management
    System," www.appellate.courts.state.ak.us

Trial Courts

CourtView, "Trial Court Records Search,"
    www.courtrecords.alaska.gov

Legislative

State Legislative Process

Alaska Department of Commerce, Community,
    and Economic Development, "Legislative
    Process in Alaska," www.commerce.state.ak.us/
    oed/ardor/pub/legprocess.pdf

Statutes

By Subject (Code)—Alaska Statutes

[1993–]: Alaska State Legislature, "Infobases,"
    www.legis.state.ak.us/basis/folio.asp

In Chronological Order (Session Laws)—
Session Laws

[1981–]: Alaska State Legislature, "Infobases,"
www.legis.state.ak.us/basis/folio.asp

Legislative History

Research Guides

Alaska State Legislature, "Legislative History,"
http://w3.legis.state.ak.us/misc/leg_history.php

Alaska State Court Library, "Alaska Legislative
History," www.courts.alaska.gov/library/
akleghistory.pdf

Alaska State Legislature, Legislative Reference
Library, "Tips for Researching Alaska
Legislative History Using Alaska State
Legislature Web Site," http://w3.legis.state.ak.us/
docs/pdf/Tips_for_researching_ak_leg_hist_using_
ak_state_leg_web_site.pdf

Executive

Directory of State Departments/Agencies

State of Alaska, "My Government,"
www.alaska.gov/akdir1.html

State Rulemaking Process

USLegal, "Administrative Procedure Act—
Alaska," http://administrativelaw.uslegal.com/
administrative-procedure-acts/alaska/

Regulations

By Agency (Code)—Alaska Administrative Code

Alaska State Legislature, "The Alaska
Administrative Code," www.legis.state.ak.us/
basis/folioproxy.asp?url=wwwjnu01.legis.state.ak.us/
cgi-bin/folioisa.dll/aac

Alaska State Legislature, "Infobases,"
www.legis.state.ak.us/basis/folio.asp

In Chronological Order (Register)—
Alaska State Administrative Journal

[1999–]: Alaska State Legislature, "The Alaska
Administrative Journal," www.legis.state.ak.us/
basis/folioproxy.asp?url=wwwjnu01.legis.state.ak.us/
cgi-bin/folioisa.dll/adjr

[1999–]: Alaska State Legislature, "Infobases,"
www.legis.state.ak.us/basis/folio.asp

Local Laws

Directories of State Counties/Municipalities

National Association of Counties, "Find a County,"
www.naco.org/Counties/Pages/FindACounty.aspx

State and Local Government on the Net,
"Alaska State and Local Government,"
www.statelocalgov.net/state-ak.cfm

Ordinances

Alaska Court System, "Alaska Municipal Codes,"
www.courts.alaska.gov/aklegal.htm#muni

Municode Code Corporation, "Alaska,"
www.municode.com/library/AK

Practice Materials and Self-Help Resources

Research Guides

N/A

Court Rules

Alaska Court System, "Alaska Rules of Court,"
www.courts.alaska.gov/rules.htm

Forms

Alaska Court System, "Forms, Instructions, and
Publications," www.courts.alaska.gov/forms.htm

Alaska Court System, "Self-Help Center: Family
Law Forms," www.courts.alaska.gov/shcforms.htm

State Bar Association Consumer Brochures

N/A

Court Brochures/Self-Help Centers

Alaska Court System, "Self-Help Center: Family
Law," www.courts.alaska.gov/selfhelp.htm

Looking for an Attorney (for free or for a fee)

Legal Aid/Advocacy Groups/Pro Bono

Alaska Legal Services Corporation, www.alsc-law.org
Pro Bono Net, AlaskaLawHelp.org, www.alaskalawhelp.org/AK/

Finding an Attorney/Lawyer Referrals

Alaska Bar Association, "Lawyer Referral Service," https://www.alaskabar.org/servlet/content/lawyer_referral_serv.html
Cornell University Law School, Legal Information Institute, "Legal Services & Lawyers," http://lawyers.law.cornell.edu

Miscellaneous

Alaska Department of Labor and Workforce Development, Employment Security Division [for Alaska Workers' Compensation Board decisions], http://uiappeals.labor.alaska.gov
Disability Law Center of Alaska, www.dlcak.org

Reference

Alaska State Legislature, "Glossary of Legislative Terms," http://w3.legis.state.ak.us/docs/pdf/glossary.pdf

ARIZONA

Research Guides

University of Arizona, John E. Rogers College of Law, "Research Guides and Portals," www.law.arizona.edu/Library/Research/guides.cfm
Arizona State University, Sandra Day O'Connor College of Law, "Research Guides and Portals," www.law.asu.edu/library/RossBlakleyLawLibrary/ResearchNow/ResearchGuides.aspx#AZ
AALL LISP, "Public Library Toolkit: Arizona," www.aallnet.org/sections/lisp/Public-Library-Toolkit

Judicial

State Court Structure

Arizona Judicial Branch, "How Arizona Courts Are Organized," www.azcourts.gov/guidetoazcourts/HowArizonaCourtsareOrganized.aspx
Court Statistics Project, "Arizona" [diagram], www.courtstatistics.org/Other-Pages/State_Court_Structure_Charts/Arizona.aspx

Directory of State Courts

Arizona Judicial Branch, "AZ Courts Locator," www.azcourts.gov/AZCourts/AZCourtsLocator.aspx

Opinions

Research Guide

Arizona State University, Sandra Day O'Connor College of Law, "Arizona Cases and Court Rules," www.law.asu.edu/library/RossBlakleyLawLibrary/ResearchNow/ResearchGuides/ArizonaCasesandCourtRules.aspx

Highest Court—Supreme Court

[1998–]: Arizona Judicial Branch, "Opinions," www.azcourts.gov/Default.aspx?alias=www.azcourts.gov/opinions
[1997–]: FindLaw, "Supreme Court of Arizona Cases," http://caselaw.findlaw.com/court/az-supreme-court/years/

Intermediate Appellate Court—Court of Appeals

"Arizona Court of Appeals, Division One" [recent], http://azcourts.gov/coa1/DivisionOne.aspx
"Arizona Court of Appeals, Division Two" [recent], www.apltwo.ct.state.az.us
[1997–]: FindLaw, "Court of Appeals of Arizona Cases," http://caselaw.findlaw.com/court/az-court-of-appeals

Dockets/Court Records

Trial Courts

Arizona Court of Appeals, Division Two, "Case Information," www.apltwo.ct.state.az.us/ODSPlus/caseInfo.cfm

Arizona Judicial Branch, "Public Access to Court Information," http://apps.supremecourt.az.gov/publicaccess/caselookup.aspx

Legislative

State Legislative Process

Randall Gnant, "From Idea to Bill to Law: The Legislative Process in Arizona" (2000), www.azleg.gov/alisPDFs/BillToLaw.pdf

Bob Richards, "Arizona Bill" (1977) [diagram], www.azleg.gov/alisPDFs/hbillaw.pdf

Statutes

Research Guide

Arizona State University, Sandra Day O'Connor College of Law, "Arizona Legislation and Statutes," www.law.asu.edu/library/RossBlakleyLawLibrary/ResearchNow/ResearchGuides/ArizonaLegislationandStatutes.aspx

By Subject (Code)—Arizona Revised Statutes

Arizona State Legislature, "Arizona Revised Statutes," www.azleg.state.az.us/ArizonaRevisedStatutes.asp

In Chronological Order (Session Laws)—
Chaptered Bills

[1997–]: Arizona State Legislature, "Session Laws (Chaptered Bills)," www.azleg.gov/SessionLaws.asp

Legislative History

Research Guides

Arizona State University, Sandra Day O'Connor College of Law, "Arizona Legislative History: Research Guide," www.law.asu.edu/library/RossBlakleyLawLibraryResearchNow/ResearchGuides/ArizonaLegislative History Research Guide.aspx

Arizona State Library, Archives, and Public Records, "Guide to Arizona Legislative History at Arizona's Capitol," www.lib.az.us/is/lr/leghist.cfm

Jacquelyn Kasper, Cracchiolo Law Library, James E. Rogers College of Law, University of Arizona, "Arizona Legislative History: A Step-By-Step Research Guide," www.law.arizona.edu/Library/Research/Guides/AZlegHist.pdf

Executive

Directory of State Departments/Agencies

AZ.gov, "State Agency Directory," http://az.gov/app/contactaz/a-b.xhtml

State Rulemaking Process

Arizona Department of State, Office of the Secretary of State, "Arizona Rulemaking Manual," www.azsos.gov/public_services/rulemakingmanual/manual.htm

Regulations

Research Guide

Arizona State University, Sandra Day O'Connor College of Law, "Administrative Law: Regulations and Executive Orders," www.law.asu.edu/library/RossBlakleyLawLibrary/ResearchNow/ResearchGuides/AdministrativeLawRegulationsandExecutiveOrde.aspx

By Agency (Code)—Arizona Administrative Code

Arizona Department of State, Office of the Secretary of State, "Arizona Administrative Code," www.azsos.gov/public_services/Table_of_Contents.htm

In Chronological Order (Register)—Arizona
Administrative Register

[1995–]: Arizona Department of State, Office of the Secretary of State, "Arizona Administrative Register," www.azsos.gov/aar/contents.htm

Local Laws

Directory of State Counties/Municipalities

AZ.gov, "Arizona Cities & Counties," http://az.gov/government_county_statemap.html

Ordinances

Municipal Code Corporation, "Arizona,"
www.municode.com/library/AZ

Sterling Codifiers Inc., "Codes Online,"
www.sterlingcodifiers.com/codes-online

Code Publishing Co., "Arizona,"
www.codepublishing.com/elibrary.html#arizona

Practice Materials and Self-Help Resources

Research Guides

University of Arizona, John E. Rogers College of Law, "A Guide To Arizona Practice Materials at the Cracchiolo Law Library,"
www.law.arizona.edu/Library/Research/Guides/azpractice.cfm

University of Arizona, John E. Rogers College of Law, "Legal Self-Help Publications,"
www.law.arizona.edu/Library/Research/Guides/Selfhelp/self_help_bib.cfm

Court Rules

Arizona Judicial Branch, "Rules,"
www.azcourts.gov/rules/

Forms

Arizona State University, Sandra Day O'Connor College of Law, "Arizona Legal Forms,"
www.law.asu.edu/library/RossBlakleyLawLibrary/ResearchNow/ResearchGuides/ArizonaLegalForms.aspx

State Bar Association Consumer Brochures

N/A

Court Brochures/Self-Help Centers

N/A

Looking for an Attorney (for a fee or for free)

Legal Aid/Advocacy Groups/Pro Bono

Coconino County, Arizona, "Law Library,"
www.coconino.az.gov/index.aspx?nid=863

State Bar of Arizona, "Lawyers on Call,"
www.azbar.org/legalhelpandeducation/lawyersoncall

Arizona Foundation for Legal Services and Education et al., www.azlawhelp.org

Finding an Attorney/Lawyer Referrals

Arizona State University, Sandra Day O'Connor College of Law, "Legal Advice in the Phoenix Area," www.law.asu.edu/library/RossBlakleyLawLibrary/ResearchNow/ResearchGuides/LegalAdviceinthePhoenixArea.aspx

State Bar of Arizona, "Find a Lawyer,"
www.azbar.org/LegalResources/findlawyer.cfm

Miscellaneous

Arizona State University, Sandra Day O'Connor College of Law, "Maricopa County Municipal and Justice Courts," www.law.asu.edu/library/RossBlakleyLawLibrary/ResearchNow/ResearchGuides/MaricopaCountyMunicipalandJusticeCourts.aspx

References

Westlaw, "Glossary for Legal Research Basics," http://lawschool.westlaw.com/shared/marketinfodisplayasp?code=RE&id=17&mainpage=23&rtid=116&rtcode=re

Cornell University Law School, Legal Information Institute, *Wex* [dictionary and encyclopedia], www.law.cornell.edu/wex/

ARKANSAS

Research Guides

University of Arkansas at Little Rock, William H. Bowen School of Law, "Research Guides," http://ualr.edu/law/library/research-guides/

Judicial

State Court Structure

Arkansas Judiciary, "Arkansas Court Structure" [diagram], https://courts.arkansas.gov/sites/default/files/Arkansas%20Court%20Structure.pdf

Directories of State Courts

Arkansas Judiciary, "Circuit Courts,"
https://courts.arkansas.gov/courts/circuit-courts

Arkansas Judiciary, "District Courts,"
https://courts.arkansas.gov/courts/district-courts

Opinions

Highest Court—Supreme Court

[1837–]: Arkansas Judiciary, "Opinions and Disciplinary Decisions," https://courts.arkansas.gov/opinions-and-disciplinary-decisions

Intermediate Appellate Court—Court of Appeals

[1981–]: Arkansas Judiciary, "Opinions and Disciplinary Decisions," https://courts.arkansas.gov/opinions-and-disciplinary-decisions

Dockets/Court Records

Appellate Courts

[last ninety days]: Arkansas Judiciary, "Docket Search," https://courts.arkansas.gov/docket-search

Trial Courts

Court.us, "Courts in Arkansas,"
www.court.us/arkansas_court_records.htm

BentonCountyAR.gov, "Circuit Clerk Public Records," http://bentoncountyar.gov/BCAdminSecond.aspx?m=CircuitPublicRecords

Legislative

State Legislative Process

Arkansas House of Representatives, "How a Bill Becomes a Law," www.arkansashouse.org/about-the-house/information-resources

Statutes

By Subject (Code)—Arkansas Code of 1987

LexisNexis, "Arkansas Code—Unannotated," www.lexisnexis.com/hottopics/arcode/

In Chronological Order (Session Laws)—
Acts of Arkansas

[1987–]: Arkansas State Legislature, "Historical Acts," www.arkleg.state.ar.us/SearchCenter/Pages/historicalact.aspx

Legislative History

Research Guide

Kathryn C. Fitzhugh, "Arkansas Legislative History Research" (2006), William H. Bowen School of Law Library, http://ualr.edu/law/files/2011/03/Arkansas_Legislative_Research.pdf

Executive

Directory of State Departments/Agencies

Arkansas.gov, "Government: Agencies," www.arkansas.gov/government/agencies

State Rulemaking Process

USLegal, "Administrative Procedure Act—Arkansas," http://administrativelaw.uslegal.com/administrative-procedure-acts/arkansas/

Regulations

By Agency (Code)—
Arkansas Administrative Rules

Arkansas Secretary of State, "Arkansas Administrative Rules," www.sosweb.state.ar.us/rules_and_regs/index.php/rules/search/new

In Chronological Order (Register)—
Arkansas Register

[2001–]: Arkansas Secretary of State, "Arkansas Register," www.sos.arkansas.gov/rules_regs.html#register

Local Laws

Directory of State Counties/Municipalities

Arkansas.gov, "Local Services," www.arkansas.gov/services/list/category/government-local

Ordinances

Municipal Code Corporation, "Arkansas,"
www.municode.com/library/AR

Justia.com, "Arkansas City Websites & City Codes," http://law.justia.com/arkansas/cities

Practice Materials and Self-Help Resources

Research Guide

Arkansas Legal Services Partnership, "Legal Library," www.arlegalservices.org/legal_library

Court Rules

Arkansas Judiciary, "Court Rules," https://courts.arkansas.gov/rules-and-administrative-orders/court-rules

Forms

Arkansas Judiciary, "Court Forms," https://courts.arkansas.gov/forms-and-publications

Arkansas Legal Services Partnership, "Free Self-Help Forms," www.arlegalservices.org/interactiveforms

Arkansas Bar Association, "Legal Pamphlets for the Public," www.arkbar.com/pages/legal_pamphlets_public.aspx

Court Brochures/Self-Help Centers

N/A

Looking for an Attorney (for a fee or for free)

Legal Aid/Advocacy Groups/Pro Bono

American Bar Association, Division for Legal Services, "Arkansas," http://apps.americanbar.org/legalservices/findlegalhelp/freehelp.cfm?id=AR

Arkansas Legal Services Partnership, "Contacting the HelpLine," www.arlegalservices.org/helpline

Finding an Attorney/Lawyer Referrals

Arkansas Bar Association, "Find a Lawyer," www.arkansasfindalawyer.com

Arkansas Judiciary, "Attorney Search," https://attorneyinfo.aoc.arkansas.gov/info/attorney_search/info/attorney/attorneysearch.aspx

Reference

Arkansas Legal Services Partnership, "Free Law Dictionary," www.arlegalservices.org/Dictionary

CALIFORNIA

Research Guides

Southern California Association of Law Libraries, *Locating the Law*, 5th ed. (2011), www.aallnet.org/chapter/scall/locating.htm

University of California, Berkeley Law Library, "California Guides," www.law.berkeley.edu/library/dynamic/online.php?node=19

University of San Francisco School of Law, "California Research Guides," www.usfca.edu/law/library/research/california/

University of San Diego School of Law, "LRC Research Guides—California," www.sandiego.edu/law/lrc/find_resources/california_guides.php

UCLA School of Law, LibGuides, "California Law," http://libguides.law.ucla.edu/cat.php?cid=7686

University of California, Hastings College of the Law, "California Law," http://librarysource.uchastings.edu/sp/subjects/guide.php?subject=cal-law

Santa Clara University, Santa Clara Law, "LawGuides," http://lawguides.scu.edu

Judicial

State Court Structure

Superior Court of California, Santa Clara County, "Overview of the State Court System," www.scscourt.org/general_info/community/courtsystem.shtml

Directory of State Courts

Judicial Branch of California, California Courts, "Courts," www.courts.ca.gov/courts.htm

Opinions

Research Guides

University of Southern California, Gould School of Law, "How to Find Cases," http://lawweb.usc.edu/library/research/basic/cases.cfm

UCLA School of Law, "California Case Materials Checklist," http://libguides.law.ucla.edu/californiacases

Highest Court—Supreme Court

[last 120 days]: Judicial Branch of California, California Courts, "Opinions," www.courts.ca.gov/opinions.htm

[1934–]: FindLaw, "California Supreme and Appellate Court Cases," www.findlaw.com/cacases/

[1850–]: LexisNexis, "California Official Reports," www.lexisnexis.com/clients/CACourts/

[2000–]: FindLaw, "Browse Supreme Court of California Opinion Summaries," http://caselaw.findlaw.com/summary/court/ca-supreme-court/years/

Intermediate Appellate Court—Court of Appeals

[last 120 days]: Judicial Branch of California, California Courts, "Opinions," www.courts.ca.gov/opinions.htm

[1934–]: FindLaw, "California Supreme and Appellate Court Cases," www.findlaw.com/cacases/

[1905–]: LexisNexis, "California Official Reports," www.lexisnexis.com/clients/CACourts/

[2000–]: FindLaw, "Browse California Court of Appeal Opinion Summaries," http://caselaw.findlaw.com/summary/court/ca-court-of-appeal/years/

Dockets/Court Records

All Courts

LLRX, "Court Rules, Forms, and Dockets" [browse by jurisdiction/state = "California" and type = "dockets"], www.llrx.com/courtrules/

Court.us, "Courts in California," www.court.us/california_court_records.htm

NCSC, "Privacy/Public Access to Court Records: State Links," www.ncsc.org/Topics/Access-and-Fairness/Privacy-Public-Access-to-Court-Records/State-Links.aspx#California

Legislative

State Legislative Process

State of California, Legislative Counsel, "Overview of Legislative Process," www.leginfo.ca.gov/bil2lawx.html

Statutes

Research Guides

University of Southern California, Gould School of Law, "Finding California Statutes," http://lawweb.usc.edu/library/research/uslaw/californialaw/statues.cfm#sec1 [sic]

UCLA School of Law, "Finding California Statutes," http://libguides.law.ucla.edu/californiastatutes

By Subject (Code)—California Law

State of California, Legislative Counsel, "California Law," www.leginfo.ca.gov/calaw.html

In Chronological Order (Session Laws)—Chapter Laws

[1993–]: State of California, Legislative Counsel, "Statutes," www.leginfo.ca.gov/statute.html

Legislative History

Research Guides

Jan Raymond, Legislative History & Intent, "Information & Services on California Law," http://najfiles.net/Web/CA.php

Legislative Research & Intent, "California Links," www.lrihistory.com/RESOURCES/CaliforniaLinks.aspx

University of Southern California, Gould School of Law, "California Legislative History Research," http://lawweb.usc.edu/library/research/uslaw/californialaw/history.cfm

University of San Francisco School of Law, "Finding California Legislative History, Guide and Checklist," www.usfca.edu/law/library/research/california/history/

UCLA School of Law, "California Legislative History," http://libguides.law.ucla.edu/callegislativehistory

University of San Diego School of Law, "California Legislative History," www.sandiego.edu/law/documents/lrc/research_guides/GS03.pdf

LA Law Library, "California Legislative History Information," www.lalawlibrary.org/research/pathfinders/califleghistory/

Executive

Directory of State Departments/Agencies

StateInformation.com, "California State Agencies," www.stateinformation.com/stateagencies.html

State Rulemaking Process

California Office of Administrative Law, "How to Participate in the Rulemaking Process," www.oal.ca.gov/res/docs/pdf/HowToParticipate.pdf

Regulations

Research Guides

University of Southern California, Gould School of Law, "Finding California Regulations," http://lawweb.usc.edu/library/research/uslaw/californialaw/statues.cfm#sec5 [sic]

University of San Francisco School of Law, "California Regulations," www.usfca.edu/law/library/research/california/finding/#california_regulations

UCLA School of Law, "California Administrative Law," http://libguides.law.ucla.edu/caladminlaw

University of San Diego School of Law, "Locating California Administrative Regulations," www.sandiego.edu/law/documents/lrc/research_guides/GS09.pdf

By Agency (Code)—
California Code of Regulations

Westlaw/California Office of Administrative Law, "California Code of Regulations," www.calregs.com

In Chronological Order (Register)—
California Regulatory Notice Register

[2002–]: California Office of Administration Law, "The California Regulatory Notice Register Online,"www.oal.ca.gov/California_Regulatory_Notice_Online.htm

Local Laws

Directories of State Counties/Municipalities

California State Association of Counties, "County Profile Information," www.csac.counties.org/county-websites-profile-information

CA.gov, "City Government," www.ca.gov/About/Government/Local/cities/

Ordinances

Municipal Code Corporation, "California," www.municode.com/library/CA

University of California, Berkeley, Institute of Governmental Studies, "California Local Codes and Charters," http://igs.berkeley.edu/node/11317

American Legal Publishing Corporation, "State of California Code Library," www.amlegal.com/nxt/gateway.dll?f=templates&fn=default.htm&vid=amlegal:ca

Quality Code Publishing, "Online Codes," www.qualitycodepublishing.com/codes.htm

Sterling Codifiers Inc., "Codes Online," www.sterlingcodifiers.com/codes-online

Practice Materials and Self-Help Resources

Research Guides

University of San Francisco School of Law, "California Practice Guides & Formbooks," www.usfca.edu/law/library/research/california/guides/

UCLA School of Law, "Online Legal Research: Beyond LexisNexis & Westlaw" ["Self-Help" tab], http://libguides.law.ucla.edu/onlinelegalresearch

UC Davis School of Law, "California Practice Materials," www.law.ucdavis.edu/library/research-guides/california-practice-materials.html

Court Rules

Judicial Branch of California, California Courts, "Rules of Court," www.courts.ca.gov/rules.htm

Forms

Judicial Branch of California, California Courts, "Browse All Forms," www.courts.ca.gov/forms.htm

State Bar of California, "Consumer Information [Pamphlets]," http://calbar.ca.gov/Public/Pamphlets.aspx

Court Brochures/Self-Help Centers

Judicial Branch of California, California Courts, "Online Self-Help Center," www.courts.ca.gov/selfhelp.htm

Looking for an Attorney (for a fee or for free)

Legal Aid/Advocacy Groups/Pro Bono

University of San Diego School of Law, "Free Legal Assistance," www.sandiego.edu/law/free_legal_assistance/

University of San Diego School of Law, "Referrals for Pro Bono Services," www.sandiego.edu/law/documents/lrc/information_guides/IS09.pdf

University of San Diego School of Law, "Referrals for Legal Advice," www.sandiego.edu/law/documents/lrc/information_guides/IS06.pdf

Finding an Attorney/Lawyer Referrals

State Bar of California, "Lawyer Referral Services," www.calbar.ca.gov/Public/LawyerReferralServicesLRS.aspx

LA Law Library, "Find A Lawyer," www.lalawlibrary.org/research/lawyers/

Miscellaneous

ABA Division for Bar Services, "State & Local Bar Associations: California," www.americanbar.org/groups/bar_services/resources/state_local_bar_associations/ca.html

References

American Association of Law Libraries, "Glossary of Legal Terms," www.aallnet.org/chapter/scall/locating/app_a.pdf

American Association of Law Libraries, "How to Read a Legal Citation," www.aallnet.org/chapter/scall/locating/ch2.pdf

COLORADO

Research Guides

AALL LISP, "Public Library Toolkit: Colorado," www.aallnet.org/sections/lisp/Public-Library-Toolkit

Colorado Association of Law Libraries, "Legal Research Corner," www.aallnet.org/chapter/coall/lrc.asp

University of Denver, Sturm College of Law, "Colorado Legal Research," http://libguides.law.du.edu/cat.php?cid=10931

Judicial

State Court Structure

Colorado Judicial Branch, "Colorado's State Court System," www.courts.state.co.us/Courts/

Court Statistics Project, "Arizona" [diagram], www.courtstatistics.org/Other-Pages/State_Court_Structure_Charts/Colorado.aspx

Directories of State Courts

Colorado Judicial Branch, "Courts by County," www.courts.state.co.us/Courts/County/Choose.cfm

Colorado Judicial Branch, "Courts by District," www.courts.state.co.us/Courts/District/Choose.cfm

Opinions

Research Guide

University of Denver, Sturm College of Law, Westminster Law Library, "Colorado Case Resources," http://law.du.edu/images/uploads/library/28COCaseResources.pdf

Highest Court—Supreme Court

[2009–]: Colorado Judicial Branch, "Colorado Supreme Court Case Announcements," www.courts.state.co.us/Courts/Supreme_Court/Case_Announcements/

[past twelve months]: Colorado Bar Association, "Colorado Supreme Court Decisions," www.cobar.org/opinions/index.cfm?courtid=2

Intermediate Appellate Court—Court of Appeals

[2009–]: Colorado Judicial Branch, "Court of Appeals Court Case Announcements," www.courts.state.co.us/Courts/Court_Of_Appeals/Case_Announcements/

[past twelve months]: Colorado Bar Association, "Colorado Court of Appeals Opinions," www.cobar.org/opinions/index.cfm?courtid=1

Dockets/Court Records

Trial Courts

LexisNexis, "Colorado Courts Record Search" [fee-based], https://www.cocourts.com/cocourts/

Legislative

State Legislative Process

Colorado.gov, "The Legislative Process," www.colorado.gov/cs/Satellite?blobcol=urldata&blobheader=application%2Fpdf&blobkey=id&blobtable=MungoBlobs&blobwhere=1231572728402&ssbinary=true

Colorado General Assembly, Office of Legislative Legal Services, "How a Bill Becomes a Colorado Law," [diagram], www.state.co.us/gov_dir/leg_dir/olls/PDF/Bill%20becomes%20law%20chart.pdf

Statutes

Research Guides

University of Denver, Sturm College of Law, "Colorado Statutes," http://libguides.law.du.edu/colostatutes

University of Colorado Boulder, Colorado Law, "How to Find Colorado Statutes," www.colorado.edu/law/lawlib/howto/statutes-guide.pdf

By Subject (Code)—Colorado Revised Statutes

LexisNexis, Colorado Legal Resources, "Colorado Revised Statutes," www.lexisnexis.com/hottopics/colorado/

In Chronological Order (Session Laws)—Session Laws of Colorado

[1993–]: Colorado General Assembly, Office of Legislative Legal Services, "Session Laws of Colorado," http://tornado.state.co.us/gov_dir/leg_dir/olls/session_laws_of_colorado.htm

Legislative History

Research Guide

University of Denver, Sturm College of Law, "Colorado Legislative History," http://libguides.law.du.edu/coloradolegislativehistory

Executive

Directory of State Departments/Agencies

Colorado.gov, "State Agencies," www.colorado.gov/government/government/state-agencies.html

State Rulemaking Process

Colorado Secretary of State, "Administrative Rules of State Agencies," www.sos.state.co.us/pubs/CCR/rules.html

Regulations

Research Guide

University of Denver, Sturm College of Law, "Federal Administrative & Executive Law," http://libguides.law.du.edu/administrative

By Agency (Code)—Code of Colorado Regulations

Colorado Secretary of State, "Code of Colorado Regulations," www.sos.state.co.us/CCR/Welcome.do

In Chronological Order (Register)—Colorado Register

[2006–]: Colorado Secretary of State, "Colorado Register," www.sos.state.co.us/CCR/RegisterHome.do

Local Laws

Directory of State Counties/Municipalities

Colorado Department of Local Affairs, "Active Colorado Local Governments," https://dola.colorado.gov/lgis/

Ordinances

Colorado Code Publishing Company, "Codebooks," www.colocode.com/codebooks.html
Municode Code Corporation, "Colorado," www.municode.com/library/CO
Code Publishing Co., "Colorado," www.codepublishing.com/elibrary.html#colorado

Practice Materials and Self-Help Resources

Research Guide

University of Denver, Sturm College of Law, "Court Rules and Related Trial Practice Materials (Federal and Colorado)," http://libguides.law.du.edu/courtrules

Court Rules

Research Guides

University of Denver, Sturm College of Law, Westminster Law Library, "Colorado State Court Rules of Procedure and Trial Practice," http://law.du.edu/images/uploads/library/17_a_CourtRulesColoradostate.pdf
LexisNexis, Colorado Legal Resources, "Colorado Court Rules," www.lexisnexis.com/hottopics/Colorado/

Forms

University of Denver, Sturm College of Law, "Legal Forms" [research guide], http://libguides.law.du.edu/content.php?pid=92430&sid=722940
Colorado Judicial Branch, "Forms and Instructions by Category," www.courts.state.co.us/Forms/

State Bar Association Consumer Brochures

Colorado Bar Association, "For the Public," www.cobar.org/index.cfm/ID/20004/dpwfp/For-the-Public/

Court Brochures/Self-Help Centers

Colorado Judicial Branch, "Self Help Center," www.courts.state.co.us/Self_Help/

Looking for an Attorney (for a fee or for free)

Legal Aid/Advocacy Groups/Pro Bono

University of Denver, Sturm College of Law, "Colorado Legal Services and Organizations," http://law.du.edu/index.php/the-colorado-law-project/colorado-legal-services-and-organizations
Pro Bono Net, ColoradoLegalServices.org, "Legal Aid Directory," www.coloradolegalservices.org/lawhelp/find-legal-help/directory

Finding an Attorney/Lawyer Referrals

Colorado Bar Association, "Find a Lawyer," www.cobar.org/directory/index.cfm?ID=20036

Miscellaneous

University of Denver, Sturm College of Law, "Colorado Law Libraries and Law Librarians," http://law.du.edu/index.php/the-colorado-law-project/colorado-law-libraries-and-law-librarians
University of Denver, Sturm College of Law, "Colorado Legislative Council Research Publications" [1954–], www.law.du.edu/index.php/library/library-services/digital-collections/colorado-legislative-process

References

Westlaw, "Glossary for Legal Research Basics," http://lawschool.westlaw.com/shared/marketinfodisplay.asp?code=RE&id=17&mainpage=23&rtid=116&rtcode=re
Cornell University Law School, Legal Information Institute, *Wex* [dictionary and encyclopedia], www.law.cornell.edu/wex/

CONNECTICUT

Research Guides

General

AALL LISP, "Public Library Toolkit: Connecticut," www.aallnet.org/sections/lisp/Public-Library-Toolkit

Connecticut Judicial Branch Law Libraries, "Research Guides," www.jud.ct.gov/lawlib/selfguides.htm

University of Connecticut School of Law Library, "Connecticut Resources," www.law.uconn.edu/system/files/private/connecticut.pdf

Topical

Connecticut Judicial Branch Law Libraries, "Connecticut Law by Subject," www.jud.ct.gov/lawlib/Law/

Judicial

State Court Structure

Connecticut Judicial Branch, "Organization of Connecticut Courts," www.jud.ct.gov/ystday/orgcourt.html

Connecticut Judicial Branch, "Connecticut Court Structure" [diagram], www.jud.ct.gov/external/media/court_structure.htm

Directory of State Courts

Connecticut Judicial Branch, "Connecticut Courts," www.jud.ct.gov/courts.htm

Opinions

Highest Court—Supreme Court

[2000–]: Connecticut Judicial Branch, "Archive of Supreme Court Opinions," www.jud.ct.gov/external/supapp/archiveAROsup.htm

Intermediate Appellate Court—Appellate Court

[2000–]: Connecticut Judicial Branch, "Archive of Appellate Court Opinions," www.jud.ct.gov/external/supapp/archiveAROap.htm

Dockets/Court Records

Trial Courts

Connecticut Judicial Branch, "Case Look-up," www.jud.ct.gov/jud2.htm

Legislative

State Legislative Process

Connecticut State Library, "Legislative Process in Connecticut," www.cslib.org/legtutorial/

Connecticut General Assembly, "How a Bill Becomes a Law in Connecticut" [diagram], www.cga.ct.gov/html/bill.pdf

Statutes

Research Guide

Connecticut Judicial Branch, "How to Find Connecticut Statutes Online," www.jud.ct.gov/lawlib/Notebooks/HowTo/FindConnecticutStatutes/findcga.htm

By Subject (Code)—
General Statutes of Connecticut

Connecticut Judicial Branch Law Libraries, "Connecticut General Statutes," www.jud.ct.gov/lawlib/statutes.htm

Connecticut General Assembly, "Statutes," http://cga.ct.gov/asp/menu/Statutes.asp

Connecticut State Library, "Public & Special Acts and General Statutes of Connecticut," www.cslib.org/psaindex.htm

In Chronological Order (Session Laws)—
Public Acts

[2004–]: Connecticut State Library, "Public & Special Acts by Effective Date," www.cslib.org/actseffective.htm

Legislative History

Research Guide

Connecticut Judicial Branch, "How to Compile a Connecticut Legislative History," www.jud.ct.gov/lawlib/Notebooks/HowTo/CompileLegislativeHistories/cgaleghist.htm

Executive

Directory of State Departments/Agencies

CT.gov, "State of Connecticut Agencies Listing,"
www.ct.gov/ctportal/cwp/view.asp?a=843&q
=489944

State Rulemaking Process

USLegal, "Administrative Procedure Act—
Connecticut," http://administrativelaw.uslegal
.com/administrative-procedure-acts/connecticut/

Regulations

By Agency (Code)—
Regulations of Connecticut State Agencies

N/A

In Chronological Order (Register)

N/A

Local Laws

Directory of State Counties/Municipalities

CT.gov, "Towns & Cities in Connecticut,"
www.ct.gov/ctportal/cwp/view.asp?a=843&q=257266

Ordinances

Connecticut Judicial Branch Law Libraries,
"Connecticut Ordinances and Charters by
Town," www.jud.ct.gov/lawlib/ordinances.htm

Practice Materials and Self-Help Resources

Research Guides

Connecticut Judicial Branch, "Connecticut
Practice Book," www.jud.ct.gov/PB.htm
Connecticut Judicial Branch Law Libraries,
"Research Guides," www.jud.ct.gov/lawlib/
selfguides.htm
Quinnipiac University School of Law, "Research
Guides + Aids," www.quinnipiac.edu/academics/
colleges-schools-and-departments/school-of-law/
about-us/facilities/school-of-law-library/research/
research-guides--aids/

Court Rules

Connecticut Judicial Branch, "Connecticut
Practice Book," www.jud.ct.gov/PB.htm

Forms

Connecticut Judicial Branch, "Official Court
Webforms," www.jud.ct.gov/webforms/
University of Connecticut School of Law, "Legal
Forms," www.law.uconn.edu/school-law-library/
library-guides/legal-forms

State Bar Association Consumer Brochures

N/A

Court Brochures/Self-Help Centers

Connecticut Judicial Branch, "Self-Help
Section," www.jud.ct.gov/selfhelp.htm

Looking for an Attorney (for a fee or for free)

Legal Aid/Advocacy Groups/Pro Bono

Connecticut Bar Association, "Pro Bono," https://
www.ctbar.org/For%20the%20Public/ProBono.aspx

Finding an Attorney/Lawyer Referrals

Connecticut Judicial Branch Law Libraries,
"Find a Lawyer," www.jud.ct.gov/lawlib/
referral.htm
Connecticut Bar Association, "Legal Resources,"
https://www.ctbar.org/For%20the%20Public/
LegalResources.aspx

Miscellaneous

Connecticut Judicial Branch Law Libraries,
"Connecticut State Administrative Decisions,"
www.jud.ct.gov/lawlib/state.htm#Administrative
Connecticut Judicial Branch Law Libraries,
"Lawyer Associations," www.jud.ct.gov/lawlib/
state.htm#associations
Connecticut Judicial Branch, "Civil Jury
Instructions," www.jud.state.ct.us/JI/Civil/
Connecticut Judicial Branch, "Criminal Jury
Instructions," www.jud.state.ct.us/JI/Criminal/

Reference

Connecticut Judicial Branch, "Common Legal Words," www.jud.ct.gov/legalterms.htm

DELAWARE

Research Guides

Widener Law, "Delaware Resources," http://law .widener.edu/LawLibrary/Research/OnlineResources/ DelawareResources.aspx

University of Delaware Library, "Delaware Legal Information," http://guides.lib.udel.edu/ delawarelaw/

Judicial

State Court Structure

Delaware State Courts, "Overview of the Delaware Court System," http://courts.state .de.us/overview.stm

Delaware State Courts, "The Delaware Court System" [diagram], http://courts.state.de.us/ AOC/Outreach/DelawareCourts.pdf

Directory of State Courts

Delaware State Courts, "Court Hours & Locations," http://courts.state.de.us/Locations/

Opinions

Research Guide

University of Delaware Library, "Delaware Legal Information: Case Law," http://guides.lib.udel .edu/delawarelaw/

Highest Court—Supreme Court

[2000–]: Delaware State Courts, "Supreme Court Opinions and Orders," http://courts.state.de.us/ opinions/List.aspx?ag=Supreme%20Court

Intermediate Appellate Court—None

Trial Courts (General Jurisdiction)

[2000–]: Delaware State Courts, "Court of Chancery Opinions and Orders," http://courts. state.de.us/opinions/List.aspx?ag=Court%20of%20 Chancery

[1996–]: Delaware State Courts, "Superior Court Opinions and Orders," http://courts.state.de.us/ opinions/List.aspx?ag=Superior%20Court

Dockets/Court Records

Trial Court Civil Cases

Delaware State Courts, "Online Civil Docket Search in the Delaware State Courts," http://courts.state.de.us/docket.stm

Legislative

State Legislative Process

Delaware General Assembly, "Legislative Process" [diagram], http://legis.delaware.gov/ legislature.nsf/Lookup/Bill_Process

Statutes

By Subject (Code)—Delaware Code

Delaware.gov, "Online Delaware Code," http://delcode.delaware.gov

In Chronological Order (Session Laws)— Laws of Delaware

[1991–]: Delaware.gov, "Laws of Delaware," http://delcode.delaware.gov/sessionlaws/

Legislative History

Research Guide

Widener Law, "Delaware Legislative History," http://libguides.law.widener.edu/content.php?pid =332096

Executive

Directory of State Departments/Agencies

Delaware.gov, "Alphabetical List of State Agencies," http://delaware.gov/egov/portal.nsf/ portal/agencylist_alpha

State Rulemaking Process

USLegal, "Administrative Procedure Act— Delaware," http://administrativelaw.uslegal.com/ administrative-procedure-acts/delaware/

Regulations

By Agency (Code)—
Delaware's Administrative Code

Delaware General Assembly, "Delaware's Administrative Code," http://regulations .delaware.gov/AdminCode/

In Chronological Order (Register)—
Delaware Register of Regulations

[1997–]: Delaware General Assembly, "Register of Regulations," http://regulations.delaware.gov/ services/register.shtml

Local Laws

Directory of State Counties/Municipalities

Delaware League of Local Governments, "Delaware Municipal and County Websites," www.ipa.udel.edu/localgovt/dllg/websites.asp

Ordinances

Municode Code Corporation, "Delaware," www.municode.com/library/DE

Practice Materials and Self-Help Resources

Research Guide

Widener University School of Law, "Delaware Practice Aids," http://law.widener.edu/LawLibrary/ Research/OnlineResources/DelawareResources/~/ media/Files/lawlibrary/researchguides/depractice .ashx

Court Rules

Delaware State Courts, "Rules of the Delaware State Courts," http://courts.state.de.us/Rules/

Forms

Widener Law, "Delaware Legal Forms" [research guide], http://law.widener.edu/LawLibrary/ Research/OnlineResources/DelawareResources/ DelawareLegalForms.aspx
Delaware State Courts, "Forms," http://courts .state.de.us/forms/

State Bar Association Consumer Brochures

Delaware State Bar Association, Committee on Law and the Elderly, "Legal Handbooks for Older Delawareans," www.delawareelderlawhandbook.com

Court Brochures/Self-Help Centers

Delaware State Courts, "Citizen Help," http://courts.state.de.us/help/

Looking for an Attorney (for a fee or for free)

Legal Aid/Advocacy Groups/Pro Bono

Delaware State Bar Association, "Access to Justice Program," www.dsba.org/index.php/ access-to-justice-program.html
Delaware State Courts, "Legal Assistance," http:// courts.state.de.us/help/legalassistance.stm

Finding an Attorney/Lawyer Referrals

Delaware Volunteer Legal Services, "Lawyer Referral Service," www.dvls.org/LRS_Public.htm

Miscellaneous

Delaware General Assembly, "Landlord-Tenant Code," http://legis.delaware.gov/legislature.nsf/ Lookup/Landlord_Tenant_Code

References

Westlaw, "Glossary for Legal Research Basics," http://lawschool.westlaw.com/shared/marketin fodisplay.asp?code=RE&id =17&mainpage=23&rtid =116&rtcode=re
Cornell University Law School, Legal Information Institute, *Wex* [dictionary and encyclopedia], www.law.cornell.edu/wex/

FLORIDA

Research Guides

AALL LISP, "Public Library Toolkit: Florida," www.aallnet.org/sections/lisp/Public-Library-Toolkit

Florida Coastal School of Law, Library and Technology Center, "Research Guides," www.fcsl.edu/ltc/resources/research_guides

University of Miami School of Law, "Research Guides: Florida Guides," www.law.miami.edu/library/guides.php

University of Florida Libraries, "Florida Research Guides," http://guides.uflib.ufl.edu/content.php?pid=44432&sid=328901

Stetson Law, "Legal Research Tools and Strategies," www.law.stetson.edu/library/legal-research-tools-and-strategy.php

Florida State University College of Law, "Research Guides & Pathfinders," www.law.fsu.edu/library/researchguides.html

Judicial

State Court Structure

Florida State Courts, "Brief Description of the District Courts," www.flcourts.org/courts/dca/dca_description.shtml

Florida State Courts, "Jurisdiction Chart" [diagram], www.flcourts.org/courts/bin/Jurisdiction_chart.pdf

Directories of State Courts

Florida State Courts, "Florida's Circuit Courts," www.flcourts.org/courts/circuit/circuit.shtml

Florida State Courts, "Florida's County Courts," www.flcourts.org/courts/county/county.shtml

Opinions

Research Guide

University of Florida Libraries, "Florida Caselaw," http://guides.uflib.ufl.edu/content.php?pid=44432&sid=357500

Highest Court—Supreme Court

[1999–]: Florida Supreme Court, "Opinions, Rules & Other Court Documents," www.floridasupremecourt.org/decisions/opinions.shtml

Intermediate Appellate Court—
District Courts of Appeal

[2003–]: Florida First District Court of Appeal, http://opinions.1dca.org

[2001–]: Florida Second District Court of Appeal, www.2dca.org/opinions/ArchivedOpinions.shtml

[2001–]: Florida Third District Court of Appeal, www.3dca.flcourts.org/Opinions/opinions.shtml

[2005–]: Florida Fourth District Court of Appeal, www.4dca.org/opinions.shtml

[2001–]: Florida Fifth District Court of Appeal, www.5dca.org/opinions.shtml

Dockets/Court Records

Supreme Court

[1973–]: Florida Supreme Court, "Online Docket," http://jweb.flcourts.org/pls/docket/ds_docket_search

District Courts of Appeal

[1987–]: Florida State Courts, "Florida District Courts of Appeal Online Docket," http://199.242.69.70/pls/ds/ds_docket_search

Trial Courts

MyFloridaCounty.com, "Official Records" [via the Florida Clerks of Courts; fee-based], https://www.myfloridacounty.com/official_records/

Legislative

State Legislative Process

Florida House of Representatives, "How an Idea Becomes a Law (Advanced)," www.myfloridahouse.gov/Sections/PublicGuide/PublicGuide.aspx

Florida Senate, "How an Idea Becomes a Law" [diagram], www.flsenate.gov/data/civics/idea_to_law_chart.pdf

Florida House of Representatives, "How an Idea Becomes a Law (Intermediate)," www.myfloridahouse.gov/Sections/PublicGuide/PublicGuide.aspx

Statutes

Research Guide

University of Florida Libraries, "Guide to Using Florida Statutes," http://guides.uflib.ufl.edu/content.php?pid=44432&sid=357468

By Subject (Code)—Florida Statutes

Florida Legislature, "Florida Statutes," www.leg.
state.fl.us/Statutes/

Florida House of Representatives, "Statutes,"
www.myfloridahouse.gov/Sections/Search/StatRev/
StatRev.aspx?ViewType=Statutes

Florida Senate, "Florida Statutes," www.flsenate.
gov/Laws/Statutes

In Chronological Order (Session Laws)—
Laws of Florida

[1997–]: State Library and Archives of Florida,
"Laws of Florida," http://laws.flrules.org/
node?field_list_year_nid=5212

Legislative History

Research Guides

University of Florida Libraries, "Florida
Legislative History," http://guides.uflib.ufl.edu/
content.php?pid=44432&sid=344380

Florida State University College of Law Research
Center, "Florida Legislative History Sources,"
www.law.fsu.edu/library/databases/PDF/florida_leg
_history.pdf

Florida International University, "FIU Law
Library Florida Legislative History Research
& Resources Guide," http://law.fiu.edu/
wp-content/uploads/2011/09/research_guide
_on_fl_legis_hist1.pdf

University of Miami School of Law, "FL
Legislative History Guide," www.law.miami.edu/
library/flhistguide.php

Executive

Directory of State Departments/Agencies

MyFlorida.com, "State of Florida Agencies,"
www.myflorida.com/directory/

State Rulemaking Process

USLegal, "Administrative Procedure Act—
Florida," http://administrativelaw.uslegal.com/
administrative-procedure-acts/florida/

Regulations

Research Guides

University of Miami School of Law, "Florida
Administrative Law Research," www.law.miami
.edu/library/fladminguide.php

University of Florida Libraries, "Florida
Administrative Law," http://guides.uflib.ufl.edu/
FLAdminLaw

By Agency (Code)—Florida Administrative Code

Florida Department of State, "Florida
Administrative Register & Florida
Administrative Code" [browse by agencies],
https://www.flrules.org

In Chronological Order (Register)—
Florida Administrative Weekly

[1999–]: Florida Department of State,
"Florida Administrative Register & Florida
Administrative Code" [browse by FAR
issues], https://www.flrules.org

Local Laws

Directories of State Counties/Municipalities

MyFlorida.com, "Florida County Government,"
www.myflorida.com/counties/

MyFlorida.com, "Florida City Government,"
www.myflorida.com/cities/

Ordinances

Municode Code Corporation, "Florida,"
www.municode.com/library/FL

Practice Materials and Self-Help Resources

Research Guide

University of Florida Libraries, "Florida Self-
Help Books," http://guides.uflib.ufl.edu/content
.php?pid=44432&sid=734341

Court Rules

Florida Supreme Court, "Florida Rules of Court
Maintained by the Florida Bar," www.florida
supremecourt.org/decisions/barrules.shtml

Florida Bar, "Florida Rules of Court Procedure," www.floridabar.org/tfb/TFBLegalRes.nsf/

Forms

Research Guide

Florida State University College of Law Library "Finding Legal Forms," www.law.fsu.edu/library/ databases/pdf/legalforms.pdf

State Bar Association Consumer Brochures

Florida Bar, "Consumer Information," www.floridabar.org/tfb/TFBConsum.nsf/

Court Brochures/Self-Help Centers

Florida State Courts, "Family Law Self-Help Centers," www.flcourts.org/gen_public/family/ self_help/map.shtml

Looking for an Attorney (for a fee or for free)

Legal Aid/Advocacy Groups/Pro Bono

Florida State Courts, "Legal Aid," www.flcourts .org/gen_public/family/self_help/legal_aid.shtml

Finding an Attorney/Lawyer Referrals

Florida Bar, "Lawyer Referral Service—Information for Consumers," www.floridabar .org/tfb/TFBConsum.nsf/48E76203493B82AD85 2567090070C9B9/EC2322E512B83D1E85256B 2F006CC812?OpenDocument

Miscellaneous

Florida Senate Website Archive, http://archive.flsenate.gov

Reference

Florida Senate, "Glossary," www.flsenate.gov/Reference/Glossary

GEORGIA
Research Guides

AALL LISP, "Public Library Toolkit: Georgia," www.aallnet.org/sections/lisp/Public-Library-Toolkit

Mercer University School of Law, "Georgia Research," www.law.mercer.edu/library/research/ georgia

Georgia State University College of Law, "Georgia Law," http://libguides.law.gsu.edu/ cat.php?cid=30570

Anne E. Burnett, "Georgia Legal Resources on the Internet" (2003), http://digitalcommons .law.uga.edu/speeches/19/

Emory University School of Law, "For Law Students," http://library.law.emory.edu/ index.php?id=6656

Superior Court of Fulton County, "Fulton County Law Library," www.fultoncourt.org/library/

Judicial
State Court Structure

Judicial Branch of Georgia, "Self Help Resources: Courts," www.georgiacourts.org/aoc/ selfhelp/courts.html

Administrative Office of the Courts, "Georgia Courts" [diagram], www.georgiacourts.org/ index.php/georgia-courts/learn-about-the-courts

Directory of State Courts

Administrative Office of the Courts, "Local Courts" [finding aid], www.georgiacourts.org/ index.php/georgia-courts/find-your-court

Opinions

Research Guide

Emory University School of Law, "Georgia Caselaw," http://library.law.emory.edu/for-law -students/emory-law-subject-guides/georgia-and -state-law/georgia-caselaw/

Highest Court—Supreme Court

[past three terms]: Supreme Court of Georgia, "Opinions," www.gasupreme.us/sc-op/ forthcoming.php

Intermediate Appellate Court—Court of Appeals

N/A

Dockets/Court Records

Supreme Court

[past three terms]: Supreme Court of Georgia, "Computerized Docketing System and Case Types," www.gasupreme.us/docket_search/

Court of Appeals

[2003–]: Court of Appeals of the State of Georgia, "Docket/Case Inquiry System," www.gaappeals.us/docket/

Trial Courts

Please refer to the individual court website.

Legislative

State Legislative Process

Georgia General Assembly, "Tracking a Bill through the General Assembly," www.legis.ga.gov/Legislation/en-US/default.aspx

Digital Library of Georgia, GeorgiaInfo, "Passing a Law in the Georgia General Assembly" [diagram], http://georgiainfo.galileo.usg.edu/legchart/legchart.htm

Statutes

Research Guide

Emory University School of Law, "Georgia Code," http://library.law.emory.edu/for-law-students/emory-law-subject-guides/georgia-and-state-law/georgia-code/

By Subject (Code)—
Official Code of Georgia Annotated

LexisNexis, "Official Code of Georgia," www.lexis-nexis.com/hottopics/gacode/

In Chronological Order (Session Laws)—
Georgia Laws (Acts and Resolutions of the General Assembly of the State of Georgia)

[1799–1999]: Digital Library of Georgia, "Georgia Legislative Documents," www.galileo.usg.edu/express?link=zlgl

Legislative History

Research Guide

Emory University School of Law, "Georgia Legislative History," http://library.law.emory.edu/for-law-students/emory-law-subject-guides/georgia-and-state-law/georgia-legislative-history/

Executive

Directory of State Departments/Agencies

GeorgiaGov, "Agencies," www.georgia.gov/agency-list

State Rulemaking Process

University of Georgia, Carl Vinson Institute of Government, "Georgia's Administrative Rule-Making Process," http://georgiainfo.galileo.usg.edu/pdf/adminruleprocess.pdf

Regulations

Research Guide

Emory University School of Law, "Georgia Administrative, Executive, and Municipal Law," http://library.law.emory.edu/for-law-students/emory-law-subject-guides/georgia-and-state-law/georgia-administrative-law/

By Agency (Code)—
Rules and Regulations of the State of Georgia

Georgia Secretary of State, "Rules and Regulations of the State of Georgia," http://sos.georgia.gov/rules_regs.htm

In Chronological Order (Register)

N/A

Local Laws

Directory of State Counties/Municipalities

GeorgiaGov, "Cities & Counties," http://georgia.gov/municipality-list

Ordinances

Municode Code Corporation, "Georgia," www.municode.com/library/GA

Practice Materials and Self-Help Resources

Research Guide

Superior Court of Fulton County, "Publications and Forms," www.fultoncourt.org/library/library-pubs.php

Court Rules

Administrative Office of the Court, "Court Rules," www.georgiacourts.org/index.php/court-rules

Judicial Branch of Georgia, "Court Rules," www.georgiacourts.org/aoc/selfhelp/rules.html

Forms

Dougherty County of Georgia, "Find a Form," www.albany.ga.us/content/1800/2889/3011/3518/

Superior Court of Fulton County, "Legal Forms," www.fultoncourt.org/library/library-pubs.php

Judicial Branch of Georgia, "Forms," www.georgiacourts.org/aoc/selfhelp/forms.html

State Bar of Georgia, "Consumer Pamphlet Series," www.gabar.org/newsandpublications/consumerpamphlets/

Court Brochures/Self-Help Centers

Judicial Branch of Georgia, "Self Help Resources," www.georgiacourts.gov/aoc/selfhelp/

Looking for an Attorney (for a fee or for free)

Legal Aid/Advocacy Groups/Pro Bono

GeorgiaLegalAid.org, www.georgialegalaid.org

Georgia Legal Services Program, www.glsp.org

Atlanta Legal Aid Society, www.atlantalegalaid.org

Atlanta Volunteer Lawyers Foundation, www.avlf.org/clients

Finding an Attorney/Lawyer Referrals

State Bar of Georgia, "How to Choose a Lawyer," www.gabar.org/newsandpublications/consumerpamphlets/chooselawyer.cfm

Miscellaneous

HG.org, "Georgia Bar Associations," www.hg.org/bar-associations-georgia.asp

References

Westlaw, "Glossary for Legal Research Basics," http://lawschool.westlaw.com/shared/marketinfodisplay.asp?code=RE&id=17&mainpage =23&rtid=116&rtcode=re

Cornell University Law School, Legal Information Institute, *Wex* [dictionary and encyclopedia], www.law.cornell.edu/wex/

HAWAII
Research Guides

AALL LISP, "Public Library Toolkit: Hawaii," www.aallnet.org/sections/lisp/Public-Library-Toolkit

Hawaiʻi State Law Library System, "Subject Guides," www.state.hi.us/jud/library/subjectguide.htm

University of Hawaiʻi at Mānoa, William S. Richardson School of Law, "Research Links," www.law.hawaii.edu/library/node/17/dup/1725

Judicial

State Court Structure

Court.us, "Courts in Hawaii," www.court.us/hawaii_court_records.htm

Court Statistics Project, "Hawaii" [diagram], www.courtstatistics.org/Other-Pages/State_Court_Structure_Charts/Hawaii.aspx

Directories of State Courts

Hawaii State Judiciary, "Circuit Courts," www.courts.state.hi.us/courts/circuit/circuit_courts.html

Hawaii State Judiciary, "District Courts" www.courts.state.hi.us/courts/district/district_courts.html

Opinions

Highest Court—Supreme Court

[1998–]: Hawaii State Judiciary, "Hawaii Appellate Court Opinions and Orders," www.courts.state.hi.us/opinions_and_orders/

Intermediate Appellate Court— Intermediate Court of Appeals

[1998–]: Hawaii State Judiciary, "Hawaii Appellate Court Opinions and Orders," www.courts.state.hi.us/opinions_and_orders/

Dockets/Court Records

Trial Courts

Hawaii State Judiciary, "Search Court Records," www.courts.state.hi.us/legal_references/records/search_court_records.html

Legislative

State Legislative Process

Hawaii State Legislature, "Legislative Process," www.capitol.hawaii.gov/session2011/docs/citizensguide/LegislativeProcess.pdf

Hawaii State Legislature, "How a Bill Becomes a Law" [diagram], www.capitol.hawaii.gov/session2011/docs/citizensguide/HowaBillBecomesLaw.pdf

Statutes

Research Guide

Hawaii State Legislature [instructions on using the Hawaii Revised Statutes], http://lrbhawaii.info/hrstrn/

By Subject (Code)—Hawaii Revised Statutes

Hawaii State Legislature, "Hawaii Revised Statutes," www.capitol.hawaii.gov/docs/HRS.htm

In Chronological Order (Session Laws)— Hawaii Session Laws

[1997–]: Hawaii Legislative Reference Bureau, "Systems Office Session Reports," http://hawaii.gov/lrb/reports/bill.html

Legislative History

Research Guides

Richard F. Kahle Jr., "How to Research Constitutional, Legislative, and Statutory History in Hawaii" (2001), http://hawaii.gov/lrb/how2/how2.pdf

Hawai'i State Law Library System, "Subject Guides," www.state.hi.us/jud/library/subjectguide.htm

University of Hawai'i at Mānoa, William S. Richardson School of Law, "Research Links," www.law.hawaii.edu/library/node/17/dup/1725

Executive

Directory of State Departments/Agencies

Hawaii Legislative Reference Bureau, "Hawaii Government Directory and the Guide to Government in Hawaii," http://hawaii.gov/lrb/capitoli/dirguide/

State Rulemaking Process

USLegal, "Administrative Procedure Act— Hawaii," http://administrativelaw.uslegal.com/administrative-procedure-acts/administrative-procedure-act-hawaii/

Regulations

Research Guide

University of Hawai'i at Mānoa, William S. Richardson School of Law, "Finding Hawaii Administrative Law," https://www.law.hawaii.edu/sites/www.law.hawaii.edu/files/content/library/FindingHawaiiAdministrativeLaw.pdf

By Agency (Code)—Hawaii Administrative Rules

Lieutenant Governor, State of Hawai'i, "Administrative Rules," http://ltgov.hawaii.gov/the-office/administrative-rules/

In Chronological Order (Register)—Hawaii Government Register

N/A

Administrative Rulings

Research Guide

Hawai'i State Law Library System, "Hawai'i Administrative Decisions and Opinions," www.state.hi.us/jud/library/admindec.htm

Local Laws

Directory of State Counties/Municipalities

National Association of Counties, "Find a County," www.naco.org/Counties/Pages/FindACounty.aspx

Ordinances

Hawaii State Judiciary, "Municipal," www.courts.state.hi.us/legal_references/resources/municipal.html

Practice Materials and Self-Help Resources

Research Guide

Legal Aid Society of Hawaii, "Brochures," www.legalaidhawaii.org/BROCHURES.html

Court Rules

Hawaii State Judiciary, "Court Rules," www.courts.state.hi.us/legal_references/resources/court_rules.html

Forms

Hawaii State Judiciary, "Court Forms," www.courts.state.hi.us/self-help/courts/forms/court_forms.html

State Bar Association Consumer Brochures

N/A

Court Brochures/Self-Help Centers

Hawaii State Judiciary, "Helpful Information and Resources," www.courts.state.hi.us/self-help/help.html

Looking for an Attorney (for a fee or for free)

Legal Aid/Advocacy Groups/Pro Bono

Hawaii State Bar Association, "Legal Assistance," www.hsba.org/Legal_Assistance_List.aspx

Finding an Attorney/Lawyer Referrals

Hawaii State Bar Association, "Lawyer Referral & Information Service," www.hawaiilawyerreferral.com

Hawaii State Bar Association, "Find a Lawyer," www.hsba.org/Find_a_lawyer.aspx

Miscellaneous

Legislative Reference Bureau Session Reports

[1950–]: Hawaii Legislative Reference Bureau, "Studies by Session Year," http://hawaii.gov/lrb/reports/

References

Hawaii Legislative Reference Bureau, "Glossary of Hawai'i Legislative Terms," http://hawaii.gov/lrb/reports/lglos.html

Hawai'i State Law Library System, "How to Read a Legal Citation," www.state.hi.us/jud/library/legalcite.pdf

IDAHO

Research Guides

University of Idaho College of Law, "Legal Research Guides," www.law.uidaho.edu/default.aspx?pid=66157

Judicial

State Court Structure

State of Idaho Judicial Branch, "Overview of the Idaho Court System" [includes diagram], www.isc.idaho.gov/overview.pdf

Directory of State Courts

State of Idaho Judicial Branch, "Idaho's District Courts," www.isc.idaho.gov/district-courts

Opinions

Research Guide

University of Idaho College of Law, "Idaho Cases," www.uidaho.edu/~/media/Files/orgs/Law/Library/reseach-guides/IdahoCases.ashx

Highest Court—Supreme Court

[last two years]: www.isc.idaho.gov/appeals-court/opinions

[1997–]: FindLaw, "Supreme Court of Idaho Cases," http://caselaw.findlaw.com/court/id-supreme-court

Intermediate Appellate Court—Court of Appeals

[last two years]: www.isc.idaho.gov/appeals-court/opinions

[1997–]: FindLaw, "Court of Appeals of Idaho Cases," http://caselaw.findlaw.com/court/id-court-of-appeals/years/

Dockets/Court Records

Trial Courts

[1995–]: Idaho State Judiciary, "Idaho Supreme Court Data Repository," https://www.idcourts.us/repository/start.do

Legislative

State Legislative Process

Idaho Legislature, "How a Bill Becomes a Law," http://legislature.idaho.gov/about/howabillbecomesalaw.htm

Statutes

Research Guide

University of Idaho College of Law, "Idaho Statutes and Code," www.uidaho.edu/~/media/Files/orgs/Law/Library/reseach-guides/IdahoStatutes.ashx

By Subject (Code)—Idaho Code

Idaho Legislature, "Idaho Statutes," www.legislature.idaho.gov/idstat/TOC/IDStatutesTOC.htm

In Chronological Order (Session Laws)—Idaho Session Laws (Enacted Legislation)

[current assembly]: Idaho Legislature [enacted legislation], www.legislature.idaho.gov

[1998–]: Idaho Legislature, "Prior Sessions Menu," http://legislature.idaho.gov/priorsessions.htm

Legislative History

Research Guide

University of Idaho College of Law, "Idaho Legislative History," www.uidaho.edu/~/media/Files/orgs/Law/Library/reseach-guides/IdahoLegisHistory.ashx

Executive

Directory of State Departments/Agencies

Idaho.gov, "Agency & Topic Index," http://idaho.gov/agency/agency_a.html

State Rulemaking Process

Idaho Office of Administrative Rules Coordinator, "Idaho Administrative Bulletins" [consult preface of any recent volume], http://adminrules.idaho.gov/bulletin/

Regulations

Research Guide

University of Idaho College of Law, "Idaho Administrative Research," www.uidaho.edu/~/media/Files/orgs/Law/Library/reseach-guides/IdahoAdminResearch.ashx

By Agency (Code)—Idaho Administrative Code

[current]: Idaho Office of Administrative Rules Coordinator, "Idaho Administrative Code," http://adminrules.idaho.gov/rules/current/

[2000–]: Idaho Office of Administrative Rules Coordinator, "Administrative Code Archives," http://adminrules.idaho.gov/rules/archive.html

In Chronological Order (Register)—
Idaho Administrative Bulletin

[1995–]: Idaho Office of Administrative
Rules Coordinator, "Idaho Administrative
Bulletins," http://adminrules.idaho.gov/bulletin/

Administrative Rulings

Research Guide

University of Idaho College of Law, "Idaho
Administrative Research," www.uidaho.edu/~/
media/Files/orgs/Law/Library/reseach-guides/
IdahoAdminResearch.ashx

Local Laws

Directory of State Counties/Municipalities

Idaho.gov, "Counties & Cities," www.idaho.gov/
aboutidaho/counties.html

Ordinances

Idaho State Law Library, "City Codes /
Ordinances for Idaho," www.isll.idaho.gov/
citycode.htm
Municode Code Corporation, "Idaho,"
www.municode.com/library/ID

Practice Materials and Self-Help Resources

Research Guide

Idaho Legal Aid Services Inc., "Library,"
www.idaholegalaid.org/library

Court Rules

University of Idaho College of Law, "Idaho
Cases," www.uidaho.edu/~/media/Files/orgs/Law/
Library/reseach-guides/IdahoCases.ashx

Forms

University of Idaho College of Law, "Finding
Legal Forms," www.uidaho.edu/~/media/Files/
orgs/Law/Library/reseach-guides/FindingForms
.ashx
Idaho Judicial Branch, "Forms, Applications,
and Guidelines Pertaining to Idaho Court
Rules," www.isc.idaho.gov/problem-solving/forms

State Bar Association Consumer Brochures

Idaho State Bar, "Publications, Brochures &
Guides," http://isb.idaho.gov/general/brochures
.html

Court Brochures/Self-Help Centers

Idaho Judicial Branch, "Court Assistance
Office," www.courtselfhelp.idaho.gov

Looking for an Attorney (for a fee or for free)

Legal Aid/Advocacy Groups/Pro Bono

Idaho Legal Aid Services Inc.,
www.idaholegalaid.org

Finding an Attorney/Lawyer Referrals

Idaho State Bar, "Find an Attorney,"
http://isb.idaho.gov/general/findattorney.html

Miscellaneous

Idaho Judicial Branch, "Idaho Civil Jury
Instructions," www.isc.idaho.gov/problem-solving/
civil-jury-instructions
Idaho Judicial Branch, "Criminal Jury
Instructions," www.isc.idaho.gov/problem-solving/
criminal-jury-instructions
Idaho Office of the Attorney General, "Consumer
Protection: General Consumer Topics,"
www.ag.idaho.gov/consumerProtection/general
Topics/topicIndexMain.html

References

Westlaw, "Glossary for Legal Research Basics,"
http://lawschool.westlaw.com/shared/marketin
fodisplay.asp?code=RE&id =17&mainpage=23&rtid
=116&rtcode=re
Cornell University Law School, Legal
Information Institute, *Wex* [dictionary and
encyclopedia], www.law.cornell.edu/wex/

ILLINOIS

Research Guides

University of Illinois at Urbana-Champaign, "Research Guides by Area of Law," https://wiki.cites.uiuc.edu/wiki/display/legalresearch/Research+Guides+By+Area+of+Law

Northwestern Law, Pritzker Legal Research Center, "Illinois," www.law.northwestern.edu/library/research/illinoischicago/illinois/

Judicial

State Court Structure

Illinois Courts, "About the Courts in Illinois," www.state.il.us/court/General/CourtsInIL.asp

Illinois Courts, "How Cases Proceed Thru the Court System" [diagram], www.state.il.us/court/General/Proceed.asp

Directory of State Courts

Northern Illinois University College of Law, "Illinois Courts: Supreme & Appellate Courts," http://law.niu.edu/law/library/onlineresearch/legal_illinois_courts.shtml

Opinions

Highest Court—Supreme Court

[last ninety days]: Illinois Courts, "Recent Supreme Court Opinions," www.state.il.us/court/Opinions/recent_supreme.asp

[1996–]: Illinois Courts [browse by year], www.state.il.us/court/Opinions/archive.asp

Intermediate Appellate Court—Appellate Court

[last ninety days]: Illinois Courts, "Recent Appellate Court Opinions," www.state.il.us/court/Opinions/recent_appellate.asp

[1996–]: Illinois Courts [browse by year], www.state.il.us/court/Opinions/archive.asp

Dockets/Court Records

All Courts

LLRX, "Court Rules, Forms, and Dockets" [browse by jurisdiction/state = "Illinois" and type = "dockets"], www.llrx.com/courtrules/

Legislative

State Legislative Process

University of Illinois at Urbana-Champaign, University Library, "Illinois's Legislative Process," http://uiuc.libguides.com/content.php?pid=34217&sid=251270

Illinois General Assembly, Legislative Research Unit, "How a Bill Becomes a Law in Illinois" [diagram], www.ilga.gov/commission/lru/howabillbecomesalaw.pdf

Statutes

By Subject (Code)—Illinois Compiled Statutes

Illinois General Assembly, "Illinois Compiled Statutes," www.ilga.gov/legislation/ilcs/ilcs.asp

In Chronological Order (Session Laws)—Laws of the State of Illinois

[current assembly]: Illinois General Assembly, "Public Acts," www.ilga.gov/legislation/publicacts/

[1971–]: Illinois General Assembly, "Previous General Assemblies," www.ilga.gov/previousga.asp

Legislative History

Research Guides

Richard C. Edwards, Legislative Reference Bureau, "Researching Legislative History," www.ilga.gov/commission/lrb/lrbres.htm

University of Illinois at Urbana-Champaign, University Library, "Illinois Legislation," http://uiuc.libguides.com/illinoislegislation

Northwestern Law, Pritzker Legal Research Center, "Illinois Legislative History," www.law.northwestern.edu/library/research/illinoischicago/illinois/legislativehistory/

Southern Illinois University School of Law Library, "Illinois Legislative History Research," www.law.siu.edu/lawlib/guides/Ill%20leg%20hist%20handout.pdf

Southern Illinois University School of Law Library, "Comparing Federal & Illinois Legislative History Research," www.law.siu.edu/lawlib/guides/fedilllhcompared.htm

John Marshall Law School, "Illinois Legislative History Research," http://libraryguides.jmls.edu/ILlegres

Executive

State Executive Branch Organization Structure

Illinois.gov, "Executive Branch Organization Chart," www.cyberdriveillinois.com/publications/handbook/execbranch.pdf

Directories of State Departments/Agencies

Illinois.gov, "State Agencies," www.illinois.gov/SitePages/Agencies.aspx

Northern Illinois University College of Law, "Governor & Administration," http://law.niu.edu/law/library/onlineresearch/legal_illinois_governor.shtml

State Rulemaking Process

Illinois General Assembly, "Illinois Rulemaking Process," www.ilga.gov/commission/jcar/ILRulemakingProcess.pdf

Regulations

Research Guides

Southern Illinois University School of Law Library, "Researching Illinois Administrative Regulations," www.law.siu.edu/lawlib/guides/Ill%20admin%20regs%20hnd-Spring%2013.pdf

Southern Illinois University School of Law Library, "Comparing the Publication of Illinois Statutes and Regulations," www.law.siu.edu/lawlib/guides/illstatutesregscompared.htm

By Agency (Code)—Illinois Administrative Code

Joint Committee on Administrative Rules, "Administrative Code," www.ilga.gov/commission/jcar/admincode/titles.html

Illinois Secretary of State, "Administrative Code and Codification Indexes," www.cyberdriveillinois .com/departments/index/admincodeindex.html

In Chronological Order (Register)—Illinois Register

[2002–]: Illinois Secretary of State, "Illinois Register," http://ilsos.net/departments/index/register/

[last six months]: Joint Committee on Administrative Rules, "Flinn Report," www.ilga.gov/commission/jcar/flinn/flinn.asp

Administrative Rulings

Research Guide

Tom Gaylord, "Beyond the Regs: Illinois Administrative Law Online," *Illinois Bar Journal*, July 1, 2007, www.thefreelibrary.com/Illinois+Bar+Journal/2007/July/1-p52749

Local Laws

Directories of State Counties/Municipalities

National Association of Counties, "Find a County," www.naco.org/Counties/Pages/FindACounty.aspx

State and Local Government on the Net, "Illinois State and Local Government," www.statelocalgov.net/state-il.cfm

Ordinances

Municipal Codes

Northern Illinois University College of Law, "Cities & Counties," http://law.niu.edu/law/library/onlineresearch/legal_illinois_cities.shtml

County Codes

Illinois Association of County Board Members, "County Codes and Ordinances," www.ilcounty.org/news/24-1.html

Practice Materials and Self-Help Resources

Research Guides

University of Illinois at Urbana-Champaign, "Illinois Resources for the Public," https://wiki.cites.uiuc.edu/wiki/display/legalresearch/Illinois+Resources+for+the+Public

Northwestern Law, Pritzker Legal Research Center, "Practice Guides," www.law.northwestern.edu/library/research/illinoischicago/illinois/practiceguides/

Court Rules

Illinois Courts, "Illinois Supreme Court Rules," www.state.il.us/court/SupremeCourt/Rules/

Illinois Courts, "Illinois Appellate Court Local Rules by District," www.state.il.us/court/AppellateCourt/RulesDefault.asp

Forms

University of Illinois at Urbana-Champaign, "Guide to Formbooks in the Illinois Alcove," https://wiki.cites.uiuc.edu/wiki/display/legalresearch/Illinois+Formbooks

John Marshall Law School, "Illinois Forms," http://libraryguides.jmls.edu/content.php?pid=49677&sid=380786

State Bar Association Consumer Brochures

Illinois State Bar Association, IllinoisLawyerFinder, "Legal Information," www.illinoislawyerfinder.com/articles/legal-information

Court Brochures/Self-Help Centers

Illinois Courts, "Citizen Self-Help," www.state.il.us/court/citizen.asp

Looking for an Attorney (for a fee or for free)

Legal Aid/Advocacy Groups/Pro Bono

University of Illinois at Urbana-Champaign, "Legal Services Information," https://wiki.cites.uiuc.edu/wiki/display/legalresearch/Legal+Services+Information

Land of Lincoln Legal Assistance Foundation Inc., www.lollaf.org/what.html

Finding an Attorney/Lawyer Referrals

Illinois State Bar Association, IllinoisLawyerFinder, "Find a Lawyer," www.illinoislawyerfinder.com/search.html

Miscellaneous

Illinois General Assembly, Legislative Research Unit, "Publications and Selected Research by Topic," www.ilga.gov/commission/lru/pubsbytopic.html

Northern Illinois University College of Law, General Illinois Legal Web Sites," http://law.niu.edu/law/library/onlineresearch/legal_illinois.shtml

Southern Illinois University School of Law, "Self-Help," www.law.siu.edu/selfhelp/

References

Illinois General Assembly, "Illinois Legislative Glossary," http://ilga.gov/legislation/glossary.asp

Southern Illinois University School of Law Library, "Glossary of Legal Research Terms," www.law.siu.edu/lawlib/guides/glossary.htm

INDIANA

Research Guides

Georgetown University Law Library, "Indiana Resources," www.law.georgetown.edu/library/research/guides/indiana.cfm

Library of Congress, Guide to Law Online, "Indiana," www.loc.gov/law/help/guide/states/us-in.php

Indiana University Bloomington, Maurer School of Law, "Research Guides," http://law.indiana.libguides.com

Judicial

State Court Structure

Judicial Branch of Indiana, "Learn about Indiana's Court System," www.in.gov/judiciary/2646.htm

Judicial Branch of Indiana, "Organizational Chart of the Indiana Judicial System" [diagram], www.in.gov/judiciary/2681.htm

Directory of State Courts

Judicial Branch of Indiana, "Courts and Clerk's Offices," www.in.gov/judiciary/2794.htm

Opinions

Highest Court—Supreme Court

[last six days]: Judicial Branch of Indiana, "Indiana Appellate Opinions—Supreme," www.in.gov/judiciary/opinions/supreme.html

[2005–]: Judicial Branch of Indiana, "Indiana Appellate Opinions Archive—Supreme," www.in.gov/judiciary/opinions/archsup.html

[1999–2005]: Judicial Branch of Indiana, "Judicial Opinions Archive," www.in.gov/judiciary/opinions/previous/archsup.html

Intermediate Appellate Court—Court of Appeals

[last six days]: Judicial Branch of Indiana, "Indiana Appellate Opinions—Appeals," www.in.gov/judiciary/opinions/appeals.html

[2008–]: Judicial Branch of Indiana, "Indiana Appellate Opinions Archive—Appeals," www.in.gov/judiciary/opinions/archapp.html

[2005–2007]: Judicial Branch of Indiana, "Indiana Appellate Opinions Archive—Appeals," www.in.gov/judiciary/opinions/archapp2005.html

[1999–2005]: Judicial Branch of Indiana, "Judicial Opinions Archive," www.in.gov/judiciary/opinions/previous/archapp.html

Dockets/Court Records

Appellate Courts

Indiana Judicial System, "Online Docket," http://hats.courts.state.in.us/ISC3RUS/ISC2menu.jsp

Trial Courts

Doxpop Court Cases [fee-based], www.doxpop.com/prod/court/

Legislative

State Legislative Process

Indiana Governor's Council for People with Disabilities, "The Legislative Process," www.in.gov/gpcpd/2354.htm

Indiana Chamber of Commerce, "How a Bill Becomes a Law" [diagram], www.indianachamber.com/media/pdf/HowABillBecomesLaw08.pdf

Statutes

By Subject (Code)—Indiana Code

Indiana General Assembly, "Indiana Code," www.ai.org/legislative/ic/code/

In Chronological Order (Session Laws)—Laws of Indiana

[current assembly]: Indiana General Assembly, "Enrolled Acts," www.in.gov/legislative/2377.htm

[2000–]: Indiana General Assembly, "Law & Administrative Rules," www.in.gov/legislative/ic_iac/

Legislative History

Research Guide

Indiana University Law Library, "Legislative Research: Where to Locate Indiana Legislative History Sources," www.law.indiana.edu/lib/netres/govt/inleghis.pdf

Executive

Directory of State Departments/Agencies

IN.gov, "Find an Agency," www.in.gov/core/find_agency.html

State Rulemaking Process

Indiana Secretary of State, "Indiana Administrative Rules," § 7, "Rule Making Procedure," www.in.gov/sos/business/2457.htm

Regulations

By Agency (Code)—Indiana Administrative Code

[current]: Indiana General Assembly, "Indiana Administrative Code," www.in.gov/legislative/iac/

[2003–]: Indiana General Assembly, "Indiana Administrative Code: Archive," www.in.gov/legislative/iac/iacarchive.htm

In Chronological Order (Register)—Indiana Register

[current]: Indiana General Assembly, "Register Documents," www.in.gov/legislative/iac/irtoc.htm

[2000–]: Indiana General Assembly, "Register Documents: Archive," www.in.gov/legislative/iac/showIRArchive

Local Laws

Directories of State Counties/Municipalities

Judicial Branch of Indiana, "Indiana Trial Courts & Clerk's Offices," www.in.gov/judiciary/2808.htm

National Association of Counties, "Find a County," www.naco.org/Counties/Pages/FindACounty.aspx

State and Local Government on the Net, "Indiana State and Local Government," www.statelocalgov.net/state-in.cfm

Ordinances

Municode Code Corporation, "Indiana," www.municode.com/library/IN

Code Publishing Co., "Indiana," www.codepublishing.com/elibrary.html#indiana

Practice Materials and Self-Help Resources

Research Guides

Indiana Legal Services Inc., "Library," www.indianalegalservices.org/library

Indiana University Law Library, "How to File for Divorce, Child Custody, Visitation, and Child Support in Indiana," www.law.indiana.edu/lawlibrary/research/guides/doc/divorce.pdf

Court Rules

Judicial Branch of Indiana, "Rules of Court," www.in.gov/judiciary/2695.htm

Court Forms

Judicial Branch of Indiana, "Court Forms for Attorneys," www.in.gov/judiciary/2696.htm

Indiana Judicial Branch Self-Service Legal Center, "Court Forms for Self-Represented Litigants," www.in.gov/judiciary/selfservice/2333.htm

State Bar Association Consumer Brochures

N/A

Court Brochures/Self-Help Centers

Indiana Judicial Branch Self-Service Legal Center, www.state.in.us/judiciary/selfservice/

Looking for an Attorney (for a fee or for free)

Legal Aid/Advocacy Groups/Pro Bono

Indiana Judicial Branch, Indiana Pro Bono Commission, www.in.gov/judiciary/probono/

Indiana University, "Robert H. McKinney School of Law, Legal Information Gateway," "Legal Assistance Organizations," http://indylaw.indiana.edu/LIG/legal%20assistance.htm

Valparaiso University Law School, "Free Legal Help," www.valpo.edu/law/current-students/p-free-legal-help

Finding an Attorney/Lawyer Referrals

American Bar Association, Division for Legal Services, "Indiana," http://apps.americanbar.org/legalservices/findlegalhelp/lris.cfm?id=IN

Miscellaneous

Libcat: A Guide to Library Resources on the Internet, "Indiana Libraries," www.librarysites.info/states/in.htm

Indiana Law Blog, http://indianalawblog.com

References

Westlaw, "Glossary for Legal Research Basics," http://lawschool.westlaw.com/shared/marketinfodisplay.asp?code=RE&id=17&mainpage=23&rtid=116&rtcode=re

Cornell University Law School, Legal Information Institute, *Wex* [dictionary and encyclopedia], www.law.cornell.edu/wex/

IOWA

Research Guides

AALL LISP, "Public Library Toolkit: Iowa,"
www.aallnet.org/sections/lisp/Public-Library-Toolkit

University of Iowa College of Law Library,
"Legal Research Pathfinders," www.law.uiowa
.edu/library/pathfinders.php

University of Iowa College of Law Library,
"Information Resources," www.law.uiowa.edu/
library/iowa.php

Drake University Law Library, "Iowa Law,"
http://drakelaw.libguides.com/cat.php?cid=16788

Judicial

State Court Structure

Iowa Judicial Branch, "About the Courts:
Structure," www.iowacourts.gov/public_
information/about_the_courts/structure/

Westlaw, "Iowa Court Structure," [diagram],
http://wlwatch.westlaw.com/aca/west/statecrtorg
.htm#IO

Directory of State Courts

Iowa Judicial Branch, "Iowa Judicial Districts,"
www.iowacourts.gov/District_Courts/

Opinions

Research Guide

Drake University Law Library, "Case Law,"
http://drakelaw.libguides.com/content.php?pid=82911
&sid=628889

Highest Court—Supreme Court

[1998–]: Iowa Judicial Branch, "Archive of
Opinions for the Iowa Supreme Court,"
www.iowacourts.gov/Supreme_Court/Opinions
_Archive/

Intermediate Appellate Court—Court of Appeals

[1998–]: Iowa Judicial Branch, "Archive of
Opinions for the Iowa Court of Appeals,"
www.iowacourts.gov/Court_of_Appeals/Opinions
_Archive/

Dockets/Court Records

All Courts

Iowa Judicial Branch, "Online Docket Records,"
www.iowacourts.gov/Online_Court_Services/Online
_Docket_Record/

Legislative

State Legislative Process

Iowa Legislature, Legislative Services Agency,
"How a Bill Becomes a Law," https://www.legis
.iowa.gov/DOCS/Resources/HowABillBecomesALaw
.pdf

Iowa Legislature, "How an Idea Becomes a Law"
[diagram], https://www.legis.iowa.gov/DOCS/
Resources/HowAnIdeaBecomesALaw.pdf

Statutes

Research Guide

Drake University Law Library, "Constitution and
Statutes," http://drakelaw.libguides.com/content
.php?pid=82911&sid=628717

By Subject (Code)—Iowa Code

Iowa Legislature, "Statutory Law: Iowa Code,"
https://www.legis.iowa.gov/IowaLaw/statutoryLaw
.aspx

In Chronological Order (Session Laws)—
Iowa Acts

[1838–]: Iowa Legislature, "Statutory Law:
Iowa Acts," https://www.legis.iowa.gov/IowaLaw/
statutoryLaw.aspx

Legislative History

Research Guide

Drake University Law Library, "Iowa Legislative
History," http://libguides.law.drake.edu/
IowaLegHist

Executive

Directory of State Departments/Agencies

Iowa.gov, "Department Listing," http://phonebook
.iowa.gov/agency.aspx

State Rulemaking Process

Iowa.gov, "Understanding Administrative Rules in Iowa State Government," www.adminrules .iowa.gov/how_rules_work/

Iowa.gov, "Rulemaking Flowchart" [diagram], www.adminrules.iowa.gov/how_rules_work/ flowchart.html

Regulations

Research Guide

Drake University Law Library, "Administrative," http://drakelaw.libguides.com/content.php?pid=82911 &sid=628966

By Agency (Code)—Iowa Administrative Code

Iowa Legislature, "Iowa Administrative Code," www.legis.iowa.gov/IowaLaw/AdminCode/agency Docs.aspx

In Chronological Order (Register)— Iowa Administrative Bulletin

[1997–]: Iowa Legislature, "Iowa Administrative Bulletin & Code Supplement," www.legis.iowa.gov/IowaLaw/AdminCode/ bulletinSupplementListing.aspx

Administrative Rulings

Research Guide

University of Iowa College of Law, "Iowa Administrative Agency Pathfinder," www.law .uiowa.edu/documents/pathfinders/iowa_agency.pdf

Local Laws

Directory of State Counties/Municipalities

Iowa.gov, "Local Government," www.iowa.gov/ pages/local

Ordinances

Drake University Law School, "Iowa Municipal and County Law," http://libguides.law.drake.edu/ IowaLocalCodes

Practice Materials and Self-Help Resources

Research Guides

University of Iowa Law Library, "How to Find Iowa Practice Materials," www.law.uiowa.edu/ documents/iowapracticematerials.pdf

Drake University Law School, "Law-Related Forms," http://libguides.law.drake.edu/Forms

Court Rules

Iowa Legislature, "Court Rules," https://www.legis .iowa.gov/IowaLaw/courtRules.aspx

Forms

Iowa Judicial Branch, "Iowa Court Rules and Forms," www.iowacourts.gov/Court_Rules_and _Forms/

State Bar Association Consumer Brochures

Iowa State Bar Association, "Consumer Pamphlet Series," www.iowabar.org/ displaycommon.cfm?an=1&subarticlenbr=134

Court Brochures/Self-Help Centers

Iowa Judicial Branch, "Representing Yourself," www.iowacourts.gov/Representing_Yourself/

Looking for an Attorney (for a fee or for free)

Legal Aid/Advocacy Groups/Pro Bono

Iowa State Bar Association, "Legal Assistance in Iowa," http://isba.affiniscape.com/displaycommon .cfm?an=1&subarticlenbr=132

Iowa Judicial Branch, "Low Cost Legal Services," www.iowacourts.gov/Representing_Yourself/Legal _Help/Find_Low_Cost_Legal_Aid/

Finding an Attorney/Lawyer Referrals

Iowa Library Services, "Help Finding an Attorney," www.statelibraryofiowa.org/services/ law-library/help/view

Iowa State Bar Association, "Iowa Lawyers Can Do!" http://iowabar.org/associations/4664/files/ Iowa%20Lawyers%20Can%20Do.pdf

Miscellaneous

Iowa.gov, "Agency Rulemaking Dockets,"
www.adminrules.iowa.gov/tracking_rules/
rulemaking_dockets.html

Attorney General Opinions

[1977–]: Iowa Department of Justice, "Attorney
General Opinions," www.state.ia.us/government/
ag/issuing_opinions/atty_gen_opin.html

References

Iowa Legislature, Legislative Services Agency,
"Legislative Terminology," www.legis.iowa.gov/
DOCS/Resources/LegislativeTerminology.pdf

Iowa Judicial Branch, "Understanding the
Docket: Case Numbers, Abbreviations,
Glossary," www.iowacourts.gov/wfdata/
frame2981-1138/Online_records_help_docket
_terms.pdf

Iowa Judicial Branch, "Legal Glossary,"
www.iowacourts.gov/Representing_Yourself/
Common_Legal_Terms/

KANSAS

Research Guides

AALL LISP, "Public Library Toolkit: Kansas,"
www.aallnet.org/sections/lisp/Public-Library-Toolkit

University of Kansas School of Law, "Research &
Study Guides," www.law.ku.edu/research-study
-guides

Washburn University School of Law, "Research
Guides," www.washburnlaw.edu/library/research/
guides/

Judicial

State Court Structure

Kansas Judicial Branch, "You and the Courts of
Kansas—Types of Courts," www.kscourts.org/
kansas-courts/general-information/you-and-the
-courts/courts.asp

Kansas Judicial Branch, "Kansas Court System"
[diagram], www.kscourts.org/pdf/ctchart.pdf

Directory of State Courts

Kansas Judicial Branch, "Links to Judicial
District Home Pages," www.kscourts.org/kansas
-courts/district-courts/Links.asp

Opinions

Research Guide

Washburn University School of Law, "Kansas
Case Law Research Guide," www.washburnlaw
.edu/library/research/guides/kansascases.html

Highest Court—Supreme Court

[1996–]: Kansas Judicial Branch, "Kansas
Supreme Court Opinions Date of Release
List," www.kscourts.org/Cases-and-Opinions/
Date-of-Release-List/

Intermediate Appellate Court—
Court of Special Appeals

[1996–]: Kansas Judicial Branch, "Kansas Court
of Appeals Opinions Date of Release List,"
www.kscourts.org/Cases-and-Opinions/Date-of
-Release-List/

Dockets/Court Records

Appellate Courts

[1990–]: Kansas Judicial Branch, "Case Inquiry
System for the Kansas Appellate Courts,"
www.kscourts.org/inquiry-system.asp

Trial Courts

Kansas Office of Judicial Administration,
"Kansas District Court Records,"
www.accesskansas.org/countyCourts/

Legislative

State Legislative Process

Kansas Legislative Research Department,
"Legislative Procedure in Kansas," http://
skyways.lib.ks.us/ksleg/KLRD/about/legproc.pdf

Kansas Legislative Research Department, "How
a Bill Becomes a Law" [diagram], http://
skyways.lib.ks.us/ksleg/KLRD/about/how_bill_law
.pdf

Statutes

By Subject (Code)—Kansas Statutes

Kansas Legislature, "Statute," http://kslegislature
.org/li/statute/

In Chronological Order (Session Laws)—
Session Laws of Kansas

[1996–]: Kansas.gov, "Kansas Legislative
Archive," www.kansas.gov/government/legislative/
sessionlaws/

Legislative History

Research Guide

Washburn University School of Law, "Kansas
Legislative History Research Guide,"
www.washburnlaw.edu/library/research/guides/
kansasleghistory.html

Executive

Directory of State Departments/Agencies

Kansas.gov, "Agencies & Associations Listing,"
www.kansas.gov/government/agencies-associations
-listing/

State Rulemaking Process

USLegal, "Administrative Procedure Act—
Kansas," http://administrativelaw.uslegal.com/
administrative-procedure-acts/kansas/

Regulations

Research Guide

Washburn University School of Law, "Kansas
Administrative Regulations Research Guide,"
www.washburnlaw.edu/library/research/guides/
kansasadminregs.html

By Agency (Code)—
Kansas Administrative Regulations

Office of the Secretary of State, "Kansas
Administrative Regulations," www.kssos.org/
Pubs/pubs_kar.aspx

In Chronological Order (Register)—
Kansas Register

[1982–]: Office of the Secretary of State,
"Kansas Register," www.kssos.org/pubs/pubs
_kansas_register.asp

Local Laws

Directories of State Counties/Municipalities

League of Kansas Municipalities, "Kansas Cities
on the Web," www.lkm.org/links/local/cities.php

Kansas City Metropolitan Bar Association,
"County, Federal, Municipal & State Links,"
www.kcmba.org/PublicService/statelinks.htm

Ordinances

Municode Code Corporation, "Kansas,"
www.municode.com/library/KS

Practice Materials and Self-Help Resources

Research Guides

Kansas Legal Services, "Legal Library,"
www.kansaslegalservices.org/legal_library

Johnson County Kansas Law Library, "Legal
Forms," www.jocolibrary.org/templates/
JCL_InfoPage.aspx?id=13980

Douglas County Law Library, "Research
Resources" [includes criminal and juvenile
law resources], www.douglascolawlibrary.org/
research.html

Court Rules

Kansas Judicial Branch, "Rules Adopted by the
Supreme Court," www.kscourts.org/rules/

Kansas Judicial Branch, "District Court Rules,"
www.kscourts.org/kansas-courts/district-courts/
rules.asp

Forms

Kansas Judicial Council, "Legal Forms,"
www.kansasjudicialcouncil.org/legal_forms.shtml

Office of the Secretary of State, "Filings &
Forms," www.kssos.org/forms/forms.html

Johnson County Kansas Law Library, "Kansas Court Forms," http://lawlibrary.jocogov.org/pForms.htm

State Bar Association Consumer Brochures

Kansas Bar Association, "Public Information Pamphlets," www.ksbar.org/displaycommon.cfm?an=1&subarticlenbr=44

Court Brochures/Self-Help Centers

Kansas Judicial Branch, "Self-Help Information," www.kscourts.org/Programs/Self-Help/

Looking for an Attorney (for a fee or for free)

Legal Aid/Advocacy Groups/Pro Bono

Johnson County Kansas Law Library, "Local Legal Assistance Services," http://lawlibrary.jocogov.org/forms/Legal%20Assistance%20Services.pdf

Finding an Attorney/Lawyer Referrals

Kansas Bar Association, "Need to Find an Attorney?" www.ksbar.org/displaycommon.cfm?an=1&subarticlenbr=8
Wichita Bar Association, "Lawyer Referral," www.wichitabar.org/resources/lawyerreferral.php

Miscellaneous

Kansas Judicial Council, "Studies and Reports," [1991–], www.kansasjudicialcouncil.org/StudiesReports.shtml
Kansas Judicial Branch, "Kansas Appellate Practice Handbook," www.kscourts.org/appellate-clerk/appellate-handbook/

References

Westlaw, "Glossary for Legal Research Basics," http://lawschool.westlaw.com/shared/marketinfodisplayasp?code=RE&id=17&mainpage=23&rtid=116&rtcode=re
Cornell University Law School, Legal Information Institute, *Wex* [dictionary and encyclopedia], www.law.cornell.edu/wex/

KENTUCKY

Research Guide

University of Kentucky College of Law, "Kentucky Sites," www.law.uky.edu/index.php?pid=237

Judicial

State Court Structure

Kentucky Court of Justice, "Courts," http://courts.ky.gov/courts/
Kentucky Court of Justice, "The Judicial Branch at a Glance" [diagram], http://courts.ky.gov/resources/publicationsresources/Publications/P2KCOJBrochure.pdf

Directory of State Courts

Kentucky Court of Justice, "Circuit Court Clerks," http://courts.ky.gov/courts/clerks/

Opinions

Research Guide

University of Louisville, Louis D. Brandeis School of Law, "Guide to Kentucky Case Law," www.law.louisville.edu/library/research/guides/ky-law/case-law

Highest Court—Supreme Court

[last five years]: Kentucky Court of Justice, "Supreme Court Minutes," http://courts.ky.gov/courts/supreme/Pages/SupremeCourtMinutes.aspx
[1999–]: Kentucky Court of Justice, "Kentucky Supreme Court and Court of Appeals Searchable Opinions," http://apps.courts.ky.gov/supreme/sc_opinions.shtm

Intermediate Appellate Court—Court of Appeals

[last three years]: Kentucky Court of Justice, "Court of Appeals Minutes," http://courts.ky.gov/courts/coa/Pages/minutes.aspx
[1996–]: Kentucky Court of Justice, "Kentucky Supreme Court and Court of Appeals Searchable Opinions," http://apps.courts.ky.gov/supreme/sc_opinions.shtm

Dockets/Court Records

Supreme Court

Kentucky Court of Justice, "Office of the Clerk of the Supreme Court of Kentucky," http://apps.courts.ky.gov/supreme/sc_dockets.shtm

Court of Appeals

Kentucky Court of Justice, "Office of the Clerk of the Appeals Court of Kentucky," http://apps.kycourts.net/Appeals/COA_Dockets.shtm

Trial Courts

Kentucky Court of Justice, "Docket Information," http://kcoj.kycourts.net/dockets/

Legislative

State Legislative Process

Kentucky Legislature, "How a Bill Becomes a Law," www.lrc.ky.gov/legproc/how_law.htm
Kentucky Legislative Research Commission, "The Road to Passage: How a Bill Becomes a Law" [diagram], www.lrc.ky.gov/Lrcpubs/Road_to_Passage_2005.pdf

Statutes

Research Guide

University of Louisville, Louis D. Brandeis School of Law, "Guide to Kentucky Statutory Law," www.law.louisville.edu/library/research/guides/ky-law/statutes

By Subject (Code)—Kentucky Revised Statutes

Kentucky Legislature, "Kentucky Revised Statutes," www.lrc.state.ky.us/statrev/frontpg.htm

In Chronological Order (Session Laws)—
Acts of the General Assembly

[1995–]: Kentucky Legislature, "Acts of the Kentucky General Assembly," www.lrc.ky.gov/ACTS/mainacts.htm

Legislative History

Research Guides

Kentucky Legislature, "Tracing Legislative History," www.lrc.ky.gov/legproc/history.htm

University of Kentucky College of Law, Alvin E. Evans Law Library, "Tracing Legislative History," www.law.uky.edu/files/docs/library/guides/KYLegHist.pdf

Executive

Directory of State Departments/Agencies

Kentucky.gov, "The Executive, Judicial, and Legislative Branches," http://kentucky.gov/government/Pages/branches.aspx

State Rulemaking Process

LouisvilleKy.gov, "Rule Making Process," www.louisvilleky.gov/APCD/Regulations/RegProcess.htm

Regulations

Research Guides

University of Louisville, Louis D. Brandeis School of Law, "Guide to Kentucky Administrative Law," www.law.louisville.edu/library/research/guides/ky-law/regulations
University of Cincinnati, "Guide to Kentucky Administrative Law," www.law.uc.edu/sites/default/files/Kentucky%20Administrative%20Law%20Guide.pdf

By Agency (Code)—
Kentucky Administrative Regulations

Kentucky Legislature, "Kentucky Administrative Regulations," www.lrc.ky.gov/kar/frntpage.htm

In Chronological Order (Register)—
Administrative Register of Kentucky

Kentucky Legislative Research Commission, "Administrative Register of Kentucky," www.lrc.ky.gov/kar/frntpage.htm

Local Laws

Directory of State Counties/Municipalities

University of Kentucky, Kentucky Atlas & Gazetteer, "Kentucky Counties," www.uky.edu/KentuckyAtlas/kentucky-counties.html

Ordinances

University of Louisville, Louis D. Brandeis
School of Law, "Kentucky: City and County
Websites," www.law.louisville.edu/library/research/
jump-zone/ky/internet-cities

Practice Materials and Self-Help Resources

Research Guide

Legal Aid Network of Kentucky, "Law Library,"
www.kyjustice.org/legalinformation

Court Rules

Westlaw, "Kentucky Court Rules," http://
government.westlaw.com/linkedslice/default
.asp?SP=KYR-1000
Kentucky Court of Justice, "Local Rules of
Practice," http://courts.ky.gov/Pages/localrules
.aspx

Forms

Kentucky Court of Justice, "Legal Forms,"
http://courts.ky.gov/resources/legalforms/Pages/
legalformlibrary.aspx

State Bar Association Consumer Brochures

N/A

Court Brochures/Self-Help Centers

N/A

Looking for an Attorney (for a fee or for free)

Legal Aid/Advocacy Groups/Pro Bono

Kentucky Bar Association, "Legal Aid Programs
in Kentucky," www.kybar.org/418
Kentucky Legal Aid, www.klaid.org
Legal Aid Society, www.laslou.org
Legal Aid Network of Kentucky, "Pro Bono
Organizations and Opportunities,"
www.kyjustice.org/probono

Finding an Attorney/Lawyer Referrals

Kentucky Bar Association, "Lawyer Locator,"
www.kybar.org/26

Kentucky Bar Association, "Lawyer Referral
Services," www.kybar.org/291
Louisville Bar Association, "Kentucky Lawyer
Referral Service," www.loubar.org/KLRS.cfm
Northern Kentucky Bar Association, "Lawyer
Referral Services," www.nkybar.com/includes/
referral.aspx

Miscellaneous

Northern Kentucky University, Chase College
of Law, "Kentucky Appellate Court Briefs"
[1999–], http://chaselaw.nku.edu/library/
electronic_resources/briefs_search.php
Kentucky Legislature, Legislative Research
Commission, "Research Reports" [1973–],
www.lrc.ky.gov/lrcpubs/research_reports.htm
Kentucky Legislature, Legislative Research
Commission, "Informational Bulletins"
[1981–], www.lrc.ky.gov/lrcpubs/info_bulletins
.htm
Kentucky Legislature, Legislative Research
Commission, "Research Memoranda" [1980–],
www.lrc.ky.gov/lrcpubs/lrc_research_memoranda
.htm

Reference

Kentucky Legislature, "Glossary of Legislative
Terms," www.lrc.ky.gov/legproc/glossary.htm

LOUISIANA

Research Guides

AALL LISP, "Public Library Toolkit: Louisiana,"
www.aallnet.org/sections/lisp/Public-Library-Toolkit
LSU Law Center, "Research Guides: Louisiana,"
www.law.lsu.edu/index.cfm?geaux=library
.researchguides

Judicial

State Court Structure

Louisiana State Bar Association, "Court
Structure," www.lsba.org/PublicResources/
courtstructure.asp?Menu=PR

Westlaw, "Louisiana Court Structure" [diagram], http://wlwatch.westlaw.com/aca/west/statecrtorg .htm#LA

Directory of State Courts

Louisiana Supreme Court, "District Courts," www.lasc.org/links.asp#DistrictCourts

Opinions

Highest Court—Supreme Court

[1996–]: Louisiana Supreme Court, "News Releases and Opinions," www.lasc.org/news _releases/

[1995–2004]: Louisiana Supreme Court, "Opinion Search," www.lasc.org/opinion _search.asp

Intermediate Appellate Court—Courts of Appeal

N/A

Dockets/Court Records

All Courts

LLRX, "Court Rules, Forms, and Dockets" [browse by jurisdiction/state = "Louisiana" and type = "dockets"], www.llrx.com/courtrules/

Legislative

State Legislative Process

Louisiana State Legislature, "How a Bill Becomes a Law" [diagram], www.legis.la.gov/legis/ LegisInfo.aspx?opt=2

Statutes

Research Guide

Brian Huddleston, Loyola University New Orleans School of Law Library, "How to Find Louisiana Statutes," www.loyno.edu/~bhuddle/ library/docs/LouisianaStatutes.htm

By Subject (Code)—Louisiana Revised Statutes

Louisiana State Legislature, "Laws Table of Contents," www.legis.la.gov/legis/LawsContents .aspx

In Chronological Order (Session Laws)— Acts of the Legislature

[1997–]: Louisiana State Legislature [enactments/acts], www.legis.la.gov/legis/ home.aspx

Legislative History

Research Guides

LSU Law Center, "Research Guides: Louisiana: Finding Louisiana Legislative History Materials," www.law.lsu.edu/index.cfm?geaux =library.researchguides

Law Library of Louisiana, "Legislative History Research Guide," http://search.lasc.org/ law_library/RESGUID1.pdf

Executive

Directory of State Departments/Agencies

Louisiana.gov, "Agency Directory," www.louisiana .gov/Government/Agency_Index/

State Rulemaking Process

Louisiana House of Representatives, "State and Local Government in Louisiana: An Overview," chapter 2, part M, "Administrative Procedure," www.lla.state.la.us/ userfiles/file/Chapter%202%20Part%20M%20-%20 Administrative%20Procedure.pdf

Regulations

By Agency (Code)— Louisiana Administrative Code

Louisiana Division of Administration, "Online Publications of the Louisiana Administrative Code," http://doa.louisiana.gov/osr/lac/books.htm

In Chronological Order (Register)— Louisiana Register

[1975–]: Louisiana Division of Administration, "Louisiana Register," http://doa.louisiana.gov/ osr/reg/register.htm

Local Laws

Directory of State Counties/Municipalities

State and Local Government on the Net,
"Louisiana State and Local Government,"
www.statelocalgov.net/state-la.cfm

Ordinances

Municode Code Corporation, "Louisiana,"
www.municode.com/library/LA

Practice Materials and Self-Help Resources

Research Guides

LSU Law Center, "Research Guides: Louisiana:
Selected Guide to Legal Forms," www.law.lsu
.edu/index.cfm?geaux=library.researchguides

Loyola University New Orleans College of Law
Library, "Legal Forms and Form Books,"
http://law.loyno.edu/~escoggin/forms.html

Court Rules

Louisiana Supreme Court, "Rules of the
Louisiana Supreme Court," www.lasc.org/rules/
supreme.asp

Louisiana Supreme Court, "Rules of the Courts
of Appeal," www.lasc.org/rules/Appellate.asp

Louisiana Supreme Court, "Rules for Louisiana
District Courts," www.lasc.org/rules/
DistrictCourt.asp

Court Forms

Louisiana Supreme Court, "Rules of the
Louisiana Supreme Court: Forms,"
www.lasc.org/rules/supreme.asp

State Bar Association Consumer Brochures

Louisiana State Bar Association, "Consumer
Brochures," www.lsba.org/2007PublicResources/
consumerbrochures.asp?Menu=PR

Court Brochures/Self-Help Centers

N/A

Looking for an Attorney (for a fee or for free)

Legal Aid/Advocacy Groups/Pro Bono

Louisiana State Bar Association, "Access to
Justice," www.lsba.org/2007atj/

Finding an Attorney/Lawyer Referrals

Louisiana State Bar Association,
"Lawyer Referral and Information,"
www.lsba.org/2007MembershipDirectory/
LawyerReferralInformation.asp?Menu=PR

Miscellaneous

Louisiana House of Representatives, David R.
Poynter Legislative Research Library,
"Selected Internet Publications," http://house
.legis.state.la.us/legispublist/subject.htm

Louisiana Digital Library,
http://louisdl.louislibraries.org

State Library of Louisiana, "Louisiana
Documents," www.state.lib.la.us/library
-collections/louisiana-documents

References

Louisiana State Legislature, "Legislative
Glossary," www.legis.la.gov/legis/Glossary.aspx

Louisiana State Bar Association, "Legal
Terms and Procedures," www.lsba.org/2007
PublicResources/LegalTerms.asp?Menu=PR

MAINE

Research Guide

Georgetown University Law Library, "Maine
Resources," www.law.georgetown.edu/library/
research/guides/maine.cfm

Judicial

State Court Structure

Maine Judicial Branch, "The Maine Courts,"
www.courts.state.me.us/maine_courts/

Westlaw, "Maine Court Structure" [diagram],
http://wlwatch.westlaw.com/aca/west/statecrtorg.
htm#ME

Directories of State Courts

Maine Judicial Branch, "Superior Courthouse Directory," www.courts.state.me.us/maine_courts/superior/directory.shtml

Maine Judicial Branch, "District Courthouse Directory," www.courts.state.me.us/maine_courts/district/directory.shtml

Opinions

Highest Court—Supreme Court

[1997–]: Maine Judicial Branch, "Supreme Judicial Court Decisions and Orders," www.courts.state.me.us/court_info/opinions/supreme/

Intermediate Appellate Court—None

General Jurisdiction Trial Court —Superior Court

[2000–]: University of Maine School of Law, http://webapp.usm.maine.edu/SuperiorCourt/

Dockets/Court Records

N/A

Legislative

State Legislative Process

Maine State Law and Legislative Reference Library, "Maine's Path of Legislation (How a Bill Becomes a Law)," www.maine.gov/legis/lawlib/billpath.htm

Statutes

By Subject (Code)—Maine Revised Statutes

Maine Legislature, "List of Titles, Maine Revised Statutes," www.mainelegislature.org/legis/statutes/

Maine Legislature, "Statute Search by Title, Section, or Phrase," www.mainelegislature.org/legis/statutes/search.htm

In Chronological Order (Session Laws)—
Laws of the State of Maine

[1997–]: Maine Legislature, "Laws of Maine," www.mainelegislature.org/ros/LOM/LOMDirectory.htm

Legislative History

Research Guide

Maine State Law and Legislative Reference Library, "Compiling a Legislative History," www.maine.gov/legis/lawlib/leghist.htm

Executive

Directory of State Departments/Agencies

Maine.gov, "State Agencies," www.maine.gov/portal/government/state-agencies

State Rulemaking Process

Maine Department of the Secretary of State, Bureau of Corporations, Elections & Commissions, "Guide to Rule Making," www.maine.gov/sos/cec/rules/guide.html

Regulations

By Agency (Code)—Code of Maine Rules

Maine Department of the Secretary of State, Bureau of Corporations, Elections & Commissions, "Rules by Department," www.maine.gov/sos/cec/rules/rules.html

In Chronological Order (Register)

[1997–]: Maine Department of the Secretary of State, Bureau of Corporations, Elections & Commissions, "Weekly Rule-making Notices," www.maine.gov/sos/cec/rules/notices.html

Local Laws

Directory of State Counties/Municipalities

State and Local Government on the Net, "Maine State and Local Government," www.statelocalgov.net/state-me.cfm

Ordinances

Maine Municipal Association, "Home Rule," www.memun.org/public/local_govt/home_rule.htm

University of Maine School of Law, "Maine Town & City Ordinances," http://mainelaw.maine.edu/library/ordinances.htm

Practice Materials and Self-Help Resources

Research Guides

Cleaves Law Library, "Maine Practice Materials," www.cleaves.org/mepracmat.htm

University of Maine School of Law, "Maine Legal Sources Bibliography," http://mainelaw .usm.maine.edu/library/handoutmainebib.htm

Maine State Law and Legislative Reference Library, "Bibliographies," www.maine.gov/legis/ lawlib/resaids.htm

Pine Tree Legal Assistance, "Legal Library," www.ptla.org/library

Court Rules

Maine Judicial Branch, "Court Rules," www.courts.state.me.us/court_info/rules/rules.html

Forms

Maine Judicial Branch, "Court Forms," www.courts.state.me.us/fees_forms/forms/

State Bar Association Consumer Brochures

Maine State Bar Association, "Legal Information Pamphlets and Pages," www.mainebar.org/ lawyer_pamphlets.asp

Court Brochures/Self-Help Centers

Maine Judicial Branch, "Frequently Asked Questions and How Do I . . . ?" www.courts.state.me.us/citizen_info/faq.shtml

Looking for an Attorney (for a fee or for free)

Legal Aid/Advocacy Groups/Pro Bono

Pine Tree Legal Assistance, "Legal Library," www.ptla.org/library

Maine Volunteer Lawyers Project, www.vlp.org

Legal Services for the Elderly, www.mainelse.org

HelpMELaw, http://helpmelaw.org

Finding an Attorney/Lawyer Referrals

Maine State Bar Association, "Lawyer Referral and Information Service," www.mainebar.org/ lawyer_need.asp

Miscellaneous

Maine State Legislature, Office of Policy and Legal Analysis, "Legislative Studies Reports," www.state.me.us/legis/opla/reportsnew.htm

Reference

Maine Legislature, "Glossary," www.maine.gov/ legis/opla/glossary.htm

MARYLAND
Research Guides

AALL LISP, "Public Library Toolkit: Maryland," www.aallnet.org/sections/lisp/Public-Library-Toolkit

Maryland Judiciary, People's Law Library, "Understanding Legal Research," www.peoples-law.org/node/308

Thurgood Marshall Law Library, "TMLL Guide to Legal Research, 2011–2012," chapter 9, "Researching a Maryland Law Problem," www.law.umaryland.edu/marshall/researchguides/ TMLLguide/

Thurgood Marshall Law Library, "Maryland Resources," www.law.umaryland.edu/ marshall/researchguides/specialtypages/ marylandresources.html

University of Baltimore School of Law, "Maryland Law and Government," http://law.ubalt.edu/template.cfm?page=504

Baltimore County Law Library, "Publications," www.baltimorecountymd.gov/Agencies/circuit/ library/publications.html

Judicial
State Court Structure

Maryland Judiciary, "Maryland's Judicial System," http://mdcourts.gov/overview.html

Court Statistics Project, "Maryland" [diagram], www.courtstatistics.org/Other-Pages/State_Court _Structure_Charts/Maryland.aspx

Directories of State Courts

Maryland Judiciary, "Circuit Court Locations/ Clerks' Offices," http://mdcourts.gov/circuit/ directory.html

Maryland Judiciary, "District Court Locations,"
http://mdcourts.gov/district/directories/courtmap
.html

Opinions

Research Guide

Maryland Judiciary, People's Law Library,
"Finding Maryland Case Law,"
www.peoples-law.org/node/894

Highest Court—Court of Appeals

[1995–]: Maryland Judiciary, "Maryland
Appellate Court Opinions in PDF,"
http://mdcourts.gov/opinions.html

Intermediate Appellate Court—
Court of Special Appeals

[1995–]: Maryland Judiciary, "Maryland
Appellate Court Opinions in PDF,"
http://mdcourts.gov/opinions.html

Dockets/Court Records

Trial Courts

Maryland Judiciary, "Case Search,"
http://casesearch.courts.state.md.us/inquiry/
inquiry-index.jsp

Legislative

State Legislative Process

Maryland State Archives, "The Legislative
Process: How a Bill Becomes a Law,"
www.msa.md.gov/msa/mdmanual/07leg/html/
proc.html

Statutes

Research Guide

Maryland Judiciary, People's Law Library,
"Finding Maryland Statutes,"
www.peoples-law.org/node/891

By Subject (Code)—Maryland Code

Maryland General Assembly, "Statutes," http://
mlis.state.md.us/asp/web_statutes.asp

LexisNexis, "Unannotated Code of Maryland and
Rules," www.lexisnexis.com/hottopics/mdcode/

In Chronological Order (Session Laws)—
Laws of the State of Maryland

[1634–]: Archives of Maryland, Legislative
Records, "Proceedings, Acts and Public
Documents of the General Assembly,"
www.msa.md.gov/megafile/msa/speccol/sc2900/
sc2908/html/legislative.html

Legislative History

Research Guides

Maryland State Law Library, "Maryland
Legislative History," www.lawlib.state.md.us/
researchtools/guides.html

Maryland State Law Library, "Ghosthunting:
Searching for Maryland Legislative History,"
www.lawlib.state.md.us/researchtools/guides/
ghosthunting.html

Thurgood Marshall Law Library, "TMLL
Research Guide," chapter 5, "Strategies for
Researching Legislative History,"
www.law.umaryland.edu/marshall/researchguides/
tmllguide/5sec3.html

Executive

Directory of State Departments/Agencies

Maryland State Archives, "Departments,"
www.msa.md.gov/msa/mdmanual/09dept/html/
00list.html

State Rulemaking Process

USLegal, "Administrative Procedure Act—
Maryland," http://administrativelaw.uslegal.com/
administrative-procedure-acts/maryland/

Regulations

Research Guides

Maryland Judiciary, People's Law Library,
"Finding Regulations," www.peoples-law.org/
node/893

Maryland Office of the Secretary of State,
"Research Guide for Maryland Regulations,"
www.lawlib.state.md.us/researchtools/guides/
comarresearch.pdf

By Agency (Code)—
Code of Maryland Administrative Regulations

Maryland Office of the Secretary of State, "COMAR Online," www.dsd.state.md.us/comar/comar.aspx

In Chronological Order (Register)—
Maryland Register

[last four months]: Maryland Office of the Secretary of State, "Maryland Register Online," www.dsd.state.md.us/MDRegister/mdregister.aspx

Local Laws

Research Guide

Thurgood Marshall Law Library, "Researching Maryland Local Law," www.law.umaryland.edu/marshall/researchguides/specialtypages/mdlocal.html

Directory of State Counties/Municipalities

Maryland State Archives, "Local Government: Counties," www.msa.md.gov/msa/mdmanual/01glance/html/county.html

Ordinances

Maryland State Law Library, "Maryland Municipal Codes," www.lawlib.state.md.us/researchtools/codeslocal.html

Maryland State Law Library, "Maryland County Codes," www.lawlib.state.md.us/researchtools/codescounty.html

Practice Materials and Self-Help Resources

Research Guides

Maryland State Law Library, "Research Tools," www.lawlib.state.md.us/researchtools/research.html

Maryland Judiciary, People's Law Library, "Research Guides," www.peoples-law.org/node/30

Court Rules

Maryland Judiciary, People's Law Library, "Finding Court Rules," www.peoples-law.org/node/896

LexisNexis, "Unannotated Code of Maryland and Rules," www.lexisnexis.com/hottopics/mdcode/

Forms

Maryland Judiciary, Department of Family Administration, "Family Law Forms," www.mdcourts.gov/family/formsindex.html

District Court of Maryland, "Fees, Fines Schedules, Brochures, and Forms Index," www.courts.state.md.us/district/dctcivforms.html

State Bar Association Consumer Brochures

Maryland State Bar Association, "Legal Information Brochures," www.msba.org/departments/commpubl/publications/brochures/

Court Brochures/Self-Help Centers

District Court of Maryland, "Self-Help Information and Brochures," www.courts.state.md.us/district/public_brochures.html

Looking for an Attorney (for a fee or for free)

Legal Aid/Advocacy Groups/Pro Bono

Maryland Judiciary, People's Law Library, "Get Help," www.peoples-law.org/gethelp

Catherine McGuire, "Court Self-Help Programs," *Justice Matters* 12, no. 4 (2009), published by the Maryland Judiciary, www.courts.state.md.us/publications/ejusticematters/2009/summer/selfhelp.html

Finding an Attorney/Lawyer ReferralsMaryland Judiciary, People's Law Library, "Referral Services," www.peoples-law.org/referrals

Maryland State Bar Association, "Lawyer Referral Services," www.msba.org/public/referral.htm

Miscellaneous

Enoch Pratt Free Library, "Maryland Government and Law," www.prattlibrary.org/research/tools/index.aspx?id=3442

Archives of Maryland Online, www.msa.md.gov/
    megafile/msa/speccol/sc2900/sc2908/html/
    volumes.html

References

Maryland Judiciary, People's Law Library,
    "Glossary," www.peoples-law.org/glossary
Maryland State Law Library, "Glossary of Legal
    Terms and Abbreviations," www.lawlib.state
    .md.us/researchtools/glossary.html
Maryland State Law Library, "Recognizing and
    Reading Legal Citations," www.lawlib.state
    .md.us/researchtools/guides/legalcitations.pdf

MASSACHUSETTS

Research Guides

Commonwealth of Massachusetts,
    Administration and Finance, "Massachusetts
    Law," www.mass.gov/anf/research-and-tech/legal
    -and-legislative-resources/massachusetts-law.html
Boston College Law Library, "Massachusetts
    Legal Research," www.bc.edu/content/dam/
    files/schools/law_sites/library/pdf/researchguides/
    MA.pdf
Suffolk University Law School, "Legal Subjects,"
    www.law.suffolk.edu/library/research/a-z/

Judicial

State Court Structure

Massachusetts Judicial Branch, Administrative
    Office of the Trial Court, "Overview of the
    Judicial Structure," www.mass.gov/courts/
    courtsandjudges/courts/overviewofjudicialstructure
    .html
Massachusetts Judicial Branch, Administrative
    Office of the Trial Court, "Massachusetts
    Court System" [diagram], www.mass.gov/
    courts/courtsandjudges/courts/structure_color.pdf

Directory of State Courts

Massachusetts Judicial Branch, Administrative
    Office of the Trial Court, "Courts—
    by Department," www.mass.gov/courts/
    courtsandjudges/courts/courtsdept.html

Opinions

Research Guides

Western New England University School of Law,
    "Massachusetts Appeals Court: A Pathfinder,"
    www1.law.wne.edu/library/index.cfm?selection
    =doc.627
Suffolk University School of Law, "Massachusetts
    Case Finding Guide," www.law.suffolk.edu/
    library/research/a-z/resguides/masscase.cfm

Highest Court—Supreme Judicial Court

[1804–]: Massachusetts Trial Court Law
    Libraries, "Massachusetts Court Cases,"
    www.lawlib.state.ma.us/source/mass/cases/

Intermediate Appellate Court—Appeals Court

[1804–]: Massachusetts Trial Court Law
    Libraries, "Massachusetts Court Cases,"
    www.lawlib.state.ma.us/source/mass/cases/

Dockets/Court Records

Appellate Courts

[1988–]: Supreme Judicial Court and Appeals
    Court of Massachusetts, "Public Case
    Information," http://ma-appellatecourts.org

Trial Courts

Massachusetts Administrative Office of the Trial
    Court, "Trial Court Information Center,"
    www.ma-trialcourts.org/tcic/welcome.jsp

Legislative

State Legislative Process

Massachusetts Bar Association, "The Legislative
    Process," www.massbar.org/legislative-activities/
    the-legislative-process

Statutes

By Subject (Code)—
General Laws of Massachusetts

General Court of Massachusetts, "General Laws,"
    www.malegislature.gov/Laws/GeneralLaws
General Court of Massachusetts, "Search Laws,"
    www.malegislature.gov/Laws/Search

Massachusetts Trial Court Law Libraries, "Massachusetts Laws by Popular Name," www.lawlib.state.ma.us/subject/popname/

In Chronological Order (Session Laws)— Acts and Resolves of Massachusetts

[1997–]: General Court of Massachusetts, "Session Laws," www.malegislature.gov/Laws/SessionLaws/

[1998–]: Social Law Library Research Portal, "Massachusetts Laws & Constitution," www.socialaw.com/content.htm?sec=Laws Constitution

[1692–]: State Library of Massachusetts, "Acts and Resolves," http://archives.lib.state.ma.us/handle/123456789/2

Legislative History

Research Guides

Commonwealth of Massachusetts, Administration and Finance, "Massachusetts Legislative History," www.mass.gov/anf/research-and-tech/legal-and-legislative-resources/tracing-ma-law.html

Social Law Library Research Guide, "Massachusetts Legislative History," www.socialaw.com/guides/res01.pdf

Executive

Directory of State Departments/Agencies

Commonwealth of Massachusetts, "State Offices & Courts," www.mass.gov/portal/global-agency-list.html

State Rulemaking Process

USLegal, "Administrative Procedure Act—Massachusetts," http://administrativelaw.uslegal.com/administrative-procedure-acts/massachusetts/

Regulations

Research Guide

Suffolk University Law School, "Guide to Massachusetts Administrative Law," www.law.suffolk.edu/library/research/a-z/resguides/massadmin.cfm

By Agency (Code)— Code of Massachusetts Regulations

Massachusetts Trial Court Law Libraries, "Code of Massachusetts Regulations," www.lawlib.state.ma.us/source/mass/cmr/

In Chronological Order (Register)— Massachusetts Register

N/A

Local Laws

Directories of State Counties/Municipalities

Secretary of the Commonwealth of Massachusetts, "County Government," www.sec.state.ma.us/cis/cislevelsofgov/ciscounty.htm

Secretary of the Commonwealth of Massachusetts, "City and Town Governments," www.sec.state.ma.us/cis/cislevelsofgov/ciscitytown.htm

Ordinances

Municode Code Corporation, "Massachusetts," www.municode.com/library/MA

Practice Materials and Self-Help Resources

Research Guides

Western New England School of Law, "Massachusetts Practice Materials: A Selected Bibliography," www1.law.wne.edu/library/index.cfm?selection=doc.746

Suffolk University School of Law, "Civil Procedure in Massachusetts," www.law.suffolk.edu/library/research/a-z/resguides/masscivpro.cfm

Suffolk University School of Law, "Massachusetts Legal Forms," www.law.suffolk.edu/library/research/a-z/resguides/massforms.cfm

Court Rules

Research Guide

Boston University School of Law, "Clinical Programs: Massachusetts Court Resources," www.bu.edu/lawlibrary/research/clinics/courtsystem.html

Text of Rules

Supreme Judicial Court of Massachusetts, "Massachusetts Court Rules,"
http://massreports.com/courtrules/

Massachusetts Trial Court Law Libraries, "Massachusetts Rules of Court,"
www.lawlib.state.ma.us/source/mass/rules/

Forms

Massachusetts Trial Court Law Libraries, "Massachusetts Legal Forms," www.lawlib.state .ma.us/subject/forms/

Massachusetts Court System, "Forms," www.mass .gov/courts/formsandguidelines/forms.html

State Bar Association Consumer Brochures

Massachusetts Bar Association, "Public and Community Services," www.massbar.org/for -the-public

Court Brochures/Self-Help Centers

Massachusetts Trial Court Law Libraries, "Massachusetts Law About . . . ,"
www.lawlib.state.ma.us/subject/about/

Massachusetts Court System, "Self-Help Center," www.mass.gov/courts/selfhelp/

Looking for an Attorney (for a fee or for free)

Legal Aid/Advocacy Groups/Pro Bono

Massachusetts Court System, "Organizations Providing General Civil Legal Assistance,"
www.mass.gov/courts/admin/ji/rsresourcesd.html

Massachusetts Court System, "Organizations Providing Topic-Specific or Group-Specific Civil Legal Assistance," www.mass.gov/courts/ admin/ji/rsresourcese.html

Finding an Attorney/Lawyer Referrals

Massachusetts Bar Association, "Lawyer Referral Service," www.massbar.org/for-the-public/ need-a-lawyer

Boston Bar Association, "Lawyer Referral Service," www.bostonbarlawyer.org

Massachusetts Court System, "Organizations Providing General Referral or Consultation Services," www.mass.gov/courts/admin/ji/ rsresourcesf.html

Miscellaneous

Massachusetts Lawyers Weekly, "Opinions" [subscription-based; includes appellate court and state agency decisions from the last ninety days], http://masslawyersweekly.com/ category/opinions/

Secretary of the Commonwealth of Massachusetts, Division of Public Records, "A Guide to Massachusetts Public Records Law,"
www.sec.state.ma.us/pre/prepdf/guide.pdf

References

Massachusetts Court System, "Glossary of Legal Terms," www.mass.gov/courts/admin/ji/ repyourselfappbglossary.pdf

General Court of Massachusetts, "Glossary,"
www.malegislature.gov/Site/Glossary

Massachusetts Trial Court Law Libraries, "Massachusetts Legal Writing and Citations,"
www.lawlib.state.ma.us/subject/about/citations.html

MICHIGAN
Research Guides

AALL LISP, "Public Library Toolkit: Michigan,"
www.aallnet.org/sections/lisp/Public-Library-Toolkit

Thomas M. Cooley Law School, "Michigan Major Legal Web Resources," http://cooleylawlibguides .com/michiganweb

Michigan State University College of Law, "Michigan Legal Resources," www.law.msu.edu/ library/substantive/michigan.html

Wayne State University, "Law—Michigan Legal Resources," http://guides.lib.wayne.edu/michlaw

Wayne State University, "Browse by Subject: Law," http://guides.lib.wayne.edu/cat.php?cid =19197

Judicial

State Court Structure

Michigan Judiciary, "Courts," http://courts.mi.gov/ Courts/Pages/

Michigan Judiciary, "Michigan Judicial System" [diagram], http://courts.mi.gov/education/ learning-center/Documents/One-Court-of-Justice .pdf

Directory of State Courts

Michigan Judiciary, "Trial Court Directory," http://courts.mi.gov/Self-help/Directories/Pages/Trial-Court-Directory-Results.aspx

Opinions

Research Guide

Wayne State University, "Law—Finding Michigan Cases," http://guides.lib.wayne.edu/findingcases_mi

Highest Court—Supreme Court

[2001–]: Michigan Judiciary, "Opinion & Order Search," http://courts.mi.gov/opinions_orders/opinions_orders/pages

Intermediate Appellate Court—Court of Appeals

[1996–]: Michigan Judiciary, "Opinion & Order Search," http://courts.mi.gov/opinions_orders/opinions_orders/pages

Dockets/Court Records

Court of Appeals

[1980s–]: Michigan Judiciary, "Case Search," http://courts.mi.gov/opinions_orders/case_search/pages/

Trial Courts

N/A

Legislative

State Legislative Process

Michigan Legislative Service Bureau, "How a Bill Becomes a Law," www.legislature.mi.gov/documents/Publications/HowBillBecomesLaw.pdf

Statutes

Research Guide

Library of Michigan, "How to Find Current Michigan Statutes," www.michigan.gov/mde/0,1607,7-140-54504_50206_18639-52423--,00.html

By Subject (Code)—Michigan Compiled Laws

Michigan Legislature, "Michigan Compiled Laws: Advanced Search," www.legislature.mi.gov/mileg.aspx?page=MCLAdvancedSearch

In Chronological Order (Session Laws)—Public Acts

[2006–]: State Bar of Michigan, "Legislation Recently Signed into Public Acts," www.michbar.org/publicpolicy/recentlegislation.cfm

[1995–]: Michigan Legislature, "Public Acts," www.legislature.mi.gov/mileg.aspx?page=publicacts

Legislative History

Research Guides

Library of Michigan, "Sources of Michigan Legislative History," www.michigan.gov/mde/0,1607,7-140-54504_50206_18639-52439--,00.html

University of Michigan Law Library, "Sources of Legislative History for Michigan," www.law.umich.edu/library/students/research/Documents/michigan.pdf

University of Detroit Mercy School of Law, "Researching Michigan Legislative History," www.law.udmercy.edu/index.php/component/content/article/10-law-library/46-researching-michigan-legislative-history

Executive

Directory of State Departments/Agencies

Michigan.gov, "State of Michigan Departments," www.michigan.gov/som/0,1607,7-192-29701_29702_30045--,00.html

State Rulemaking Process

Michigan.gov, "Administrative Rules Process in a Nutshell," http://michigan.gov/documents/lara/Admin_Rules_Process_353271_7.pdf

Regulations

By Agency (Code)—
Michigan Administrative Code

Michigan Department of Licensing and Regulatory Affairs, "Michigan Administrative Code," www.michigan.gov/dleg/0,1607,7-154-10576_35738_5698--,00.html

In Chronological Order (Register)—
Michigan Register

[current year]: Michigan Department of
  Licensing and Regulatory Affairs, "Michigan
  Register," www.michigan.gov/dleg/0,1607,7-154
  -10576_35738_40280--,00.html

[2000–]: OCLC WorldCat / Library of Michigan,
  "Michigan Register," http://worldcat.org/
  oclc/49676477/viewonline

Local Laws

Directory of State Counties/Municipalities

Michigan.gov, "Michigan Counties List,"
  www.michigan.gov/som/0,1607,7-192-29701_31713
  _31714_31720-97053--,00.html

Ordinances

Michigan State University College of Law,
  "Michigan Ordinances & Code," www.law.msu
  .edu/library/substantive/local.html

Practice Materials and Self-Help Resources

Research Guides

Thomas M. Cooley Law School, "Useful
  Resources for Practicing Attorneys," http://
  cooleylawlibguides.com/usefulresourcespractice

Thomas M. Cooley Law School, "Form Books,"
  http://cooleylawlibguides.com/formbooks

Thomas M. Cooley Law School, "Family Law,"
  http://cooleylawlibguides.com/familylaw

Wayne State University, "Law—Landlord
  Tenant—Michigan," http://guides.lib.wayne.edu/
  content.php?hs=a&pid=72303

Court Rules

Michigan Judiciary, "Michigan Court Rules,"
  http://courts.mi.gov/Courts/MichiganSupremeCourt/
  rules/Pages/current-court-rules.aspx

Michigan Judiciary, "Administrative Matters,"
  http://courts.mi.gov/courts/michigansupremecourt/
  rules/court-rules-admin-matters/

Forms

Michigan Judiciary, "Court Forms," http://courts
  .mi.gov/administration/scao/forms/

State Bar Association Consumer Brochures

State Bar of Michigan, "Consumer Tips and
  Alerts," www.michbar.org/public_resources/
  consumertips.cfm

Court Brochures/Self-Help Centers

Michigan Judiciary, "Michigan Courts Self-Help
  Center," http://courts.mi.gov/self-help/center/

Looking for an Attorney (for a fee or for free)

Legal Aid/Advocacy Groups/Pro Bono

State Bar of Michigan, "Legal Aid Programs,"
  www.michbar.org/public_resources/legalaid.cfm

Finding an Attorney/Lawyer Referrals

Wayne State University, "Law—Michigan Legal
  Resources: Lawyers," http://guides.lib.wayne.edu/
  content.php?pid=105173&sid=791210

Michigan Judiciary, "How to Find an Attorney,"
  http://courts.mi.gov/self-help/center/legalhelp/

State Bar of Michigan, "Lawyer Referral
  Service," www.michbar.org/programs/
  lawyerreferral.cfm

Miscellaneous

Michigan Legislature, "Legislative Publications,"
  http://legislature.mi.gov/doc.aspx?Publications

Michigan Legislature, "Frequently Requested
  Laws," http://legislature.mi.gov/doc.aspx
  ?MostRequested

State Bar of Michigan, "Local and Special
  Purpose Bar Associations," www.michbar.org/
  resources/localspecialbar.cfm

Reference

Michigan Legislature, "Glossary of Legislative
  Terms," www.legislature.mi.gov/mileg.aspx
  ?page=Glossary

MINNESOTA

Research Guides

AALL LISP, "Public Library Toolkit: Minnesota," www.aallnet.org/sections/lisp/Public-Library-Toolkit

Minnesota Association of Law Libraries, "Internet Reference Guide," www.aallnet.org/chapter/mall/mnetgd.htm

University of North Dakota, Thormodsgard Law Library, "Online Legal Research Sources—Minnesota," http://web.law.und.edu/Library/research/MN.php

University of Minnesota Law Library, "Research Guides," http://library.law.umn.edu/researchguides.html

Minnesota Association of Law Libraries, "A Guide to Major Law Library Collections in the Twin Cities," www.aallnet.org/chapter/mall/tclawlib.pdf

Judicial

State Court Structure

Minnesota State Law Library, "Minnesota Courts," http://mn.gov/lawlib/selfhelp.html#cts

Westlaw, "Minnesota Court Structure" [diagram], http://wlwatch.westlaw.com/aca/west/statecrtorg.htm#MN

Directory of State Courts

Minnesota Judicial Branch, "Minnesota District Courts," www.mncourts.gov/default.aspx?page=238

Opinions

Research Guide

Minnesota State Law Library, "Skills Center: Case Reports, Free Online Sources," http://mn.gov/lawlib/casereports.html

Highest Court—Supreme Court

[1996–]: Minnesota State Law Library, "Minnesota State Court Opinions," http://mn.gov/lawlib/archive/

Intermediate Appellate Court—Court of Appeals

[1996–]: Minnesota State Law Library, "Minnesota State Court Opinions," http://mn.gov/lawlib/archive/

Dockets/Court Records

Appellate Courts

Minnesota Appellate Courts, "Case Management System (P-MACS)," http://macsnc.courts.state.mn.us/ctrack/publicLogin.jsp

Trial Courts

Minnesota Judicial Branch, "Access Case Records," www.mncourts.gov/publicaccess

Legislative

State Legislative Process

Minnesota State Legislature, "How a Bill Becomes a Law in Minnesota," www.leg.state.mn.us/leg/howbill.aspx

Statutes

Research Guide

University of Minnesota Law Library, "Researching Minnesota Law: Statutory Law," http://libguides.law.umn.edu/content.php?pid=386046&sid=3163787#statutory

By Subject (Code)—Minnesota Statutes

Minnesota Office of the Revisor of Statutes, "Minnesota Statutes," https://www.revisor.mn.gov/statutes/

In Chronological Order (Session Laws)—Laws of Minnesota

[1849–]: Minnesota Office of the Revisor of Statutes, "Minnesota Laws Search," https://www.revisor.mn.gov/search/?search=laws

[1849–]: Minnesota Office of the Revisor of Statutes, "Minnesota Session Laws," https://www.revisor.mn.gov/laws/

Legislative History

Research Guide

Minnesota Legislative Reference Library, "Minnesota Legislative History—Step by Step," www.leg.state.mn.us/leg/leghist/histstep.aspx

Executive

Directory of State Departments/Agencies

Minnesota.gov, "State Agencies, Boards, Commissions," http://mn.gov/portal/government/state/agencies-boards-commissions/

State Rulemaking Process

Paul M. Marinac, Office of the Revisor of Statutes, "Rulemaking in Minnesota: A Guide" (2006), https://www.revisor.mn.gov/revisor/pubs/arule_drafting_manual/ruleguide.htm

Regulations

Research Guide

University of Minnesota Law Library, "Minnesota Rules," http://library.law.umn.edu/researchguides/adminlaw.html#mnintro

By Agency (Code)—
Minnesota Administrative Rules

Office of the Revisor of Statutes, "Minnesota Administrative Rules," https://www.revisor.mn.gov/rules/

In Chronological Order (Register)—
Minnesota State Register

[1997–]: Minnesota's Bookstore, "Minnesota State Register Archives," www.comm.media.state.mn.us/bookstore/mnbookstore.asp?page=archives

Local Laws

Directories of State Counties/Municipalities

Minnesota.gov, "County Websites," http://mn.gov/portal/government/local/Counties/

League of Minnesota Cities, "City Directory," www.lmnc.org/page/1/city-directory.jsp

Ordinances

Minnesota State Law Library, "Minnesota County and Municipal Ordinances," http://mn.gov/lawlib/ordinance.html

LawMoose, Legal Reference Library, "Minnesota County Ordinances," www.lawmoose.com/index.cfm?Action=Library.&Topic=MN122

LawMoose, Legal Reference Library, "Minnesota City Ordinances and Charters," www.lawmoose.com/index.cfm?Action=Library.&Topic=MN6

Practice Materials and Self-Help Resources

Research Guides

University of Minnesota Law Library, "Self-Help Legal Materials," http://libguides.law.umn.edu/selfhelp

University of Minnesota Law Library, "Guide to Pretrial & Trial Practice Materials," http://library.law.umn.edu/researchguides/trialpractice.html

University of Minnesota Law Library, "Finding Forms & Form Books," http://library.law.umn.edu/researchguides/legalforms.html

William Mitchell College of Law, "Self Help Resources," http://libguides.wmitchell.edu/selfhelp

Court Rules

Minnesota Judicial Branch, "Court Rules," www.mncourts.gov/default.aspx?page=511

Forms

Minnesota State Law Library, "Form Finder," http://mn.gov/lawlib/forms.html

Minnesota Statutes, "Forms (Documents)," https://www.revisor.mn.gov/data/revisor/statutes_index/current/F/FO/forms_documents.html

Minnesota Judicial Branch, "Court Forms," www.mncourts.gov/default.aspx?page=513

State Bar Association Consumer Brochures

Minnesota State Bar Association, "Public Resources," www.mnbar.org/nav-public.asp

Court Brochures/Self-Help Centers

Minnesota Judicial Branch, "Self-Help Center," www.mncourts.gov/selfhelp/

Minnesota Judicial Branch, "Court of Appeals Self-Help Center," www.mncourts.gov/?page=3665

Minnesota Judicial Branch, "Legal Advice
Clinics & Self-Help Centers" [district courts],
www.mncourts.gov/selfhelp/?page=251

Looking for an Attorney
(for a fee or for free)

Legal Aid/Advocacy Groups/Pro Bono

William Mitchell College of Law, "Self Help
Resources: Legal Aid," http://libguides.wmitchell
.edu/content.php?pid=139719&sid=1193783

Minnesota Legal Services State Support, "Civil
Legal Services Directory," www.mnlegalservices
.org/LocalResources.cfm?pagename=Quick%20
Reference%20Guide

LawMoose, Legal Reference Library,
"Minnesota Legal Aid & Pro Bono
Lawyers," www.lawmoose.com/index.cfm?Action
=Library.&Topic=MN38

LawHelpMN.org, "Legal Aid Directory,"
www.lawhelpmn.org/find-legal-help/directory

Finding an Attorney/Lawyer Referrals

Minnesota State Law Library, "Find an Attorney
and Other Referrals," http://mn.gov/lawlib/
selfhelp.html#atty

Minnesota Judicial Branch, "Find a Lawyer &
Legal Resources," www.mncourts.gov/?siteID
=4&page=1202

Miscellaneous

LawMoose, Legal Articles, "Minnesota Legal
Periodical Index" [1984–], www.lawmoose
.com/index.cfm?Action=MLPI.ShowArticle Finder
&CKS=MNLaw

Minnesota Sentencing Guidelines Commission,
"Guidelines and Grids," www.msgc.state.mn.us/
msgc5/guidelines.htm

LawMoose, Home of the Minnesota Legal Web,
"Minnesota Legal Reference Library,"
www.lawmoose.com

Minnesota Judicial Branch, "High Profile Cases,"
www.mncourts.gov/?page=508

References

Minnesota Judicial Branch, "Glossary of Court-
Related Terms," www.mncourts.gov/?page=1320

Minnesota Judicial Branch, Fifth District,
"Legal Terms," www.mncourts.gov/district/5/
?page=490

United States District Court, District of
Minnesota, "Glossary of Terms," www.mnd
.uscourts.gov/Pro-Se/Glossary.shtml

MISSISSIPPI
Research Guide

Mississippi College School of Law, "Mississippi
Resources," http://law.mc.edu/index.php/library/
public/miss/

Judicial

State Court Structure

Mississippi Judiciary, "About the Courts,"
http://courts.ms.gov/aboutcourts/aboutcourts.html

Westlaw, "Mississippi Court Structure"
[diagram], http://wlwatch.westlaw.com/aca/west/
statecrtorg.htm#MS

Directory of State Courts

Mississippi Judiciary, "Circuit Court,"
http://courts.ms.gov/trialcourts/circuitcourt/
circuitcourt.html

Opinions

Research Guide

Mississippi State University Libraries, "Case Law
Research Guide," http://guides.library.msstate
.edu/content.php?pid=15507

Highest Court—Supreme Court

[1996–]: Mississippi Judiciary, "Supreme Court
Decisions," http://courts.ms.gov/appellate_courts/
sc/scdecisions.html

Intermediate Appellate Court—
Court of Appeals

[1996–]: Mississippi Judiciary, "Court of
Appeals Decisions," http://courts.ms.gov/
appellate_courts/coa/coadecisions.html

Dockets/Court Records

Appellate Courts

Mississippi Judiciary, "Appellate Courts General Docket," http://courts.ms.gov/appellate_courts/generaldocket.html

Trial Courts

N/A

Legislative

State Legislative Process

Mississippi Legislature, "How a bill becomes law in Mississippi" [diagram], http://billstatus.ls.state.ms.us/htms/billlaw.htm

Statutes

By Subject (Code)—Mississippi Code of 1972

LexisNexis, "Mississippi Code of 1972 Unannotated," www.lexisnexis.com/hottopics/mscode/

In Chronological Order (Session Laws)—Mississippi Session Laws

[1999–]: Mississippi Legislature, "Mississippi Legislative Bill Status System Global Text Search," http://index.ls.state.ms.us

Legislative History

Research Guides

N/A

Executive

Directory of State Departments/Agencies

MS.gov, "Agency Directory," www.ms.gov/agency_directory/

State Rulemaking Process

USLegal, "Administrative Procedure Act—Mississippi," http://administrativelaw.uslegal.com/administrative-procedure-acts/administrative-procedures-act---mississippi

Regulations

By Agency (Code)—Code of Mississippi Rules

N/A

In Chronological Order (Register)—Mississippi Government Register

N/A

Local Laws

Directory of State Counties/Municipalities

MS.gov, "Local Governments," www.ms.gov/content/Pages/Local-Governments.aspx

Ordinances

Municode Code Corporation, "Mississippi," www.municode.com/library/MS

Practice Materials and Self-Help Resources

Research Guide

MSLegalServices.org, www.mslegalservices.org

Court Rules

Mississippi Judiciary, "Rules," http://courts.ms.gov/rules/msrules.html

Forms

Mississippi Judiciary, "Forms," http://courts.ms.gov/forms/forms.html

State Bar Association Consumer Brochures

Mississippi Bar, "Consumer Information," www.msbar.org/for-the-public/consumer.information.aspx

Court Brochures/Self-Help Centers

N/A

Looking for an Attorney (for a fee or for free)

Legal Aid/Advocacy Groups/Pro Bono

Mississippi Bar, "Pro Bono Resources," https://www.msbar.org/for-the-public/pro-bono-resources.aspx

North Mississippi Rural Legal Services,
www.nmrls.com

MSLegalServices.org, "Legal Aid Directory,"
www.mslegalservices.org/find-legal-help/directory

Finding an Attorney/Lawyer Referrals

Mississippi Bar, "How to Select a Lawyer,"
https://www.msbar.org/for-the-public/how-to
-select-a-lawyer.aspx

Miscellaneous

HG.org, "Mississippi Bar Associations,"
www.hg.org/bar-associations-mississippi.asp

Reference

Mississippi Bar, "Legal Terms & Procedures,"
https://www.msbar.org/for-the-public/legal-terms
-procedures.aspx

MISSOURI

Research Guides

AALL LISP, "Public Library Toolkit: Missouri,"
www.aallnet.org/sections/lisp/Public-Library-Toolkit

University of Missouri–Kansas City School of
Law, "Missouri State and City Page,"
www1.law.umkc.edu/library/molaw.htm

Judicial

State Court Structure

Missouri Judicial Branch, "About Your Courts,"
www.courts.mo.gov/page.jsp?id=258

Westlaw, "Missouri Court Structure" [diagram],
http://wlwatch.westlaw.com/aca/west/statecrtorg
.htm#MO

Directory of State Courts

Missouri Judicial Branch, "Circuit Courts of
Missouri," www.courts.mo.gov/page.jsp?id=321

Opinions

Highest Court—Supreme Court

[1997–]: Missouri Judicial Branch, "Supreme
Court of Missouri Opinions," www.courtsmo.
gov/page.jsp?id=1983

Intermediate Appellate Court—Court of Appeals

[1997–]: Missouri Judicial Branch, "Court of
Appeals," www.courts.mo.gov/page.jsp?id=261

Dockets/Court Records

Trial Courts

Case.net [state courts automated case
management system], https://www.courts
.mo.gov/casenet/

Legislative

State Legislative Process

Missouri Senate, "How a Bill Becomes a Law"
[diagram], www.senate.mo.gov/bill-law.htm

Statutes

By Subject (Code)—Missouri Revised Statutes

Missouri General Assembly, "MO Statutes:
Statute Search," www.moga.mo.gov

Missouri General Assembly, "MO Statutes: View
All Statutes," www.moga.mo.gov

In Chronological Order (Session Laws)—
Session Laws of Missouri

[2000–]: Missouri General Assembly, "Session
Laws," www.moga.mo.gov

Legislative History

Research Guide

MU Libraries, University of Missouri-Columbia,
"Missouri Law and Legislative Source
Guide," http://mulibraries.missouri.edu/collections/
documents/mo/laws.htm

Executive

Directory of State Departments/Agencies

MO.gov, "State Agencies," www.mo.gov/search
-results?mode=state_agencies

State Rulemaking Process

Missouri Secretary of State, "Rulemaking Manual," www.sos.mo.gov/adrules/manual/manual.asp

Regulations

By Agency (Code)—Code of State Regulations

Missouri Secretary of State, "Code of State Regulations," www.sos.mo.gov/adrules/csr/current/1csr/1csr.asp

In Chronological Order (Register)—
Missouri Register

[1999–]: Missouri Secretary of State, "Missouri Register," www.sos.mo.gov/adrules/moreg/moreg.asp

Local Laws

Directories of State Counties/Municipalities

Missouri Association of Counties, "MAC Member Counties," www.mocounties.com/list-of-counties.php

Official City Sites.org, "Missouri," http://officialcitysites.org/us/states/missouri/

Ordinances

Municode Code Corporation, "Missouri," www.municode.com/library/MO

Saint Louis Public Library, "Laws of the City of Saint Louis," www.slpl.lib.mo.us/cco/

Practice Materials and Self-Help Resources

Research Guides

Washington University Law, "Missouri Practice Materials," http://law.wustl.edu/library/pages.aspx?id=1381

University of Missouri School of Law, "Self-Help Legal Research Guide," http://libraryguides.missouri.edu/SelfHelpResearch

Court Rules

Missouri Judicial Branch, "Supreme Court Rules and Supreme Court Operating Rules," www.courts.mo.gov/page.jsp?id=46

Forms

Missouri Judicial Branch, "Court Forms," www.courts.mo.gov/page.jsp?id=525

State Bar Association Consumer Brochures

Missouri Bar, "Public Information Brochures," www.mobar.org/publicinformation/

Court Brochures/Self-Help Centers

Missouri Judicial Branch, "Representing Yourself in Missouri Courts: Access to Family Courts," www.courts.mo.gov/page.jsp?id=5240

Looking for an Attorney (for a fee or for free)

Legal Aid/Advocacy Groups/Pro Bono

Missouri Judicial Branch, "Representing Yourself in Missouri Courts: Local County Resources & Services," www.courts.mo.gov/page.jsp?id=3773

Gateway Legal Services Inc., www.gatewaylegal.org

Legal Services of Eastern Missouri, www.lsem.org

Legal Aid of Western Missouri, www.lawmo.org

Legal Advocates for Abused Women, www.laawstl.org

Finding an Attorney/Lawyer Referrals

Missouri Bar Lawyer Referral Service, www.mobar.org/lrs/clients.htm

Miscellaneous

Missouri Lawyers Media, http://molawyersmedia.com

Reference

Missouri Judicial Branch, "Legal Terms," www.courts.mo.gov/page.jsp?id=3772

MONTANA

Research Guides

State Law Library of Montana, "A Guide to Montana Legal Research," http://courts.mt.gov/content/library/guides/guide.pdf

Montana Judicial Branch, "Montana Laws,"
http://courts.mt.gov/library/montana_laws.mcpx

University of Montana, Jameson Law Library,
"Legal Research Guides," www.umt.edu/law/
library/researchguides.php

Judicial

State Court Structure

State Bar of Montana, "The Montana Citizen's
Guide to the Courts," www.montanabar.org/
associations/7121/files/Guide%20to%20Montana%20
Courts.pdf

Westlaw, "Montana Court Structure" [diagram],
http://wlwatch.westlaw.com/aca/west/statecrtorg
.htm#MT

Directory of State Courts

Montana Judicial Branch, "Court Locator,"
http://courts.mt.gov/locator/

Opinions

Highest Court—Supreme Court

[1980–]: State Law Library of Montana,
"Montana Supreme Court Cases,"
http://searchcourts.mt.gov

Intermediate Appellate Court—None

Dockets/Court Records

Supreme Court

Montana Office of the Clerk of the Supreme
Court, "Public View Docket,"
http://supremecourtdocket.mt.gov

Trial Courts

N/A

Legislative

State Legislative Process

Montana Legislature, "From Bill to Law,"
http://leg.mt.gov/css/About-the-Legislature/
Lawmaking-Process/from-bill-to-law.asp

Montana Legislature, "From Bill to Law
Illustration" [diagram], http://leg.mt.gov/css/
About-the-Legislature/Lawmaking-Process/bill-to
-law-diagram.asp

Statutes

Research Guide

State Law Library of Montana, "A Guide to
Montana Legal Research" [pp. 25–32],
http://courts.mt.gov/content/library/guides/
guide.pdf

By Subject (Code)—Montana Code Annotated

Montana Legislature, "Montana Code
Annotated," http://leg.mt.gov/bills/mca_toc/
index.htm

In Chronological Order (Session Laws)—
Laws and Resolutions of the State of Montana

[1997–]: Montana Legislature, "Past Sessions,"
http://leg.mt.gov/css/Sessions/default.asp

Legislative History

Research Guide

Montana Judicial Branch, "Legal Research
Guides," http://courts.mt.gov/library/guides/

Executive

Directory of State Departments/Agencies

MT.gov, "State of Montana Agency Listings,"
http://mt.gov/govt/agencylisting.mcpx

State Rulemaking Process

USLegal, "Administrative Procedure Act—
Montana," http://administrativelaw.uslegal.com/
administrative-procedure-acts/montana/

Regulations

By Agency (Code)—
Administrative Rules of Montana

Montana Secretary of State, "Administrative
Rules of Montana," www.mtrules.org

In Chronological Order (Register)—
Montana Administrative Register

[2007–]: Montana Secretary of State, "Montana Administrative Register" [search], www.mtrules.org

[2000–]: Montana Secretary of State, "Montana Administrative Register" [browse], http://sos.mt.gov/ARM/Register/

Local Laws

Directories of State Counties/Municipalities

Montana Association of Counties, "County Information," www.mtcounties.org/counties/county-information

Montana League of Cities and Towns, "Montana Incorporated Cities and Towns," www.mlct.org/members/municipalities.html

Ordinances

Municode Code Corporation, "Montana," www.municode.com/library/MT

Practice Materials and Self-Help Resources

Research Guide

Cornell University Law School, Legal Information Institute, "Montana Legal Materials," www.law.cornell.edu/states/montana

Court Rules

Montana Judicial Branch, "Montana Court Rules," http://courts.mt.gov/library/montana_laws.mcpx#judicial

Forms

Montana Judicial Branch, "Law by Topic," http://courts.mt.gov/library/topic/

State Bar Association Consumer Brochures

State Bar of Montana, "Legal Research," http://montanabar.org/displaycommon.cfm?an=1&subarticlenbr=179

Court Brochures/Self-Help Centers

Montana Judicial Branch, "Court Help Program," http://courts.mt.gov/selfhelp/

Looking for an Attorney (for a fee or for free)

Legal Aid/Advocacy Groups/Pro Bono

State Bar of Montana, "Summary of Statewide & County Montana Legal Resources," www.montanabar.org/associations/7121/files/Montana%20Legal%20Resources.PDF

Montana Judicial Branch, "Montana Legal Resource Directory," http://courts.mt.gov/library/directory.mcpx

Finding an Attorney/Lawyer Referrals

State Bar of Montana, "Lawyer Referral & Information Service," www.montanabar.org/displaycommon.cfm?an=1&subarticlenbr=19

State Bar of Montana, "I Want to Hire a Lawyer!" http://montanabar.org/displaycommon.cfm?an=1&subarticlenbr=255

Miscellaneous

Montana State University, "Local Government Center," www.msulocalgov.org

Montana Department of Labor and Industry, "Workers' Compensation Court Decisions" [1993–], http://wcc.dli.mt.gov/cases.asp

Montana State Law Library, Montana Indian Law Portal, http://indianlaw.mt.gov

Reference

Montana Judicial Branch, "Common Legal Terms," http://courts.mt.gov/library/legal_terms.mcpx

NEBRASKA

Research Guides

Creighton University School of Law, "Nebraska," http://lawguides.creighton.edu/nebraska

University of Nebraska College of Law, "Nebraska State Law Resources," http://law.unl.edu/library/neresources/

Judicial

State Court Structure

Nebraska Judicial Branch, "The Nebraska Judicial System," www.supremecourt.ne.gov/4853/nebraska-judicial-system

Westlaw, "Nebraska Court Structure," [diagram], http://wlwatch.westlaw.com/aca/west/statecrtorg.htm#NE

Directories of State Courts

Nebraska Judicial Branch, "County Court Contacts and Addresses," http://supremecourt.ne.gov/cc/clerks

Nebraska Judicial Branch, "District Court Contacts and Addresses," http://supremecourt.ne.gov/dc/clerks

Opinions

Highest Court—Supreme Court

[last ninety days]: Nebraska Judicial Branch, "Supreme Court Opinions," http://supremecourt.ne.gov/sc/opinions

Intermediate Appellate Court—Court of Appeals

[last ninety days]: Nebraska Judicial Branch, "Court of Appeals Opinions," http://supremecourt.ne.gov/coa/opinions

Dockets/Court Records

Trial Courts

Nebraska Supreme Court, "Nebraska Trial Courts Online Case Search," www.nebraska.gov/justicecc/ccname.cgi

Legislative

State Legislative Process

Nebraska Legislature, "Lawmaking in Nebraska," http://uniweb.legislature.ne.gov/about/lawmaking.php

Statutes

By Subject (Code)—Nebraska Revised Statutes

Nebraska Legislature "Search Laws," http://uniweb.legislature.ne.gov/laws/laws.php

Nebraska Legislature, "Nebraska Revised Statutes by Chapter," http://uniweb.legislature.ne.gov/laws/browse-statutes.php

Nebraska Legislature "Books for Download: Index," http://nebraskalegislature.gov/laws/laws.php

In Chronological Order (Session Laws)—Laws of Nebraska

N/A

Legislative History

Research Guide

Creighton University School of Law, "Nebraska Legislative History," http://lawguides.creighton.edu/NebLegisHist

Executive

Directory of State Departments/Agencies

Nebraska.gov, "All Nebraska State Agencies, Boards, and Commissions," www.nebraska.gov/allagencies.html

State Rulemaking Process

Nebraska Secretary of State, "Overview of Regulation Process," www.sos.ne.gov/rules-and-regs/reg_process.html

Regulations

By Agency (Code)—Nebraska Rules

Nebraska Secretary of State, "Rules and Regulations" [search], www.sos.state.ne.us/rules-and-regs/regsearch/

Nebraska Secretary of State, "Rules and Regulations" [browse], www.sos.ne.gov/rules-and-regs/regsearch/Rules/

In Chronological Order (Register)—Nebraska Government Register

N/A

Local Laws

Directory of State Counties/Municipalities

State and Local Government on the Net, "Nebraska State and Local Government," www.statelocalgov.net/state-ne.cfm

Ordinances

NebraskAccess, "Where Can I Find Nebraska Municipal and County Codes?" http://nebraskaccess.ne.gov/municipalcodes.asp

Practice Materials and Self-Help Resources

Research Guides

Creighton University School of Law, "Pro Se Assistance in Simple Divorce," http://lawguides.creighton.edu/ProSeAssSimpDiv

Creighton University School of Law, "Forms," http://lawguides.creighton.edu/content.php?pid=112426

Court Rules

Nebraska Judicial Branch, "Supreme Court Rules," www.supremecourt.ne.gov/rules

Nebraska Judicial Branch, "External Court Rules," www.supremecourt.ne.gov/rules/external

Forms

Nebraska Judicial Branch, "Forms," www.supremecourt.ne.gov/forms/

State Bar Association Consumer Brochures

Nebraska State Bar Association, "For the Public: Free Legal Information," http://nebar.com/displaycommon.cfm?an=1&subarticlenbr=74

Court Brochures/Self-Help Centers

Nebraska Online Legal Self-Help Center, http://court.nol.org/self-help/

Looking for an Attorney (for a fee or for free)

Legal Aid/Advocacy Groups/Pro Bono

Nebraska State Bar Association, "For the Public: Low Income Legal Services," http://nebar.com/displaycommon.cfm?an=1&subarticlenbr=83

Finding an Attorney/Lawyer Referrals

Nebraska State Bar Association, "For the Public: Lawyer Search," http://nebar.com/displaycommon.cfm?an=1&subarticlenbr=151

Miscellaneous

Nebraska Legislature, "General Research Reports" [1997–], http://uniweb.legislature.ne.gov/reports/research.php

References

Nebraska Judicial System, "Glossary of Legal Terms" www.supremecourt.ne.gov/sites/supremecourt.ne.gov/files/misc/citizens/glossary-eng.pdf

Nebraska Legislature, "Glossary of Legislative Terms," http://uniweb.legislature.ne.gov/about/glossary.php

NEVADA

Research Guides

General

AALL LISP, "Public Library Toolkit: Nevada," www.aallnet.org/sections/lisp/Public-Library-Toolkit

Supreme Court of Nevada Law Library, "Nevada Legal Resources," http://lawlibrary.nevadajudiciary.us/selfHelp/nevadaLegalResources.php

UNLV Boyd School of Law, Wiener-Rogers Law Library, "Bridge the Gap: February 2010," http://law.unlv.edu/law-library/services/bridge-the-gap.html

Washoe County Law Library, Legal Electronic Assistance for Nevadans, "Guide to Finding Nevada Law on the Web," www.nvlawdirectory.org/bysubresearchguide.html

Topical

UNLV Boyd School of Law, Wiener-Rogers Law
Library, "Resource Guides," http://law.unlv.edu/
law-library/resource-guides.html

Judicial

State Court Structure

Supreme Court of Nevada, "About the Nevada
Judiciary," http://nevadajudiciary.us/index.php/
aboutthenevadajudiciary

Westlaw, "Nevada Court Structure" [diagram],
http://wlwatch.westlaw.com/aca/west/statecrtorg.
htm#NV

Directory of State Courts

Supreme Court of Nevada, "Find a Court,"
www.nevadajudiciary.us/index.php/findtrialcourt

Opinions

Highest Court—Supreme Court

[last six months]: Supreme Court of Nevada,
"Advance Opinions," www.nevadajudiciary.us/
index.php/advance-opinions

Intermediate Appellate Court—None

Dockets/Court Records

Trial Courts

Clark County Clerk of the Court, "Records
Search and Viewing," www.clarkcountycourts.us/
clerk/records-search.html

Legislative

State Legislative Process

Nevada Legislature, "How a Bill Is Passed,"
www.leg.state.nv.us/General/AboutLeg/im_just_a
_bill.cfm

Nevada Legislature, "Nevada's Legislative
Process" [diagram], www.leg.state.nv.us/Division/
Research/Publications/LegManual/2009/AppC.pdf

Statutes

By Subject (Code)—Nevada Revised Statutes

Nevada Legislature, "Nevada Law Library:
Nevada Revised Statutes," www.leg.state.nv.us/
law1.cfm

In Chronological Order (Session Laws)—
Statutes of the State of Nevada

[1989–]:Nevada Legislature, "Nevada
Law Library: Statutes of Nevada,"
www.leg.state.nv.us/law1.cfm

Legislative History

Research Guides

Nevada Legislature, "Legislative History
Tutorial," www.leg.state.nv.us/Division/Research/
Library/LegHistory/Tutorial/Start.cfm

Nevada Legislature, "Legislative History FAQs,"
www.leg.state.nv.us/Division/Research/Library/
LegHistory/Tutorial/HistoryFAQs.cfm

Executive

Directory of State Departments/Agencies

NV.gov, "State Agencies and Departments,"
http://nv.gov/agency/department/

State Rulemaking Process

Nevada Office of the Attorney General,
"Administrative Rulemaking: A Procedural
Guide," http://ag.nv.gov/uploadedFiles/agnvgov/
Content/Publications/RulemakingManualComplete
.pdf

Regulations

By Agency (Code)—Nevada Administrative Code

Nevada Legislature, "Nevada Law Library:
Nevada Administrative Code,"
www.leg.state.nv.us/law1.cfm

In Chronological Order (Register)—Nevada
Register of Administrative Regulations

[1997–]: Nevada Legislature, "Register
of Administrative Regulations,"
www.leg.state.nv.us/Register/

Local Laws

Directory of State Counties/Municipalities

NV.gov, "County and City Governments," http://nv.gov/government/county-city/

Ordinances

Supreme Court of Nevada Law Library, "Local Codes," http://lawlibrary.nevadajudiciary.us/legalCommunity/localCodes.php

Nevada Legislature, "Nevada County and City Codes," www.leg.state.nv.us/Division/Research/Library/Links/Codes.cfm

Practice Materials and Self-Help Resources

Research Guide

Washoe County Law Library, Legal Electronic Assistance for Nevadans, "Web Links Organized by Subject," www.nvlawdirectory.org/links.html

Court Rules

Nevada Legislature, Legislative Counsel Bureau, "Court Rules of Nevada," www.leg.state.nv.us/Division/Legal/LawLibrary/CourtRules/

Forms

Supreme Court of Nevada Law Library, "Form Links," http://lawlibrary.nevadajudiciary.us/forms/formsDirectory.php

State Bar Association Consumer Brochures

State Bar of Nevada, "Legal Information Brochures," www.nvbar.org/node/116

Court Brochures/Self-Help Centers

Supreme Court of Nevada Law Library, "Self Help Resources," http://lawlibrary.nevadajudiciary.us/selfHelp/nvProSe.php

Clark County Courts, "Self-Help Centers," www.clarkcountycourts.us/self-help.html

Looking for an Attorney (for a fee or for free)

Legal Aid/Advocacy Groups/Pro Bono

Legal Aid Center of Southern Nevada, www.lacsn.org

Washoe County Law Library, Legal Electronic Assistance for Nevadans, www.nvlawdirectory.org

Clark County Bar Association, "Legal Resource Guide for Southern Nevada," www.clarkcountybar.org/index.php?option=com_content&task=blogcategory&id=48&Itemid=101

Washoe County Bar Association, "Public Information," www.wcbar.org/public.html

Finding an Attorney/Lawyer Referrals

State Bar of Nevada, "Lawyer Referral & Information Service," www.nvbar.org/content/lawyer-referral-information-service

Clark County Bar Association, "CCBA Member Directory," www.clarkcountybar.org/index.php?option=com_cb_search&Itemid=148

Washoe County Bar Association, "Public Information," www.wcbar.org/public.html

Miscellaneous

Washoe County Law Library, Legal Electronic Assistance for Nevadans, "Public Law Libraries in Nevada," www.nvlawdirectory.org/bysubresearchlawlibmain.html

Nevada Legislature, "Summaries of Enacted Legislation" [1975–], www.leg.state.nv.us/Division/Research/Publications/SoL/

References

Westlaw, "Glossary for Legal Research Basics," http://lawschool.westlaw.com/shared/marketinfodisplay.asp?code=RE&id=17&mainpage=23&rtid=116&rtcode=re

Cornell University Law School, Legal Information Institute, *Wex* [dictionary and encyclopedia], www.law.cornell.edu/wex/

NEW HAMPSHIRE

Research Guides

AALL LISP, "Public Library Toolkit: New Hampshire," www.aallnet.org/sections/lisp/Public-Library-Toolkit

New Hampshire Law Library, "Online Legal Research," www.courts.state.nh.us/lawlibrary/

Judicial

State Court Structure

New Hampshire Judicial Branch Self-Help Center, "The New Hampshire Court System at a Glance," www.courts.state.nh.us/selfhelp/find_your_court.htm

New Hampshire Judicial Branch, "Court Structure" [diagram], www.courts.state.nh.us/images/courtstructure.jpg

Directory of State Courts

New Hampshire Judicial Branch, "Find Your Court," www.courts.state.nh.us/courtlocations/

Opinions

Highest Court—Supreme Court

[1995–]: New Hampshire Judicial Branch, "Supreme Court—Opinions," www.courts.state.nh.us/supreme/opinions/

Intermediate Appellate Court—None

Dockets/Court Records

Trial Courts

New Hampshire Judicial Branch, "Superior Court—Daily Docket," www.courts.state.nh.us/superior/dailydocket/

Legislative

State Legislative Process

NH.gov, "How a Bill Becomes a Law," www.nh.gov/nhinfo/bills.html

New Hampshire Municipal Association, "How a Bill Becomes a Law" [diagram], www.nhlgc.org/attachments/nhma/BillBecomesLaw_Cartoon.pdf

Statutes

By Subject (Code)—Revised Statutes Annotated

New Hampshire General Court, "Revised Statutes Online," www.gencourt.state.nh.us/rsa/html/indexes/

In Chronological Order (Session Laws)—Laws of the State of New Hampshire

N/A

Legislative History

Research Guides

New Hampshire Law Library, "Compiling a New Hampshire Legislative History," www.courts.state.nh.us/lawlibrary/nhlegislativehistory.pdf

University of New Hampshire School of Law, "New Hampshire Legislative History," http://library.law.unh.edu/NHLegHistory

Executive

Directory of State Departments/Agencies

NH.gov, "State Agencies," www.nh.gov/government/agencies.html

State Rulemaking Process

New Hampshire General Court, "Summary of Procedure for Adoption of Regular Rules," http://gencourt.state.nh.us/rules/process/flowchart.pdf

Regulations

By Agency (Code)—
New Hampshire Code of Administrative Rules

New Hampshire Office of Legislative Services, "Administrative Rules: Rules Listed by State Agency according to Rule Title and Subtitle Prefixes Currently in Use," http://gencourt.state.nh.us/rules/About_Rules/listagencies.htm

In Chronological Order (Register)—
New Hampshire Rulemaking Register

[1998–]: New Hampshire Office of Legislative Services, "Administrative Rules: New Hampshire Rulemaking Register," http://gencourt.state.nh.us/rules/register/

Local Laws

Directory of State Counties/Municipalities

NH.gov, "Local Government,"
www.nh.gov/government/local.html

Ordinances

Municode Code Corporation, "New Hampshire,"
www.municode.com/library/NH
General Code, "New Hampshire eCode360
Library," www.generalcode.com/ecode360/NH

Practice Materials and Self-Help Resources

Research Guide

New Hampshire Law Library [search
for "Hampshire practice"],
http://nhll.ipac.dynixasp.com

Court Rules

New Hampshire Judicial Branch,
"New Hampshire Court Rules,"
www.courts.state.nh.us/rules/

Forms

New Hampshire Law Library, "Online Legal
Research" [follow link and choose "Forms"
under New Hampshire, Judicial Branch],
www.courts.state.nh.us/lawlibrary/

State Bar Association Consumer Brochures

New Hampshire Bar Association, "For the
Public," www.nhbar.org/for-the-public/

Court Brochures/Self-Help Centers

New Hampshire Judicial Branch, "The NH
Judicial Branch Self-Help Center,"
www.courts.state.nh.us/selfhelp/
New Hampshire Judicial Branch, "Superior
Court—Domestic Relations Cases,"
www.courts.state.nh.us/superior/selfhelp/

Looking for an Attorney (for a fee or for free)

Legal Aid/Advocacy Groups/Pro Bono

New Hampshire Bar Association, "New
Hampshire Legal Services Programs,"
www.nhbar.org/for-the-public/legalservices.asp
New Hampshire Law Library, "Online Legal
Research" [follow link and choose "Libraries
& Legal Services"], www.courts.state.nh.us/
lawlibrary/

Finding an Attorney/Lawyer Referrals

New Hampshire Bar Association,
"Lawyer Referral Service,"
www.nhbar.org/lawyer-referral/

Reference

New Hampshire Bar Association, "Glossary
of Legal Terms," www.nhbar.org/uploads/pdf/
GlossaryLegalTerms.pdf

NEW JERSEY

Research Guides

General

Rutgers University Law Library, "Basic New
Jersey Legal Materials," http://law-library
.rutgers.edu/basicnjpf.html
Rutgers University Law Library, "New Jersey
Law," http://law-library.rutgers.edu/ilg/njlaw.html
New Jersey State Library, "New Jersey Legal
Resources," http://law.njstatelib.org/#njlaw

Topical

New Jersey State Bar Foundation, "For the
Public: Find a Publication," www.njsbf.org/
for-the-public/public-publications.html

Judicial

State Court Structure

New Jersey Judiciary, "Welcome to the New
Jersey Court System," www.judiciary.state.nj.us/
process.htm

Westlaw, "New Jersey Court Structure" [diagram], http://wlwatch.westlaw.com/aca/west/statecrtorg.htm#NJ

Directory of State Courts

New Jersey Judiciary, "Local Courthouse Addresses," www.judiciary.state.nj.us/trial.htm

Opinions

Highest Court—Supreme Court

[last ten business days]: New Jersey Judiciary, "Supreme and Appellate Opinions," www.judiciary.state.nj.us/opinions/

[1994–]: Rutgers University School of Law–Newark, "New Jersey Courts Search Page," http://njlaw.rutgers.edu/collections/courts/

Intermediate Appellate Court—
Appellate Division of Superior Court

[last ten business days]: New Jersey Judiciary, "Supreme and Appellate Opinions," www.judiciary.state.nj.us/opinions/

[1995–]: Rutgers University School of Law–Newark, "New Jersey Courts Search Page," http://njlaw.rutgers.edu/collections/courts/

Dockets/Court Records

Trial Courts—Civil

Superior Court of New Jersey, "Motion Calendar Search Page," www.judiciary.state.nj.us/acms/MOTN/CV0390W0E.ASP

Legislative

State Legislative Process

New Jersey Office of Legislative Services, "The Legislative Process in New Jersey," www.njleg.state.nj.us/legislativepub/Legislative_Process.pdf

New Jersey Legislature, "How a Bill Becomes a Law in New Jersey" [diagram], www.njleg.state.nj.us/legislativepub/legprocess.asp

Statutes

By Subject (Code)—
New Jersey Permanent Statutes

New Jersey State Legislature, "Laws and Constitution: Statutes," www.njleg.state.nj.us

In Chronological Order (Session Laws)—
New Jersey Session Laws (Chapter Laws)

[1996–]: New Jersey Legislature, "Chapter Laws," www.njleg.state.nj.us/lawsconstitution/chapter.asp

[1776–1999]: Rutgers University School of Law–Camden, "New Jersey Session Laws Online," http://camlaw.rutgers.edu/new-jersey-session-laws-online

Legislative History

Research Guide

Rutgers University Law Library, "Guide to New Jersey Legislative History," http://law-library.rutgers.edu/leghist.html

Compiled Legislative History

[1970–]: New Jersey State Law Library, "New Jersey Legislative Histories," http://law.njstatelib.org/njlh

Executive

Directory of State Departments/Agencies

State of New Jersey, "Departments & Agencies," www.state.nj.us/nj/gov/deptserv/

State Rulemaking Process

USLegal, "Administrative Procedure Act—New Jersey," http://administrativelaw.uslegal.com/administrative-procedure-acts/administrative-procedure-act-new-jersey/

Regulations

By Agency (Code)—
New Jersey Administrative Code

LexisNexis, "New Jersey Administrative Code," www.lexisnexis.com/hottopics/njcode/

In Chronological Order (Register)—
New Jersey Register

[1969–1995]: New Jersey State Library, "New Jersey Register," http://law.njstatelib.org/slic_home/law_library/new_jersey_legal_resources/new_jersey_register

Administrative Rulings

[1997–]: Rutgers University School of Law–Newark, "New Jersey Administrative Law Decisions," http://njlaw.rutgers.edu/collections/oal/

[1979–1991]: Rutgers University, New Jersey Digital Library, "New Jersey Administrative Reports [First Series]," http://njlegallib.rutgers.edu/njar/njarhome.htm

Local Laws

Directory of State Counties/Municipalities

State of New Jersey, "County and Municipal Web Sites," www.state.nj.us/nj/govinfo/county/localgov.html

Ordinances

Coded Systems LLC, "New Jersey," www.codedsystems.com/codelibrary/newjersey.html

Municode Code Corporation, "New Jersey," www.municode.com/library/NJ

Practice Materials and Self-Help Resources

Research Guides

Rutgers University Law Library, "Legal Forms in the Library," http://law-library.rutgers.edu/resources/forms.php

Rutgers University Law Library, "Public Patron Guide to New Jersey Sources," http://law-library.rutgers.edu/resources/publicpatron.php

Legal Services of New Jersey, "LSNJ Publications," www.lsnj.org/PublicationsVideos.aspx

Court Rules

New Jersey Judiciary, "Rules Governing the Courts of the State of New Jersey," www.judiciary.state.nj.us/rules/

Forms

New Jersey Judiciary, "Legal Practice Forms," www.judiciary.state.nj.us/forms.htm

State Bar Association Consumer Brochures

New Jersey State Bar Foundation, "For the Public: Find a Publication," www.njsbf.org/for-the-public/public-publications.html

Court Brochures/Self-Help Centers

New Jersey Judiciary, "Represent Yourself in Court (Pro Se): Self-Help Resource Center," www.judiciary.state.nj.us/prose/

Looking for an Attorney (for a fee or for free)

Legal Aid/Advocacy Groups/Pro Bono

Legal Services of New Jersey, "Legal Services Offices," www.lsnj.org/LegalServicesOffices.aspx

Camden Center for Law and Social Justice, www.cclsj.org

Finding an Attorney/Lawyer Referrals

New Jersey State Bar Association, "Lawyer Referral Service," www.njsba.com/for-the-public/lawyer-referral-service.html

Miscellaneous

New Jersey Department of State, "Organizational Chart for Pre-1948 Court System," www.nj.gov/state/archives/catcourtstructure.html

Paul Axel-Lute, "New Jersey Legal Research Handbook 6th Edition [2012] Supplement," http://law-library.rutgers.edu/ilg/NJLR6.php

New Jersey Judiciary, "A Guide to Filing for Litigants without Lawyers," www.judiciary.state.nj.us/supreme/guide.htm

New Jersey Judiciary, "Trial Court Unpublished Decisions" [last six weeks], www.judiciary.state.nj.us/decisions/

New Jersey Legislature, "New Jersey Legislative Digest—Past Issues" [1997–], www.njleg.state.nj.us/legislativepub/digest-past_dyn.asp

Reference

New Jersey Legislature, "Glossary of Terms," www.njleg.state.nj.us/legislativepub/glossary.asp

NEW MEXICO

Research Guides

AALL LISP, "Public Library Toolkit: New Mexico," www.aallnet.org/sections/lisp/Public-Library-Toolkit

New Mexico Supreme Court Law Library, www.supremecourtlawlibrary.org

University of New Mexico School of Law Library, "New Mexico Law Research," http://lawlibrary.unm.edu/nm/

Judicial

State Court Structure

University of New Mexico School of Law, Judicial Education Center, "A Flow Chart of the New Mexico Court System" [diagram], http://jec.unm.edu/manuals-resources/new -mexico-court-system

Directory of State Courts

University of New Mexico School of Law Library, "Courts & Opinions," http://lawlibrary .unm.edu/legal-webs/new-mexico/courts/

Opinions

Highest Court—Supreme Court

[last year]: New Mexico Compilation Commission, "New Mexico Appellate Opinions," www.nmcompcomm.us/nmcases/ NMCases.aspx

[1998–2013]: New Mexico Supreme Court Law Library, "Case Law" [follow links to "Table of Cases"], www.supremecourtlawlibrary.org

Intermediate Appellate Court—Court of Appeals

[last year]: New Mexico Compilation Commission, "New Mexico Appellate Opinions," www.nmcompcomm.us/nmcases/ NMCases.aspx

[1998–2013]: New Mexico Supreme Court Law Library, "Case Law" [follow links to "Table of Cases"], www.supremecourtlawlibrary.org

Dockets/Court Records

Trial Courts

New Mexico Courts, "Case Lookup," www2.nmcourts.gov/caselookup/app

Legislative

State Legislative Process

New Mexico Legislature, "The Birth of a Notion: How an Idea Becomes a Law," www.nmlegis .gov/lcs/Employment/house/Birth%20of%20a%20 Notion%20for%20Web.pdf

Statutes

By Subject (Code)—New Mexico Statutes

New Mexico Compilation Commission, "New Mexico Public Access Law—Statutes and Court Rules," http://public.nmcompcomm.us/ nmnxtadmin/NMPublic.aspx

In Chronological Order (Session Laws)— Laws of New Mexico

[1996–]: New Mexico Legislature, "Session Publications," www.nmlegis.gov/lcs/session pub.aspx

Executive

Directory of State Departments/Agencies

New Mexico.gov, "Government: A to Z Directory," www.newmexico.gov/government/ A_to_Z_state_Agency_Listings.aspx

State Rulemaking Process

New Mexico Commission of Public Records, Administrative Law Division, "Explanation of the New Mexico Administrative Code," www.nmcpr.state.nm.us/nmac/_explanation/ explanation.htm

Regulations

By Agency (Code)—
New Mexico Administrative Code

New Mexico Commission of Public Records, Administrative Law Division, "New Mexico Administrative Code," www.nmcpr.state.nm.us/nmac/

In Chronological Order (Register)—
New Mexico Register

[current year]: New Mexico Commission of Public Records, Administrative Law Division, "New Mexico Register," www.nmcpr.state.nm.us/nmregister/

[2001–]: New Mexico Commission of Public Records, Administrative Law Division, "New Mexico Register: Previous Issues," www.nmcpr.state.nm.us/nmregister/prev_issues.htm

Local Laws

Directories of State Counties/Municipalities

New Mexico Association of Counties, www.nmcounties.org

New Mexico Municipal League, "New Mexico Municipal Websites," http://nmml.org/new-mexico-municipal-websites/

Ordinances

University of New Mexico School of Law Library, "Ordinances," http://lawlibrary.unm.edu/legal-webs/new-mexico/ordinances/

Practice Materials and Self-Help Resources

Research Guide

University of New Mexico School of Law, Judicial Education Center, "Manuals," http://jec.unm.edu/manuals-resources/manuals

Court Rules

New Mexico Compilation Commission, "New Mexico Public Access Law—Statutes and Court Rules," www.nmonesource.com/nmnxtadmin/NMPublic.aspx

Forms

University of New Mexico School of Law Library, "Forms," http://lawlibrary.unm.edu/legal-webs/new-mexico/rules/

State Bar Association Consumer Brochures

State Bar of New Mexico, "Public Publications," www.nmbar.org/Public/publicpubs.html

Court Brochures/Self-Help Centers

Administrative Office of the Courts, "NM State Judiciary Self Representation Website: Family Law," http://www.nmcourts.gov/cgi/prose_lib/

Looking for an Attorney (for a fee or for free)

Legal Aid/Advocacy Groups/Pro Bono

State Bar of New Mexico, "Legal Service Providers," www.nmbar.org/Public/legalserviceproviders.html

American Bar Association, "Pro Bono Program Listings: New Mexico," http://apps.americanbar.org/legalservices/probono/directory/newmexico.html

University of New Mexico School of Law Library, "Community Legal Resources," http://lawlibrary.unm.edu/research-guides/nm/helpful-numbers.pdf

Finding an Attorney/Lawyer Referrals

State Bar of New Mexico, "Referral Programs," www.nmbar.org/Public/referralprograms.html

State Bar of New Mexico, "Find an Attorney," www.nmbar.org/findattorney/attorneyfinder.aspx

Miscellaneous

University of New Mexico School of Law, Judicial Education Center, "Manuals & Resources," http://jec.unm.edu/manuals-resources

New Mexico Legislature, "Legislative Publications: Committee Reports" [2003–], www.nmlegis.gov/lcs/reports.aspx

New Mexico Legislature, "Session Publications" [subject index to bills, 1996–], www.nmlegis.gov/lcs/sessionpub.aspx

References

University of New Mexico School of Law, Judicial Education Center, "Glossary of Legal Terms," http://jec.unm.edu/manuals-resources/glossary-of-legal-terms

State Bar of New Mexico, "Common Legal Terms," www.nmbar.org/Public/commonlegalterms.html

NEW YORK

Research Guides

General

Georgetown University Law Library, "New York Research In-Depth," www.ll.georgetown.edu/states/newyork-in-depth.cfm

Albany Law School, untitled document [starting on page 10 of 15], www.albanylaw.edu/media/user/librarypdfs/guides/free_internet_resources.pdf

Topical

SUNY Buffalo Law School, Charles B. Sears Law Library, "New York Workers' Compensation," http://law.lib.buffalo.edu/PDFs/nys/NYWorker.pdf

SUNY Buffalo Law School, Charles B. Sears Law Library, "New York Environmental Law," http://law.lib.buffalo.edu/PDFs/nys/NYEnvironmental.pdf

Albany Law School, "Schaffer Law Library's Guide on New York State Environmental Law," www.albanylaw.edu/media/user/librarypdfs/guides/nyenvir.pdf

Pace Law Library, "Health Law Research Guide," http://libraryguides.law.pace.edu/healthlaw

Albany Law School, "Schaffer Law Library's Guide on NYS Tax Law Materials," www.albanylaw.edu/media/user/librarypdfs/guides/nystax.pdf

Albany Law School, "Schaffer Law Library's Guide on Federal & NYS Public Sector Labor Management Relations" [starting on page 4], www.albanylaw.edu/media/user/librarypdfs/guides/public_sector.pdf

Judicial

State Court Structure

New York State Unified Court System, "The New York State Courts: An Introductory Guide," www.nycourts.gov/reports/ctstrct99.pdf

New York State Unified Court System, "Structure of the Courts" [diagram], www.nycourts.gov/courts/structure.shtml

New York Court of Appeals, "Court System Outline" [diagram], www.courts.state.ny.us/ctapps/outline.htm

Directory of State Courts

New York State Unified Court System, "Court Guides," www.nycourts.gov/litigants/courtguides/

Opinions

Research Guide

New York University School of Law, "New York Court System," www.law.nyu.edu/library/research/researchguides/newyorkcourtsystem/

Highest Court—Court of Appeals

[2003–]: New York State Law Reporting Bureau, "Court of Appeals," www.nycourts.gov/reporter/slipidx/cidxtable.shtml

Intermediate Appellate Court—Appellate Divisions of Supreme Court

[2003–]: New York State Law Reporting Bureau, "Decisions," www.nycourts.gov/reporter/Decisions.htm

Intermediate Appellate Court— Appellate Terms of Supreme Court

[2003–]: New York State Law Reporting Bureau, "Decisions," www.nycourts.gov/reporter/Decisions.htm

Trial Court Decisions

[2003–]: New York State Law Reporting Bureau, "Other Court Decisions," www.nycourts.gov/reporter/slipidx/miscolo.shtml

[2001–]: New York State Unified Court System, "Search Decisions," http://decisions.courts.state.ny.us/search/query3.asp

Dockets/Court Records

All Courts

New York State Unified Court System, "UCS eCourts," https://iapps.courts.state.ny.us/webcivil/ecourtsMain

Legislative

State Legislative Process

New York State Senate, "How a Bill Becomes a Law," www.nysenate.gov/How_a-Bill_Becomes_a_Law

Statutes

By Subject (Code)—Consolidated Laws

New York State Legislature, "Laws of New York," http://public.leginfo.state.ny.us/menugetf.cgi?COMMONQUERY=LAWS

In Chronological Order (Session Laws)—
Laws of the State of New York

[1995–]: New York State Legislature, "Legislative Information," http://public.leginfo.state.ny.us/menugetf.cgi

Legislative History

Research Guides

New York State Library, "The Legislative History of a New York State Law: A Tutorial and Guide to Library Sources," www.nysl.nysed.gov/leghist/

New York State Library Publications and Reports, *Legislative Intent in New York State: Materials, Cases and Annotated Bibliography,* by Robert Allan Carter, 2nd ed. [e-book, 2001], www.nysl.nysed.gov/nyslpubs.htm

Syracuse University College of Law, H. Douglas Barclay Law Library, "New York State Legislative History," www.law.syr.edu/Pdfs/0NYS%20Leghis.pdf

SUNY Buffalo Law School, Charles B. Sears Law Library, "New York Legislative History," http://law.lib.buffalo.edu/PDFs/nys/NYLegHist.pdf

Albany Law School, "Schaffer Law Library's Guide on New York State Legislative History Materials," www.albanylaw.edu/media/user/librarypdfs/guides/nyleghist.pdf

Executive

Directory of State Departments/Agencies

New York State, "Agency Listing (State Agencies)," www.nysegov.com/citGuide.cfm?superCat=102&cat=449&content=main

State Rulemaking Process

New York Department of State, Division of Administrative Rules, "Rule Making in New York Manual," www.dos.state.ny.us/info/rulemakingmanual.html

Regulations

Research Guides

SUNY Buffalo Law School, Charles B. Sears Law Library, "New York Administrative Law," http://law.lib.buffalo.edu/PDFs/nys/NYAdmin.pdf

Albany Law School, "Schaffer Law Library's Guide on NYS Regulations and Executive Orders," www.albanylaw.edu/media/user/librarypdfs/guides/nyreg.pdf

By Agency (Code)—
New York Codes, Rules and Regulations

Westlaw, "New York Codes, Rules and Regulations," http://government.westlaw.com/linkedslice/default.asp?SP=nycrr-1000

In Chronological Order (Register)—
New York State Register

[2003–]: New York Department of State, Division of Administrative Rules, "NYS Register," www.dos.state.ny.us/info/register.htm

[1979–]: New York Department of State, "New York State Register" [e-text from New York State Library], http://purl.org/net/nysl/nysdocs/4877826

Local Laws

Research Guides

New York University School of Law, "Sources of New York City Law and Regulations," www.law.nyu.edu/library/research/researchguides/newyorkcitylaw/

Fordham University School of Law, Leo T. Kissam Memorial Library, "New York City Legal Research," http://lawlib1.lawnet.fordham.edu/research/nycresearch.pdf

Directory of State Counties/Municipalities

New York State, "Municipality Websites Listed by County," www.nysegov.com/citguide.cfm?context=citguide&content=munibycounty2

Ordinances

General Code, "New York eCode360 Library," www.generalcode.com/ecode360/NY

Municode Code Corporation, "New York," www.municode.com/library/NY

Fordham University School of Law, Leo T. Kissam Memorial Library, "Electronic Resources by Subject: New York City: Legislative," http://lawlib1.lawnet.fordham.edu/eresources/eresources.html

Practice Materials and Self-Help Resources

Research Guides

Fordham University School of Law, Leo T. Kissam Memorial Library, "New York Forms," http://lawlib1.lawnet.fordham.edu/research/nyforms.pdf

Albany Law School, "Schaffer Law Library's Guide on New York Materials" [topical], www.albanylaw.edu/media/user/librarypdfs/guides/nymaterials.pdf

SUNY Buffalo Law School, Charles B. Sears Law Library, "New York Civil Procedure," http://law.lib.buffalo.edu/PDFs/nys/NYCivPro.pdf

SUNY Buffalo Law School, Charles B. Sears Law Library, "New York Criminal Law," http://law.lib.buffalo.edu/PDFs/nys/NYCrim.pdf

SUNY Buffalo Law School, Charles B. Sears Law Library, "New York Evidence," http://law.lib.buffalo.edu/PDFs/nys/NYEvidence.pdf

Court Rules

New York State Unified Court System, "Administrative Rules of the Unified Court System & Uniform Rules of the Trial Courts," www.courts.state.ny.us/rules/

Forms

New York State Unified Court System, CourtHelp, "Forms," www.nycourts.gov/courthelp/forms.html

New York State Unified Court System, "Forms," www.nycourts.gov/forms/

State Bar Association Consumer Brochures

New York State Bar Association, "For the Community," www.nysba.org/?Section=Public_Resources

Court Brochures/Self-Help Centers

New York State Unified Court System, "Landlord/Tenant Guides," www.nycourts.gov/litigants/landlordTenantGuides.shtml

Civil Court of the City of New York, "How to Try or Defend a Civil Case When You Don't Have a Lawyer," www.nycourts.gov/publications/GuideforProSes.pdf

New York State Unified Court System, "Litigants: Criminal Justice System Handbook," www.nycourts .gov/litigants/crimjusticesyshandbk .shtml

Looking for an Attorney (for a fee or for free)

Legal Aid/Advocacy Groups/Pro Bono

Pro Bono Net, LawHelpNY.org, www.lawhelpny.org

Finding an Attorney/Lawyer Referrals

New York State Bar Association Lawyer Referral and Information Service, www.nysba.org/AM/Template.cfm?Section=Find_a_Lawyer&Template=/CustomSource/LegalInfobyCounty.cfm&cty=lrs

Miscellaneous

New York State Unified Court System, "Public Access Law Libraries," www.nycourts.gov/lawlibraries/publicaccess.shtml

New York State Attorney General, "Tenants' Rights Guide" [e-text from New York State Library], http://purl.org/net/nysl/nysdocs/298553885

Goldfarb Abrandt Salzman & Kutzin LLP,
"Senior Law: Information for Seniors,
Advocates & Other Professionals,"
www.seniorlaw.com/senior.htm

Reference

New York State Unified Court System, CourtHelp,
"Glossary of Common Legal Terms,"
www.nycourts.gov/courthelp/TermsGlossary.html

NORTH CAROLINA

Research Guides

General

AALL LISP, "Public Library Toolkit: North
Carolina," www.aallnet.org/sections/lisp/
Public-Library-Toolkit
North Carolina State University Libraries,
"NC and U.S. Legal Resources Guide,"
www.lib.ncsu.edu/guides/uslegal/primary.html

Topical

Wake Forest University School of Law,
Professional Center Library, "Advanced Legal
Research Pathfinders," http://library.law.wfu
.edu/student-learning/advanced-legal-research
-pathfinders/
Duke Law, "Legal Research for Non-Lawyers,"
www.law.duke.edu/lib/researchguides/nonlaw

Judicial

State Court Structure

North Carolina Administrative Office of the
Courts, "The North Carolina Judicial
System," 2008 ed. [includes diagram],
www.nccourts.org/Citizens/Publications/Documents/
JudicialSystem.pdf

Directory of State Courts

North Carolina Court System, "North Carolina
Trial Courts," www.nccourts.org/County/

Opinions

Highest Court—Supreme Court

[1998–]: North Carolina Court System, "N.C.
Supreme Court Opinions," http://appellate
.nccourts.org/opinions/

Intermediate Appellate Court—
Court of Special Appeals

[1998–]: North Carolina Court System, "N.C.
Court of Appeals Opinions," http://appellate
.nccourts.org/opinions/

Dockets/Court Records

Appellate Courts

North Carolina Supreme Court and Court of
Appeals Electronic Filing Site and Document
Library, www.ncappellatecourts.org

Trial Courts

North Carolina Court System, "District and
Superior Court Query, www1.aoc.state.nc.us/
www/calendars/CriminalQuery.html

Legislative

State Legislative Process

North Carolina General Assembly, "How a Law
Is Made" [includes diagram], www.ncleg.net/
NCGAInfo/Bill-Law/bill-law.html

Statutes

By Subject (Code)—
North Carolina General Statutes

North Carolina General Assembly, "North
Carolina General Statutes" [browse],
www.ncleg.net/gascripts/Statutes/StatutesTOC.pl
North Carolina General Assembly, "NC General
Statutes" [search], www.ncleg.net/gascripts/
statutes/Statutes.asp

In Chronological Order (Session Laws)—State of
North Carolina Session Laws and Resolutions

[1959–]: North Carolina General Assembly,
"Session Laws," www.ncleg.net/gascripts/
EnactedLegislation/ELTOC.pl?sType=Law

Legislative History

Research Guides

Wake Forest School of Law, "North Carolina Legal Research: Statutes and Legislative History," http://libguides.law.wfu.edu/content .php?pid=223642&sid=1855611

University of North Carolina, Kathrine R. Everett Law Library, "Researching North Carolina Historical and Current Legislation," http:// library.law.unc.edu/documents/researchguides/ nc_legislative_history.pdf

North Carolina General Assembly Legislative Library, "North Carolina Legislative History Step by Step," www.ncleg.net/library/Documents/ LegisHistGuide2010.pdf

Executive

Directory of State Departments/Agencies

NC.gov, "Agencies," www.ncgov.com/government/ agencies/

State Rulemaking Process

USLegal, "Administrative Procedure Act—North Carolina," http://administrativelaw.uslegal.com/ administrative-procedure-acts/north-carolina/

Regulations

By Agency (Code)—
North Carolina Administrative Code

North Carolina Office of Administrative Hearings, "NCAC Table of Contents," http://reports.oah.state.nc.us/ncac.asp

In Chronological Order (Register)—
North Carolina Register

[1986–]: North Carolina Office of Administrative Hearings, "Rules Division—North Carolina Register," www.oah.state.nc.us/rules/register/

Local Laws

Directories of State Counties/Municipalities

University of North Carolina School of Government, Knapp Library, "Counties in North Carolina," www.sog.unc.edu/node/724

University of North Carolina School of Government, Knapp Library, "Cities in North Carolina," www.sog.unc.edu/node/723

Ordinances

Municode Code Corporation, "North Carolina," www.municode.com/library/NC

Practice Materials and Self-Help Resources

Research Guides

Duke Law, "North Carolina Practice," www.law.duke.edu/lib/researchguides/ncprac

Legal Aid of North Carolina, "Brochures, Handbooks & Fliers," www.legalaidnc.org/public/ learn/publications/Brochures/

University of North Carolina, Kathrine R. Everett Law Library, "Form Books," http://library.law .unc.edu/documents/researchguides/form_books _2009.pdf

University of North Carolina, Kathrine R. Everett Law Library, "A Selected Bibliography of North Carolina Practice Materials for Legal Professionals and Students," http://library.law .unc.edu/documents/researchguides/nc_practice _materials.pdf

Court Rules

Office of the North Carolina Appellate Reporter, "Rules & Resources," www.aoc.state.nc.us/www/ public/html/ARResources.asp

Forms

North Carolina Administrative Office of the Courts, "Forms Manual," www.nccourts.org/ Forms/Documents/CompleteIndex.pdf

North Carolina Court System, "Judicial Forms," www.nccourts.org/Forms/FormSearch.asp

State Bar Association Consumer Brochures

North Carolina Bar Association, "This Is the Law Pamphlets," www.ncbar.org/public-pro-bono/ publications/this-is-the-law-pamphlets.aspx

North Carolina Bar Association, "Publications," www.ncbar.org/public-pro-bono/publications.aspx

Court Brochures/Self-Help Centers

North Carolina Court System, "Citizens,"
www.nccourts.org/Citizens/

Looking for an Attorney
(for a fee or for free)

Legal Aid/Advocacy Groups/Pro Bono

Legal Aid of North Carolina, "Brochures,
Handbooks & Fliers: Legal Aid of North
Carolina," www.legalaidnc.org/public/learn/
publications/Brochures/#LANC

Finding an Attorney/Lawyer Referrals

North Carolina Bar Association, "Lawyer
Referral Service: For the Public,"
www.ncbar.org/public-pro-bono/lawyer-referral
-service/for-the-public.aspx

26th Judicial District, SelfServe Center, "Lawyer
Referral Services," www.aoc.state.nc.us/www/
public/courts/meck/disk01/lawyeref.html

Miscellaneous

North Carolina Office of Administrative
Hearings, "Decisions,"
www.ncoah.com/hearings/decisions/

References

North Carolina General Assembly, "Action
Code Abbreviations Used in the Bill Status
System," www.ncleg.net/Legislation/abbreviations
.html

North Carolina Court System, "Glossary of Legal
Terms," www.nccourts.org/Citizens/Publications/
LegalTerms.asp

NORTH DAKOTA

Research Guides

University of North Dakota, Thormodsgard Law
Library, "Online Legal Research Sources—
North Dakota," http://web.law.und.edu/Library/
research/ND.php

North Dakota Supreme Court, "Legal Research,"
www.ndcourts.gov/court/resource/nd.htm

Judicial

State Court Structure

North Dakota Supreme Court, "The North
Dakota Judicial System," www.ndcourts.gov/
court/Brochure.htm

Westlaw, "North Dakota Court Structure"
[diagram], http://wlwatch.westlaw.com/aca/west/
statecrtorg.htm#ND

Directory of State Courts

North Dakota Supreme Court, "Courts,"
www.ndcourts.gov/Court/Courts.htm

Opinions

Highest Court—Supreme Court

[1965–]: North Dakota Supreme Court,
"Opinions," www.ndcourts.gov/search/
opinions.asp

Intermediate Appellate Court—Court of Appeals

[1998–]: North Dakota Supreme Court, "ND
App Citations," www.ndcourts.gov/opinions/cite/
NDApp.htm

Dockets/Court Records

Trial Courts

North Dakota Supreme Court, "North Dakota
Courts Records Inquiry," http://publicsearch
.ndcourts.gov

Legislative

State Legislative Process

North Dakota Legislative Council, "How a Bill
Becomes a Law," www.legis.nd.gov/files/resource/
miscellaneous/bill-law.pdf

Statutes

By Subject (Code)—North Dakota Century Code

North Dakota Legislative Branch, "North Dakota
Century Code," www.legis.nd.gov/information/
statutes/cent-code.html

In Chronological Order (Session Laws)—
Session Laws

[1997–]: North Dakota Legislative Branch,
"Session Laws," www.legis.nd.gov/information/
statutes/session-laws.html

Legislative History

Research Guides

N/A

Compiled Bill History

[2001–]: North Dakota Legislative Branch,
"Legislative History," www.legis.nd.gov/research
-center/history/

Executive

Directory of State Departments/Agencies

ND.gov, "Agencies," www.nd.gov/agency.htm

State Rulemaking Process

USLegal, "Administrative Procedure Act—North
Dakota," http://administrativelaw.uslegal.com/
administrative-procedure-acts/north-dakota/

Regulations

By Agency (Code)—
North Dakota Administrative Code

North Dakota Legislative Branch, "North Dakota
Administrative Code," www.legis.nd.gov/agency
-rules/north-dakota-administrative-code

In Chronological Order (Register)—None

Local Laws

Directories of State Counties/Municipalities

North Dakota Association of Counties,
"Interactive Map," www.ndaco.org/?id=76&page
=Interactive+Map
ND.gov, "City Website List,"
www.nd.gov/category.htm?id=122

Ordinances

Municode Code Corporation, "North Dakota,"
www.municode.com/library/ND

Practice Materials and Self-Help Resources

Research Guide

Legal Services of North Dakota, "Legal Topics
and Education Materials," www.legalassist
.org/?id=34

Court Rules

North Dakota Supreme Court, "North Dakota
Rules," www.ndcourts.gov/Rules/

Forms

North Dakota Supreme Court, "Forms for Self
Represented Parties," www.ndcourts.gov/court/
Forms/

State Bar Association Consumer Brochures

State Bar Association of North Dakota,
"Graduating into an Adult World: Your Legal
Rights and Responsibilities," https://sband
.org/UserFiles/files/pdfs/publications/GIAAW
_BookFINAL.pdf

Court Brochures/Self-Help Centers

North Dakota Supreme Court, "Website Guides,"
www.ndcourts.gov/court/Welcome.htm

Looking for an Attorney (for a fee or for free)

Legal Aid/Advocacy Groups/Pro Bono

State Bar Association of North Dakota,
"Volunteer Lawyers Program," www.sband.org/
Resources%20for%20the%20Public/Volunteers.aspx
Legal Services of North Dakota,
www.legalassist.org

Finding an Attorney/Lawyer Referrals

State Bar Association of North Dakota, "Lawyer
Referral Service" www.sband.org/Resources%20
for%20the%20Public/referralInfo.aspx
North Dakota Supreme Court, "Lawyers
Directory," www.ndcourts.gov/court/lawyers/
index/frameset.htm

Miscellaneous

State Bar Association of North Dakota, "Pattern Jury Instructions," www.sband.org/ PatternJuryInstruction/

North Dakota Supreme Court, "A Hornbook to the North Dakota Criminal Code" [50 N.D.L. Rev. 639 (1974)], www.ndcourts.gov/Research/

Reference

North Dakota Supreme Court, "Judicial System Glossary," www.ndcourts.gov/court/Glossary.htm

OHIO

Research Guides

General

Ohio State University, Moritz College of Law, "Research Guides: Introduction to the State Materials of Ohio," http://moritzlaw.osu.edu/ library/assistance/ohio_intro.php

Supreme Court of Ohio, Office of the Clerk, "Filing an Appeal in the Supreme Court of Ohio: A Pro Se Guide," www.supremecourt.ohio .gov/Publications/proSeGuide.pdf

Cleveland Law Library Association, "Basic Ohio Legal Materials in Books, CD-ROM, Online, and on the Internet," www.clelaw.lib.oh.us/ Public/Misc/REGUIDES/guide29.html

Cleveland State University, Cleveland-Marshall College of Law, "Ohio Primary Law Legal Research Guide," http://guides.law.csuohio.edu/ ohio_primary_law

Cleveland State University, Cleveland-Marshall College of Law, "Legal Research on the Web," https://www.law.csuohio.edu/lawlibrary/web

University of Akron School of Law Library, "Ohio Law," http://law.uakron.libguides.com/ ohiolaw

Topical

Cleveland State University, Cleveland-Marshall College of Law, "Research Guides: O," https://www.law.csuohio.edu/lawlibrary/guides#O

Judicial

State Court Structure

Supreme Court of Ohio, "Judicial System Structure," www.supremecourt.ohio.gov/ JudSystem/

Supreme Court of Ohio, "Ohio Judicial Structure" [diagram], www.supremecourt.ohio .gov/SCO/jurisdiction/structure.pdf

Directories of State Courts

Supreme Court of Ohio, "Ohio Courts of Appeals," www.supremecourt.ohio.gov/JudSystem/ districtCourts/

Supreme Court of Ohio, "Ohio Trial Courts & Local Rules," www.supremecourt.ohio.gov/ JudSystem/trialCourts/

Opinions

Research Guides

Cleveland State University, Cleveland-Marshall College of Law, "How to Find an Ohio Case in the Law Library," https://www.law.csuohio .edu/lawlibrary/web/faq/ocase

University of Dayton School of Law, Zimmerman Law Library, "Ohio Case Law," www.udayton .edu/law/library/ohio_case_law.php

Highest Court—Supreme Court

[last year]: Cleveland Law Library Association, "Ohio Supreme Court Opinions & Announcements," www.clelaw.lib.oh.us/public/ decision/oh_sup.html

[1992–]: Supreme Court of Ohio, "Opinions & Announcements," www.supremecourt.ohio.gov/ rod/docs/

Intermediate Appellate Court—Court of Appeals

[2001–]: Supreme Court of Ohio, "Opinions & Announcements," www.supremecourt.ohio.gov/ rod/docs/

Dockets/Court Records

Research Guide

Cleveland State University, Cleveland-Marshall College of Law, "Courts, Dockets, Rules & Briefs," https://www.law.csuohio.edu/lawlibrary/ web/dockets

Supreme Court

Supreme Court of Ohio, "Search for Supreme Court Cases" [1985–], www.supremecourt.ohio.gov/Clerk/ecms/

Trial Courts

Supreme Court of Ohio and Ohio Judicial System, "Ohio Trial Courts & Local Rules," www.sconet.state.oh.us/JudSystem/trialCourts/

Legislative

State Legislative Process

Ohio Senate, "How a Bill Becomes a Law," www.ohiosenate.gov/education/how-a-bill-becomes-a-law

Ohio General Assembly, "The Legislative Process" [diagram], www.legislature.state.oh.us/process.cfm

Statutes

By Subject (Code)—Ohio Revised Code

Lawriter LLC, Ohio Rules and Laws, "Ohio Revised Code," http://codes.ohio.gov/orc/

In Chronological Order (Session Laws)—
Laws of Ohio (Acts)

[1997–]: Ohio General Assembly, "Acts," www.legislature.state.oh.us/acts.cfm

Legislative History

Research Guides

Ohio General Assembly, "A Guide to Legislative History in Ohio," *Members Only* 128, no. 10 (January 26, 2010), www.lsc.state.oh.us/membersonly/128legislativehistory.pdf

University of Cincinnati College of Law, "Ohio Legislative History Guide," www.law.uc.edu/library/guides/ohio-legislative-history-guide

Cleveland State University, Cleveland-Marshall College of Law, "Ohio and Other States' Legislative History," https://www.law.csuohio.edu/lawlibrary/guides/legishistory/states

Executive

Directory of State Departments/Agencies

Ohio.gov, "Agencies, Departments, Boards & Commissions," www.ohio.gov/agencies/

State Rulemaking Process

Ohio Legislative Service Commission, "Register of Ohio: An Overview of Administrative Rule Making in Ohio," www.registerofohio.state.oh.us/jsps/public/overview.jsp

Regulations

Research Guide

Cleveland State University, Cleveland-Marshall College of Law, "Ohio Primary Law Legal Research Guide: Administrative Regulations," http://guides.law.csuohio.edu/ohio_primary_law

By Agency (Code)—Ohio Administrative Code

Lawriter LLC, Ohio Rules and Laws, "Ohio Administrative Code," http://codes.ohio.gov/oac/

In Chronological Order (Register)—
Register of Ohio

Ohio Legislative Service Commission, "Register of Ohio," www.registerofohio.state.oh.us

Local Laws

Research Guide

Cleveland State University, Cleveland-Marshall College of Law, "Ohio Local Government Law Resource Guide," http://guides.law.csuohio.edu/ohio_local_government

Directory of State Counties/Municipalities

Ohio.gov, "Cities, Townships & Counties," www.ohio.gov/government/localities/

Ordinances

Cleveland State University, Cleveland-Marshall College of Law, "Ordinances," https://www.law.csuohio.edu/lawlibrary/web/ord

Cleveland Law Library Association, "Ohio Municipal Codes & Ordinances," www.clelaw.lib.oh.us/public/misc/Muni_Ct.html

Practice Materials and Self-Help Resources

Research Guides

Cleveland Law Library Association, "Frequently Asked Questions," www.clelaw.lib.oh.us/Public/Misc/FAQ.html

Ohio State University, Moritz College of Law, "Subject Guide to Self-Help Law Books," http://moritzlaw.osu.edu/library/assistance/selfhelp.pdf

Cleveland State University, Cleveland-Marshall College of Law, "Forms and Practice Materials," http://guides.law.csuohio.edu/legal_forms

Claude W. Pettit College of Law, "Taggart Law Library Research Guide #1: Finding Form Books," http://law.onu.edu/sites/default/files/Form%20Books.pdf

Montgomery County Law Library, "Library Resource Guides," www.daylawlib.org/Guides.htm

Court Rules

University of Dayton School of Law, Zimmerman Law Library, "Ohio Cases and Court Rules," www.udayton.edu/law/library/ohio_cases_court_rules.php

Supreme Court of Ohio, "Ohio Rules of Court," www.supremecourt.ohio.gov/LegalResources/Rules/

Ronald L Burdge Esq., OhioCourtLinks.org, www.ohiocourtlinks.org

Cleveland Law Library Association, "Internet Legal Web Sites: Ohio Courts: Ohio Court Rules," www.clelaw.lib.oh.us/Public/Misc/Sites/Ohio.html

Forms

Ronald L Burdge Esq., OhioCourtLinks.org, www.ohiocourtlinks.org

State Bar Association Consumer Brochures

Ohio State Bar Association, "LawFacts Pamphlets," https://www.ohiobar.org/ForPublic/Resources/LawFactsPamphlets/Pages/LawFactsPamphlets.aspx

Ohio State Bar Association, *The Law and You: A Legal Handbook for Ohio Consumers and Journalists*, 14th ed. (2012),

https://www.ohiobar.org/ForPublic/PressRoom/Pages/StaticPage-276.aspx

Court Brochures/Self-Help Centers

Supreme Court of Ohio, Office of the Clerk, "Filing an Appeal in the Supreme Court of Ohio: A Pro Se Guide," www.supremecourt.ohio.gov/Publications/proSeGuide.pdf

Looking for an Attorney (for a fee or for free)

Legal Aid/Advocacy Groups/Pro Bono

Cleveland State University, Cleveland-Marshall College of Law, "Where to Go for Legal Advice in the Cleveland Area," https://www.law.csuohio.edu/lawlibrary/guides/where

Ohio Legal Services, www.ohiolegalservices.org/public/legal_problem

Finding an Attorney/Lawyer Referrals

Ohio Legal Services, "Ohio Lawyer Referral Programs," www.ohiolegalservices.org/programs/ohio-lawyer-referral-programs-1

Miscellaneous

Ohio Public Library Information Network, "Find-a-Library" [by county], www.oplin.org/content/find-a-library

Ohio Regional Association of Law Libraries, "County Law Libraries Directory," www.clelaw.lib.oh.us/public/misc/colawlib.html

Ohio Legislative Service Commission, *A Guidebook for Ohio Legislators*, chapter 6, "Tools for Understanding a Bill," www.lsc.state.oh.us/guidebook/

Cleveland State University, Cleveland-Marshall College of Law, "FAQ: Workers' Compensation Claims," https://www.law.csuohio.edu/lawlibrary/guides/faqworkers

References

Cleveland State University, Cleveland-Marshall College of Law, "How to Read a Legal Citation," http://guides.law.csuohio.edu/read_citation

Ohio Legislative Service Commission, Register of Ohio, "Abbreviation and Definitions," www.registerofohio.state.oh.us/jsps/public/abbrev.jsp

Ohio General Assembly, "Glossary of Terms," www.legislature.state.oh.us/glossary.cfm

University of Cincinnati College of Law, "Common Ohio Abbreviations," www.law.uc.edu/sites/default/files/ohiocitations.pdf

OKLAHOMA

Research Guide

Library of Congress, Guide to Law Online, "Oklahoma," www.loc.gov/law/help/guide/states/us-ok.php

Judicial

State Court Structure

Supreme Court of Oklahoma, "Oklahoma Court System," www.oscn.net/applications/oscn/start.asp?viewType=COURTS

Westlaw, "Oklahoma Court Structure" [diagram], http://wlwatch.westlaw.com/aca/west/statecrtorg.htm#OK

Directory of State Courts

Supreme Court of Oklahoma, "Oklahoma Court System," www.oscn.net/applications/oscn/start.asp?viewType=COURTS

Opinions

Highest Court—Supreme Court

[1909–]: University of Oklahoma College of Law, "Oklahoma Public Legal Research System," http://oklegal.onenet.net/sample.basic.html

[1890–]: Oklahoma State Courts Network, "Oklahoma Cases," www.oscn.net/applications/oscn/index.asp?ftdb=STOKCS&level=1

Highest Court—Court of Criminal Appeals

[1929–]: University of Oklahoma College of Law, "Oklahoma Public Legal Research System," http://oklegal.onenet.net/sample.basic.html

[1908–]: Oklahoma State Courts Network, "Oklahoma Cases," www.oscn.net/applications/oscn/index.asp?ftdb=STOKCS&level=1

Intermediate Appellate Court—Court of Civil Appeals

[1968–]: Oklahoma State Courts Network, "Oklahoma Cases," www.oscn.net/applications/oscn/index.asp?ftdb=STOKCS&level=1

Dockets/Court Records

Trial Courts

Oklahoma State Courts Network, "Dockets of Oklahoma Courts," www.oscn.net/applications/oscn/start.asp?viewType=DOCKETS

Legislative

State Legislative Process

Oklahoma State Legislature, "The Legislative Process Pages: The Course of Bills in Becoming Law," www.okhouse.gov/Information/CourseOfBills.aspx

Oklahoma State Legislature, "The Legislative Process Pages: Flow Charts" [diagram], www.okhouse.gov/Information/FlowCharts.aspx

Statutes

By Subject (Code)—Oklahoma Statutes

Oklahoma State Courts Network, "Oklahoma Statutes Citationized," www.oscn.net/applications/oscn/index.asp?ftdb=STOKST&level=1

Oklahoma State Legislature, "Oklahoma Statutes," www.oklegislature.gov/osStatuesTitle.aspx [sic]

Oklahoma State Legislature, "Oklahoma Text Search and Retrieval System: Search Oklahoma Statutes Database," www.oklegislature.gov/tsrs_os_oc.aspx

In Chronological Order (Session Laws)—Oklahoma Session Laws

[1998–]: Oklahoma State Courts Network, "Oklahoma Session Laws," www.oscn.net/applications/oscn/index.asp?ftdb=STOKLG&year=2001&level=1

Legislative History

Research Guides

Oklahoma City University Law Library, "Library User Guide—State Legislative History," www.okcu.edu/law/lawlib/pdfs/guide_statelh.pdf

Oklahoma State Legislature, "The Legislative Process Pages: Researching Legislation Topics In Oklahoma," www.okhouse.gov/Information/ResearchingLegislation.aspx

Executive

Directory of State Departments/Agencies

OK.gov, "Agencies," www.ok.gov/agency.php

State Rulemaking Process

USLegal, "Administrative Procedure Act— Oklahoma," http://administrativelaw.uslegal.com/administrative-procedure-acts/oklahoma/

Regulations

Research Guide

Oklahoma City University School of Law, "Administrative Law," http://law.okcu.libguides.com/content.php?pid=114399

By Agency (Code)—
Oklahoma Administrative Code

Oklahoma Secretary of State, "View Code," https://www.sos.ok.gov/oar/online/viewCode.aspx

Oklahoma Secretary of State, "Search the Code," https://www.sos.ok.gov/oar/online/searchCode.aspx

In Chronological Order (Register)—
Oklahoma Register

[2001–]: Oklahoma Secretary of State, "View Registers," https://www.sos.ok.gov/oar/online/viewRegisters.aspx

[2001–]: Oklahoma Secretary of State, "Search Registers," https://www.sos.ok.gov/oar/online/searchRegisters.aspx

Administrative Rulings

University of Oklahoma College of Law, "Oklahoma Public Legal Research System," http://oklegal.onenet.net/ok.agency.decisions.basic.html

Local Laws

Directories of State Counties/Municipalities

State and Local Government on the Net, "Oklahoma State and Local Government," www.statelocalgov.net/state-ok.cfm

Oklahoma Municipal League, "City Links," http://okml.webs.com/apps/links/

Ordinances

Municode Code Corporation, "Oklahoma," www.municode.com/library/OK

Coded Systems LLC, "Oklahoma," www.codedsystems.com/codelibrary/oklahoma.html

Practice Materials and Self-Help Resources

Research Guide

Pro Bono Net, OKLaw.org, http://oklaw.org

Court Rules

Oklahoma State Courts Network, "Oklahoma Court Rules," www.oscn.net/applications/oscn/index.asp?ftdb=STOKRU&level=1

Forms

Research Guide

University of Tulsa, Mabee Legal Information Center, "Legal Forms," http://mlic.utulsa.libguides.com/forms

All Courts

Oklahoma State Courts Network, www.oscn.net/static/forms/

State Bar Association Consumer Brochures

Oklahoma Bar Association, "Consumer Legal Information," www.okbar.org/public/Brochures.asp

Court Brochures/Self-Help Centers

N/A

*Looking for an Attorney
(for a fee or for free)*

Legal Aid/Advocacy Groups/Pro Bono

Oklahoma Bar Association, "Legal Services,"
www.okbar.org/public/LegalServices.aspx

Finding an Attorney/Lawyer Referrals

Oklahoma Bar Association,
"OklahomaFindALawyer,"
www.oklahomafindalawyer.com/FindALawyer

Miscellaneous

Oklahoma State Courts Network, "Uniform Jury
Instructions," www.oscn.net/applications/oscn/
index.asp?ftdb=STOKJU&level=1

Reference

Oklahoma State Legislature, "The Legislative
Process Pages: Glossary of Legislative Terms,"
www.okhouse.gov/Information/GlossaryOfTerms
.aspx

OREGON

Research Guides

AALL LISP, "Public Library Toolkit: Oregon,"
www.aallnet.org/sections/lisp/Public-Library-Toolkit
Lewis and Clark Law School, Paul L. Boley Law
Library, "Oregon Legal Research,"
http://lawlib.lclark.edu/research/oregonlaw/
Willamette University College of Law, J. W. Long
Law Library, "Oregon Law," http://willamette
.edu/wucl/longlib/oregon_law/

Judicial

State Court Structure

Oregon Judicial Department, "An Introduction
to the Courts of Oregon," http://courts.oregon
.gov/OJD/aboutus/courtsintro/
Westlaw, "Oregon Court Structure" [diagram],
http://wlwatch.westlaw.com/aca/west/statecrtorg
.htm#OR

Directory of State Courts

Oregon Judicial Department, "Trial Court
Locations," www.ojd.state.or.us/sca/ojdrefdir.nsf/
Trial%2BCourt%2BLocations

Opinions

Highest Court—Supreme Court

[1998–]: Oregon Judicial Department, "Supreme
Court Opinions," www.publications.ojd.state
.or.us/Pages/OpinionsSC.aspx

Intermediate Appellate Court—Court of Appeals

[1998–]: Oregon Judicial Department, "Court of
Appeals Opinions," www.publications.ojd.state
.or.us/Pages/OpinionsCOA.aspx

Dockets/Court Records

Trial Courts

Oregon Judicial Department, Oregon Judicial
Information Network (OJIN) Case Tracking
System [fee-based, command-based],
http://courts.oregon.gov/OJD/OnlineServices/OJIN/
getstarted.page

Legislative

State Legislative Process

Oregon State Legislature, "How an Idea Becomes
a Law," www.leg.state.or.us/process.html
Oregon State Legislature, "How an Idea
Becomes a Law: A simple View of the Oregon
Legislative Process" [diagram], www.leg.state
.or.us/faq/lawprocs.pdf

Statutes

Research Guide

Willamette University College of Law, J. W. Long
Law Library, "Oregon Revised Statutes,"
www.willamette.edu/wucl/longlib/oregon_rev
_stat.html

By Subject (Code)—Oregon Revised Statutes

Oregon State Legislature, "Oregon Revised
Statutes," www.leg.state.or.us/ors/home.htm

In Chronological Order (Session Laws)—
Oregon Laws

[1999–]: Oregon State Legislature, "Bills and Laws," www.leg.state.or.us/bills_laws/

Legislative History

Research Guides

University of Oregon, John E. Jaqua Law Library, "Researching Oregon Legislative History—About" and "Researching Oregon Legislative History—Steps," http://library .uoregon.edu/law/libraryguides.html

Lewis and Clark Law School, Paul L. Boley Law Library, "Oregon Legislative History," http://lawlib.lclark.edu/research/orleghistory8.pdf

Oregon Secretary of State, Oregon State Archives, "Oregon Legislative Records Guide," http://arcweb.sos.state.or.us/pages/ records/legislative/recordsguides/legislative_guide/ legal.html

Willamette University College of Law, J. W. Long Law Library, "Oregon Legislative Records," www.willamette.edu/wucl/longlib/oregon_legis _records.html

Executive

Directory of State Departments/Agencies

Oregon.gov, Department of Administrative Services, "State Agency Directory," http://dasapp.oregon.gov/statephonebook/

State Rulemaking Process

Oregon Secretary of State, Oregon State Archives, "Permanent Rulemaking Overview / Temporary Rulemaking Overview," http://arcweb.sos.state.or.us/doc/rules/RuleFile _Overviews.pdf

Regulations

Research Guide

Willamette University College of Law, J. W. Long Law Library, "Oregon Administrative Rules," www.willamette.edu/wucl/longlib/oregon_admin _rules.html

By Agency (Code)—Oregon Administrative Rules

Oregon Secretary of State, "Oregon Administrative Rules," http://arcweb.sos.state .or.us/banners/rules.htm

In Chronological Order (Register)—
Oregon Bulletin

[past few years]: Oregon Secretary of State, Oregon State Archives, "Oregon Bulletin," http://arcweb.sos.state.or.us/pages/rules/bulletin/

Local Laws

Directories of State Counties/Municipalities

Oregon Secretary of State, Oregon Blue Book, "County Government," http://bluebook.state .or.us/local/counties/counties.htm

Oregon Secretary of State, Oregon Blue Book, "City Government," http://bluebook.state.or.us/ local/cities/citieshome.htm

Ordinances

Willamette University College of Law, J. W. Long Law Library, "Oregon Counties," http:// willamette.edu/wucl/longlib/oregon_law/categories/ counties.html

Municode Code Corporation, "Oregon," www.municode.com/library/OR

Practice Materials and Self-Help Resources

Research Guides

University of Oregon, John E. Jaqua Law Library, "Oregon Practice Material," http:// library.uoregon.edu/sites/default/files/data/law/ orpractice-06.pdf

Willamette University College of Law, J. W. Long Law Library, "Oregon Forms," www.willamette .edu/wucl/longlib/oregon_forms.html

Court Rules

Research Guide

Willamette University College of Law, J. W. Long Law Library, "Oregon Court Rules," www .willamette.edu/wucl/longlib/oregon_court_rules .html

All Courts

Oregon Judicial Department, "Rules,"
www.ojd.state.or.us/Web/OJDPublications.nsf/Rules

Forms

Oregon Judicial Department, "Appellate Court
Forms," http://courts.oregon.gov/OJD/OSCA/acs/
records/AppellateCourtForms.page

Oregon Judicial Department, "Optional
Statewide Family Law Forms," http://courts
.oregon.gov/OJD/OSCA/cpsd/courtimprovement/
familylaw/familylawforms.page

State Bar Association Consumer Brochures

Oregon State Bar, "Legal Information Topics,"
www.osbar.org/public/legalinfo.html

Court Brochures/Self-Help Centers

Oregon Judicial Department, "Family Law
Resources," http://courts.oregon.gov/OJD/OSCA/
cpsd/courtimprovement/familylaw/AddResources
.page

*Looking for an Attorney
(for a fee or for free)*

Legal Aid/Advocacy Groups/Pro Bono

University of Oregon, John E. Jaqua Law
Library, "Law-Related Community Services,"
http://library.uoregon.edu/sites/default/files/data/
law/commlegalservices-10.pdf

Finding an Attorney/Lawyer Referrals

Oregon State Bar, "Hiring a Lawyer,"
www.osbar.org/public/ris/ris.html

Miscellaneous

Willamette University College of Law,
Willamette Law Online, "Oregon Court of
Appeals Updates" [recent case summaries],
www.willamette.edu/wucl/resources/journals/wlo/
orappeals/

References

Oregon State Capitol, Legislative Glossary,"
www.leg.state.or.us/glossary.html

Oregon Judicial Department, "The Oregon
eCourt Glossary," http://courts.oregon.gov/
oregonecourt/pages/orecourtglossary.aspx

Oregon Judicial Department, "Family Law: Legal
Terms and Definitions," http://courts.oregon
.gov/OJD/docs/OSCA/cpsd/courtimprovement/
familylaw/Terms.pdf

PENNSYLVANIA

Research Guides

University of Pittsburgh School of Law,
"Pennsylvania Legal Research,"
www.law.pitt.edu/library/PAresearch

Jenkins Law Library, "Pennsylvania Legal
Research—Getting Started," www.jenkinslaw
.org/research/resource-guides/pennsylvania-legal
-research-getting-started

Dittakavi Rao, "Pennsylvania Legal Research
Web Sites," www.pennsylvanialegalresearch.com

Judicial

State Court Structure

Unified Judicial System of Pennsylvania,
"Learn" [interactive diagram],
www.pacourts.us/learn

Directory of State Courts

Unified Judicial System of Pennsylvania,
"Courts," www.pacourts.us/courts/

Opinions

Highest Court—Supreme Court

[1996–]: Unified Judicial System of
Pennsylvania, "Court Opinions and Postings,"
www.pacourts.us/courts/supreme-court/
court-opinions/

Intermediate Appellate Court—Superior Court

[1997–]: Unified Judicial System of
Pennsylvania,"Court Opinions," www.pacourts
.us/courts/ superior-court/court-opinions/

Intermediate Appellate Court—
Commonwealth Court

[1997–]: Unified Judicial System of Pennsylvania, "Court Opinions and Postings," www.pacourts.us/courts/commonwealth-court/court-opinions/

Dockets/Court Records

Appellate Courts

Unified Judicial System of Pennsylvania Web Portal, "Appellate Courts Docket Sheets," http://ujsportal.pacourts.us/DocketSheets/Appellate.aspx

Trial Courts

Unified Judicial System of Pennsylvania Web Portal, "Common Pleas Courts Docket Sheets," http://ujsportal.pacourts.us/DocketSheets/CP.aspx

Legislative

State Legislative Process

Pennsylvania Legislative Services, "How a Bill Becomes a Law in Pennsylvania," www.wschamber.org/legislative/howabillbecomesalaw.pdf

Statutes

By Subject (Code)—
Consolidated Statutes of Pennsylvania

Westlaw, "Unofficial Purdon's Pennsylvania Statutes from West," http://government.westlaw.com/linkedslice/default.asp?SP=pac-1000

In Chronological Order (Session Laws)—
Pennsylvania Session Laws

Pennsylvania Legislative Reference Bureau, "Pennsylvania Session Laws," www.palrb.us

Legislative History

Research Guides

Jenkins Law Library, "Pennsylvania Legislative History—A How To Guide," www.jenkinslaw.org/research/resource-guides/pennsylvania-legislative-history-how-guide

Widener Law, "Pennsylvania Legal Resources: Compiling a Pennsylvania Legislative History," http://libguides.law.widener.edu/content.php?pid=159023&sid=2262881

Executive

Directory of State Departments/Agencies

Commonwealth of Pennsylvania, Enterprise Portal, "Other State Agencies," www.portal.state.pa.us/portal/server.pt/community/enterprise_portal_information/212

State Rulemaking Process

USLegal, "Administrative Procedure Act—Pennsylvania," http://administrativelaw.uslegal.com/administrative-procedure-acts/pennsylvania/

Regulations

By Agency (Code)—Pennsylvania Code

Pennsylvania Legislative Reference Bureau, "The Pennsylvania Code," www.pacode.com/about/about.html

In Chronological Order (Register)—
Pennsylvania Bulletin

[1996–]: Pennsylvania Legislative Reference Bureau, "The Pennsylvania Bulletin," www.pabulletin.com/secure/search.html

Local Laws

Directories of State Counties/Municipalities

National Association of Counties, "Find a County," www.naco.org/Counties/Pages/FindACounty.aspx

Governor's Center for Local Government Services, "Pennsylvania's Local Governments' Websites," http://sites.state.pa.us/govlocal.html

Ordinances

General Code, "Pennsylvania eCode360 Library," www.generalcode.com/ecode360/PA

Municode Code Corporation, "Pennsylvania," www.municode.com/library/PA

Practice Materials and Self-Help Resources

Research Guide

Jenkins Law Library, "Research Links: Self-Help," www.jenkinslaw.org/research/resource-guides/research-links?active_tab =299540

Court Rules

Unified Judicial System of Pennsylvania Web Portal, "Rules of Court Selection," http://ujsportal.pacourts.us/LocalRules/RuleSelection.aspx

Forms

Unified Judicial System of Pennsylvania, "Forms," www.pacourts.us/Forms/

State Bar Association Consumer Brochures

Philadelphia Bar Association, Probate and Trust Law Section, "Philadelphia Estate Practitioner Handbook," www.peph.com

Court Brochures/Self-Help Centers

Unified Judicial System of Pennsylvania, "FAQs," www.pacourts.us/learn/faqs

Looking for an Attorney (for a fee or for free)

Legal Aid/Advocacy Groups/Pro Bono

Philadelphia Bar Association, "Directory of Public Interest Legal Organizations," www.philadelphiabar.org/page/DirectoryOfPublic InterestAgencies

Finding an Attorney/Lawyer Referrals

Philadelphia Bar Association, "Lawyer Referral and Information Service," www.philadelphiabarlawyers.com

Miscellaneous

Pennsylvania Department of Education, "Library Directory" [select "Category: Law Library"], www.libdir.ed.state.pa.us/screens/wfLibrarySearch .aspx

Reference

Unified Judicial System of Pennsylvania, "Legal Glossary," www.pacourts.us/learn/legal-glossary

RHODE ISLAND

Research Guides

University of Rhode Island, University Libraries User Guides, "Rhode Island Legal Sources," www.uri.edu/library/guides/subject/govlaw/rilegal.html

Library of Congress, Guide to Law Online, "Rhode Island," www.loc.gov/law/help/guide/states/us-ri.php

Judicial

State Court Structure

Rhode Island Judiciary, "Rhode Island Court Structure" [diagram], www.courts.ri.gov/pdf/Court_Structure.pdf

Directory of State Courts

Rhode Island Judiciary, "Divisions and Contact Numbers," www.courts.ri.gov/Courts/districtcourt/PDF/District-HomeDivisonsandContacts.pdf

Opinions

Highest Court—Supreme Court

[1999–]: Rhode Island Judiciary, Supreme Court, "Opinions and Orders Issued in Supreme Court Cases," www.courts.ri.gov/Courts/SupremeCourt/Pages/Opinions%20and%20Orders%20Issued%20in%20Supreme%20Court%20Cases.aspx

Intermediate Appellate Court—None

General Trial Court—Superior Court

[2000–]: Rhode Island Judiciary, Superior Court, "Decisions," www.courts.ri.gov/Courts/SuperiorCourt/Pages/Decisions.aspx

Dockets/Court Records

Supreme Court

Rhode Island Judiciary, "Supreme Court Case Docket Search," http://rijrs.courts.ri.gov/rijrs/case.do

Trial Courts

N/A

Legislative

State Legislative Process

Rhode Island General Assembly, "How a Bill Becomes Law," http://webserver.rilin.state.ri.us/legislation/GenMisc/genbilaw.html

Statutes

By Subject (Code)—
State of Rhode Island General Laws

Rhode Island General Assembly, "State of Rhode Island General Laws," http://webserver.rilin.state.ri.us/Statutes/

Rhode Island General Assembly, "Search the Rhode Island General Assembly Website," http://webserver.rilin.state.ri.us/search/search.asp?SearchWhere=/Statutes/

In Chronological Order (Session Laws)—
Public Laws

[1994–]: Rhode Island General Assembly, "Legislation," http://webserver.rilin.state.ri.us/Legislation/

Legislative History

Research Guide

University of Rhode Island, University Libraries Research Guides, "Rhode Island Legal Sources," www.uri.edu/library/guides/subject/govlaw/rilegal.html

Executive

Directory of State Departments/Agencies

RI.gov, "Top Agencies A–Z," www.ri.gov/guide/

State Rulemaking Process

USLegal, "Administrative Procedure Act— Rhode Islands [sic]," http://administrativelaw.uslegal.com/administrative-procedure-acts/rhode-islands/ [sic]

Regulations

By Agency (Code)—Code of Rhode Island Rules

Rhode Island Secretary of State, "Final Rules and Regulations Database Search," http://sos.ri.gov/rules/

In Chronological Order (Register)—
Rhode Island Government Register

N/A

Local Laws

Directory of State Counties/Municipalities

Rhode Island Office of Library and Information Services, "Cities & Towns," www.info.ri.gov/browse.php?choice=show_area&ID_mcat=15

Ordinances

Rhode Island Office of Library and Information Services, "Cities & Towns: Ordinances," www.info.ri.gov/browse.php?choice=show_area&ID_mcat=15

Municode Code Corporation, "Rhode Island," www.municode.com/library/RI

Practice Materials and Self-Help Resources

Research Guide

Suffolk University School of Law, "Rhode Island Practice Guide," www.law.suffolk.edu/library/research/a-z/resguides/riguide.cfm

Court Rules

Rhode Island Judiciary, "Supreme Court Rules," www.courts.ri.gov/Courts/SupremeCourt/Pages/Supreme%20Court%20Rules.aspx

USLegal, "Rhode Island Rules of Civil Procedure," http://civilprocedure.uslegal.com/rules-of-civil-procedure/state-rules-of-civil-procedure/rhode-island-rules-of-civil-procedure/

Forms

Rhode Island Judiciary, "Forms,"
www.courts.ri.gov/publicresources/forms/

State Bar Association Consumer Brochures

Rhode Island Bar Association, "Information
on Common Areas of the Law,"
https://www.ribar.com/For%20the%20Public/
InformationOnCommonAreasOfTheLaw.aspx

Court Brochures/Self-Help Centers

Rhode Island Judiciary, "Self-Help Center,"
www.courts.ri.gov/Self%20Help%20Center/

*Looking for an Attorney
(for a fee or for free)*

Legal Aid/Advocacy Groups/Pro Bono

Rhode Island Bar Association, "Community
Resources, Agencies and Legal Links
Index," https://www.ribar.com/Directory/
CommunityResources.aspx

Finding an Attorney/Lawyer Referrals

Rhode Island Bar Association, "How to Choose
and Use a Lawyer," https://www.ribar.com/
For%20the%20Public/FindingAndChoosingALawyer
.aspx

Miscellaneous

Roger Williams University School of Law, "R.I.
Bar Journal Index"[1952–], http://law.rwu.edu/
library/research-resources/ri-bar-journal-index

References

Westlaw, "Glossary for Legal Research
Basics," http://lawschool.westlaw.com/shared/
marketinfodisplay.asp?code=RE&id=17&mainpage
=23&rtid=116&rtcode=re
Cornell University Law School, Legal
Information Institute, *Wex* [dictionary and
encyclopedia], www.law.cornell.edu/wex/

SOUTH CAROLINA

Research Guides

AALL LISP, "Public Library Toolkit: South
Carolina," www.aallnet.org/sections/lisp/
Public-Library-Toolkit
University of South Carolina School of Law,
Coleman Karesh Law Library, "Research
Guides & Web Resources," http://law.sc.edu/
library/research_aids/

Judicial

State Court Structure

South Carolina Judicial Department,
"The South Carolina Judicial System"
[includes diagram], www.judicial.state.sc.us/
summaryCourtBenchBook/HTML/GeneralA.htm

Directory of State Courts

South Carolina Judicial Department, "Circuit
Court Judges," www.judicial.state.sc.us/
circuitCourt/circuitMap.cfm

Opinions

Research Guide

University of South Carolina School of Law,
Coleman Karesh Law Library, "Circuit Riders
Outreach Program: Legal Research for Non-
Law Librarians: Manual 2011," chapter 6,
"Judicial Branch," www.law.sc.edu/library/
circuit_riders/manual/

Highest Court—Supreme Court

[1997–]: South Carolina Judicial Department,
"Supreme Court Published Opinions,"
www.judicial.state.sc.us/opinions/indexSCPub.cfm
[1997–]: South Carolina Judicial Department,
"Search Opinions," www.judicial.state.sc.us/
opinions/searchOpinion.cfm

Intermediate Appellate Court—Court of Appeals

[1997–]: South Carolina Judicial Department,
"Court of Appeals Published Opinions,"
www.judicial.state.sc.us/opinions/indexCOAPub.cfm
[1997–]: South Carolina Judicial Department,
"Search Opinions," www.judicial.state.sc.us/
opinions/searchOpinion.cfm

Dockets/Court Records

Trial Courts

South Carolina Judicial Department, "Case Records Search," www.judicial.state.sc.us/caseSearch/

Legislative

State Legislative Process

South Carolina Legislature, "Publications: South Carolina's Legislative Process," www.scstatehouse.gov/publications.php

Statutes

Research Guide

University of South Carolina School of Law, Coleman Karesh Law Library, "Circuit Riders Outreach Program: Legal Research for Non-Law Librarians: Manual 2011," chapter 4, "Legislative Branch," www.law.sc.edu/library/circuit_riders/manual/

By Subject (Code)—
Code of Laws of South Carolina

South Carolina Legislature, "South Carolina Code of Laws," www.scstatehouse.gov/code/statmast.php
[2000–2009]: South Carolina Legislature, "1976 South Carolina Code of Laws—Previous Versions," www.scstatehouse.gov/archives/CodeOfLaws.php

In Chronological Order (Session Laws)—
South Carolina Acts and Joint Resolutions

[1980–]: South Carolina Legislature, "Acts Archives," www.scstatehouse.gov/aacts.php

Legislative History

Research Guide

Charlotte School of Law, "South Carolina Legislative History: A Research Guide," www.charlottelaw.org/downloads/lawlibrary/research/SC%20leg%20hist.pdf

Executive

Directory of State Departments/Agencies

SC.gov, "Agency Listing," www.sc.gov/Pages/OrgList.aspx

State Rulemaking Process

USLegal, "Administrative Procedure Act—South Carolina," http://administrativelaw.uslegal.com/administrative-procedure-acts/south-carolina/

Regulations

Research Guide

University of South Carolina School of Law, Coleman Karesh Law Library, "Circuit Riders Outreach Program: Legal Research for Non-Law Librarians: Manual 2011," chapter 5, "Executive Branch," www.law.sc.edu/library/circuit_riders/manual/

By Agency (Code)—
South Carolina Code of Regulations

South Carolina Legislature, "South Carolina Code of Regulations," www.scstatehouse.gov/coderegs/statmast.php

In Chronological Order (Register)—
South Carolina State Register

[1999–]: South Carolina Legislature, "Sate Register," www.scstatehouse.gov/state_register.php

Local Laws

Directories of State Counties/Municipalities

South Carolina State Library, "S.C. Counties," www.statelibrary.sc.gov/sc-counties
South Carolina State Library, "S.C. Cities," www.statelibrary.sc.gov/sc-cities

Ordinances

Municode Code Corporation, "South Carolina," www.municode.com/library/SC

Practice Materials and Self-Help Resources

Research Guide

University of South Carolina, School of Law, "South Carolina Legal Resources—A Selected Bibliography," http://law.sc.edu/library/research_aids/tutorials/sc_legal_bibliography.pdf

Court Rules

South Carolina Judicial Department, "Court Register—Table of Contents," www.sccourts.org/courtReg/

Forms

South Carolina Judicial Department, "Court Forms," www.judicial.state.sc.us/forms/

State Bar Association Consumer Brochures

South Carolina Bar, "Public Services," www.scbar.org/PublicServices.aspx

Court Brochures/Self-Help Centers

South Carolina Judicial Department, "Self Help Resources," www.judicial.state.sc.us/selfHelp/

South Carolina Judicial Department, "Self-Represented Litigant Simple Divorce Packets," www.judicial.state.sc.us/forms/indexSRLdivorcepacket.cfm

Looking for an Attorney (for a fee or for free)

Legal Aid/Advocacy Groups/Pro Bono

South Carolina Legal Services, www.sclegal.org

South Carolina Bar, "Free Legal Clinics," www.scbar.org/PublicServices/FreeLegalClinics.aspx

Finding an Attorney/Lawyer Referrals

South Carolina Bar, "Find a Lawyer," www.scbar.org/PublicServices/FindaLawyer.aspx

Miscellaneous

University of South Carolina School of Law, Coleman Karesh Law Library, "Circuit Riders Outreach Program: Legal Research for Non-Law Librarians: Manual 2011," chapter 3,

"Secondary Sources," www.law.sc.edu/library/circuit_riders/manual/

South Carolina Appleseed Legal Justice Center, "Brochures," http://scjustice.org/brochures-and-manuals/

University of South Carolina Children's Law Center, "Legal Resources," http://childlaw.sc.edu/LegalResource.shtml

South Carolina Family Law Blog, "Category Archives: Procedure," www.scfamilylaw.com/articles/procedure/

Reference

University of South Carolina School of Law, Coleman Karesh Law Library, "Circuit Riders Outreach Program: Legal Research for Non-Law Librarians: Manual 2011," chapter 7, "What the Heck Is That? Deciphering Legal Citations," www.law.sc.edu/library/circuit_riders/manual/

SOUTH DAKOTA

Research Guide

University of South Dakota, "Legal Research: South Dakota Law," http://libguides.usd.edu/content.php?pid=154079&sid=1306266

Judicial

State Court Structure

South Dakota Unified Judicial System, "Court Information," www.sdjudicial.com/courtinfo/

Court Statistics Project, "South Dakota" [diagram], www.courtstatistics.org/Other-Pages/State_Court_Structure_Charts/South-Dakota.aspx

Directory of State Courts

South Dakota Unified Judicial System, "Circuit Court," www.sdjudicial.com/cc/circuithome.aspx

Opinions

Highest Court—Supreme Court

[1996–]: South Dakota Unified Judicial System, "Supreme Court Opinions," www.sdjudicial.com/sc/scopinions.aspx

Intermediate Appellate Court—None

Dockets/Court Records

Trial Courts

South Dakota Unified Judicial System,
"Record Search," www.sdjudicial.com/courtinfo/
cricivrecords.aspx

Legislative

State Legislative Process

South Dakota Legislative Research Council,
"2004 Guide to the Legislature: How a Bill
Becomes a Law" [includes diagram],
http://legis.state.sd.us/General/guide.htm#HowBill

Statutes

By Subject (Code)—South Dakota Codified Laws

South Dakota Legislature, "South Dakota
Codified Laws—Title List," http://legis.state
.sd.us/statutes/TitleList.aspx

South Dakota Legislature, "South Dakota
Codified Laws—Text Search," http://legis.state
.sd.us/statutes/StatutesTextSearch.aspx

In Chronological Order (Session Laws)—
Session Laws

[1997–]: South Dakota Legislature, "Session
Laws," http://legis.state.sd.us/SessionLaws.aspx

Legislative History

Research Guide

South Dakota Legislative Research Council,
"How to Compile Legislative History Using
the Legislative Research Council Web Site,"
http://legis.state.sd.us/general/leghist.htm

Executive

Directory of State Departments/Agencies

SD.gov, "Government,"
http://sd.gov/government.aspx

State Rulemaking Process

USLegal, "Administrative Procedure Act—South
Dakota," http://administrativelaw.uslegal.com/
administrative-procedure-acts/south-dakota/

Regulations

By Agency (Code)—
Administrative Rules of South Dakota

South Dakota Legislature, "Administrative Rules
List," http://legis.state.sd.us/rules/RulesList.aspx

South Dakota Legislature, "Administrative
Rules Text Search," http://legis.state.sd.us/rules/
TextSearch.aspx

In Chronological Order (Register)—Register

[1998–]: South Dakota Legislature, "Register
Archive," http://legis.state.sd.us/rules/
RegisterArchive.aspx

Local Laws

Directories of State Counties/Municipalities

South Dakota Municipal League, "SD
Municipalities Online," www.sdmunicipalleague
.org/index.asp?Type=B_BASIC&SEC={D3F8855C
-992B-4DC8-A309-BC9246FBBD64}

South Dakota Association of County Officials,
"Interactive Map," www.sdcounties.org/counties/

Ordinances

Municode Code Corporation, "South Dakota,"
www.municode.com/library/SD

Practice Materials and Self-Help Resources

Research Guides

University of South Dakota, McKusick Law
Library, "LibGuides," http://libguides.law.usd.edu

Court Rules

South Dakota Unified Judicial System, "Supreme
Court Rules," www.sdjudicial.com/sc/scrules.aspx

Forms

South Dakota Unified Judicial System, "Forms,"
www.sdjudicial.com/forms/

State Bar Association Consumer Brochures

State Bar of South Dakota, "For the Public:
Publications," www.sdbar.org/new/public/
pubs.html

Court Brochures/Self-Help Centers

South Dakota Unified Judicial System, "Going
Solo: Representing Yourself in the South
Dakota Courts," www.sdjudicial.com/uploads/
forms/UJS%20300%20-%20A%20Guide%20for%20
Representing%20Yourself.pdf

Looking for an Attorney
(for a fee or for free)

Legal Aid/Advocacy Groups/Pro Bono

Help South Dakota, www.helpsouthdakota.com
South Dakota Department of Social Services,
"Legal Services for the Elderly,"
http://dss.sd.gov/formspubs/docs/ELDERLY/
LegalServicesforElderly.pdf
Legal Services Corporation, "LSC Programs:
South Dakota," www.lsc.gov/find-legal-aid

Finding an Attorney/Lawyer Referrals

State Bar of South Dakota, "Resource Guide,"
www.sdbar.org/resource.htm
State Bar of South Dakota, "Frequently Asked
Questions," www.sdbar.org/faq.htm

Miscellaneous

South Dakota State Historical Society,
"South Dakota Digital Archives," http://
sddigitalarchives.contentdm.oclc.org

Reference

South Dakota Legislative Research Council,
"2004 Guide to the Legislature: Glossary
of Legislative Terms," http://legis.state.sd.us/
General/guide.htm#Glossary

TENNESSEE
Research Guides
General

AALL LISP, "Public Library Toolkit: Tennessee,"
www.aallnet.org/sections/lisp/Public-Library-Toolkit
University of Tennessee Knoxville, Joel A. Katz
Law Library, "Tennessee Resources,"
http://law.utk.edu/law-library/research/tennessee
-resources/

Topical

University of Memphis, Cecil C. Humphreys
School of Law, "Family Law,"
http://libguides.law.memphis.edu/familylaw

Judicial
State Court Structure

Tennessee Supreme Court, Administrative Office
of the Courts, "Understanding Your Court
System: A Guide to the Judicial Branch"
[includes diagram], www.tncourts.gov/sites/
default/files/citizenbook-revised.pdf

Directory of State Courts

Tennessee State Courts, "Clerks," http://tncourts
.gov/courts/court-clerks/clerks-list

Opinions

Highest Court—Supreme Court

[1995–]: Tennessee State Courts, "Supreme
Court Opinions," www.tncourts.gov/courts/
supreme-court/opinions

Intermediate Appellate Court—Court of Appeals

[1995–]: Tennessee State Courts, "Court of
Appeals Opinions," www.tncourts.gov/courts/
court-appeals/opinions

Intermediate Appellate Court—
Court of Criminal Appeals

[1995–]: Tennessee State Courts, "Court of
Criminal Appeals Opinions," www.tncourts.gov/
courts/court-criminal-appeals/opinions

Dockets/Court Records

Appellate Courts

Tennessee State Courts, "Public Case History,"
www.tsc.state.tn.us/courts/supreme-court/
public-case-history

Trial Courts

N/A

Legislative

State Legislative Process

Tennessee General Assembly, "How a Bill
Becomes a Law," www.capitol.tn.gov/about/
billtolaw.html

Statutes

By Subject (Code)—Tennessee Code

LexisNexis, "Tennessee Code Unannotated,"
www.lexisnexis.com/hottopics/tncode/

In Chronological Order (Session Laws)—
Acts and Resolutions

[1997–]: Tennessee Secretary of State, "Acts and
Resolutions," http://tennessee.gov/sos/acts/

Legislative History

Research Guides

Tennessee Secretary of State, "Legal &
Legislative Materials Available @ the
Tennessee State Library & Archives,"
http://state.tn.us/tsla/history/guides/guide02.htm

University of Tennessee Knoxville, "State Law,
Legislation and Regulations: The Legislative
Process," http://libguides.utk.edu/content.php?pid
=78297&sid=579757

Executive

Directory of State Departments/Agencies

TN.gov, "Directory," www.tn.gov/directory/

State Rulemaking Process

Tennessee Department of State, "Rulemaking
Guidelines, Pursuant to Tennessee Code
Annotated, Title 4, Chapter 5," www.tn.gov/
sos/pub/RulemakingGuidelines.pdf

Regulations

By Agency (Code)—Rules and Regulations

Tennessee Secretary of State, "Effective Rule
Chapters," www.state.tn.us/sos/rules/rules2.htm

In Chronological Order (Register)—
Tennessee Administrative Register

[2000–2009]: Tennessee Secretary of State,
"Administrative Register," www.state.tn.us/
sos/pub/tar/

Local Laws

Directory of State Counties/Municipalities

TN.gov, "County and City Web Sites,"
www.tn.gov/local/

Ordinances

Municode Code Corporation, "Tennessee,"
www.municode.com/library/TN

Practice Materials and Self-Help Resources

Research Guides

University of Tennessee Knoxville, Joel A. Katz
Law Library, "LibGuides," http://law.utk.edu

Court Rules

Tennessee State Courts, "Court Rules,"
www.tsc.state.tn.us/courts/rules

Tennessee State Courts, "Proposed Rules &
Amendments," www.tncourts.gov/rules/proposed/

Tennessee State Courts, "Local Rules of
Practice," www.tsc.state.tn.us/courts/court-rules2/
local-rules-practice

Forms

Tennessee State Courts, "Court Forms,"
www.tncourts.gov/node/707185

State Bar Association Consumer Brochures

Chattanooga Bar Association, "For the Public," www.chattbar.org/www/docs/3

Knoxville Bar Association, "Consumer Legal Needs," www.knoxbar.org/index.php?option =com_content&view=article&id=157&Itemid=129

Memphis Bar Association, "Frequently Asked Legal Questions & Answers," http://memphisbar .org/displaycommon.cfm?an=1&subarticlenbr=79

Court Brochures/Self-Help Centers

Tennessee State Courts, "Self Help Center," http://tncourts.gov/programs/self-help-center

Looking for an Attorney (for a fee or for free)

Legal Aid/Advocacy Groups/Pro Bono

Memphis Bar Association, "Pro Bono," http://memphisbar.org/displaycommon.cfm?an =1&subarticlenbr=160

Legal Aid Society of Middle Tennessee and the Cumberlands, "Resources," www.las.org/resources

Finding an Attorney/Lawyer Referrals

Tennessee Bar Association, "Finding an Attorney," www.tba.org/info/find-an-attorney

Knoxville Bar Association, "The Lawyer Referral & Information Service," www.knoxbar.org/index.php?option=com _content&view=article&id=152&Itemid=124

Memphis Bar Association, "LEGALHELP. memphisbar.org," http://memphisbar.org/ displaycommon.cfm?an=1&subarticlenbr=74

Nashville Bar Association, Lawyer Referral and Information Service, www.nashvillelawyer referral.org

Miscellaneous

Tennessee Bar Association, "Tennessee Legal Organizations," www.tba.org/info/tennessee -legal-organizations

Reference

Tennessee General Assembly, "Glossary of Terms," www.capitol.tn.gov/about/glossary.html

TEXAS
Research Guides
General

AALL LISP, "Public Library Toolkit: Texas," www.aallnet.org/sections/lisp/Public-Library-Toolkit

University of Texas School of Law, Tarlton Law Library, "Texas Legal Research Web Resources," http://tarltonguides.law.utexas.edu/ texas-web-resources

Topical

Southern Methodist University, Dedman School of Law, "Child Support Laws in Texas," http://library.law.smu.edu/Research-Tools/Research -Guides/Texas-Law-%28300%29/354-Child-Support -Laws-in-Texas

Southern Methodist University, Dedman School of Law, "Small Claims Court—Texas," http://library.law.smu.edu/Research-Tools/Research -Guides/Texas-Law-%28300%29/307-Small-Claims -Court--Texas

Southern Methodist University, Dedman School of Law, "Divorce in Texas," http://library.law .smu.edu/Research-Tools/Research-Guides/Texas -Law-%28300%29/355-Divorce-in-Texas

University of Texas School of Law, Tarlton Law Library, "Texas Death Penalty Law," http://tarltonguides.law.utexas.edu/texas-death -penalty

University of Texas School of Law, Tarlton Law Library, "Insurance Law," http://tarltonguides .law.utexas.edu/insurance-law

University of Texas School of Law, Tarlton Law Library, "Family Law," http://tarltonguides.law .utexas.edu/family-law

University of Houston Law Center, O'Quinn Law Library, "Texas Legal Ethics," www.law.uh.edu/libraries/Publications/ ResearchGuides/TexasLegalEthics.htm

Judicial
State Court Structure

Texas Courts Online, "Court Structure of Texas" [interactive diagram], www.courts.state.tx.us

Directories of State Courts

Texas Courts Online, "Texas Judicial System Directory," www.courts.state.tx.us/pubs/JudDir.asp

Texas Courts Online, "Courts of Appeals," www.courts.state.tx.us/courts/coa.asp

Texas Courts Online, "District Courts' Website Links," www.courts.state.tx.us/courts/dclinks.asp

Opinions

Highest Court—Supreme Court

[1997–]: Supreme Court of Texas, "Orders & Opinions," www.supreme.courts.state.tx.us/historical/recent.asp

Highest Court—Court of Criminal Appeals

[2004–]: Texas Court of Criminal Appeals, "Opinion, Order or Statement Search," www.cca.courts.state.tx.us/opinions/opinionsearch.asp

[1998–2004]: Texas Court of Criminal Appeals, "Opinions—Archives," www.cca.courts.state.tx.us/archives/ophome.asp

Intermediate Appellate Court—Courts of Appeals

Texas Courts Online, "Courts of Appeals," www.courts.state.tx.us/courts/coa.asp

Dockets/Court Records

Trial Courts

TexasDockets.com, "Texas Online Court Dockets," www.texasdockets.com

Legislative

State Legislative Process

Texas Legislative Council, Guide to Texas Legislative Information, "Process for a Bill," www.tlc.state.tx.us/gtli/legproc/process.html

Texas Legislative Council, Guide to Texas Legislative Information, "Diagram for Legislative Process" [diagram], www.tlc.state.tx.us/gtli/legproc/diagram.html

Statutes

Research Guide

University of Texas School of Law, Tarlton Law Library, "Finding a Statute," http://tarltonguides.law.utexas.edu/find-statute

By Subject (Code)—Texas Code

Texas Constitution and Statutes, "Texas Statutes," www.statutes.legis.state.tx.us

Easy Law Lookup, "Search Law: Texas," www.easylawlookup.com

In Chronological Order (Session Laws)—Session Laws

[2003–]: Legislative Reference Library of Texas, "Sessions," www.lrl.state.tx.us/sessions/

[2003–]: Texas Laws and Resolutions Archive, http://texinfo.library.unt.edu/sessionlaws/browse.htm

Legislative History

Research Guides

Legislative Reference Library of Texas, "Guide to Researching Legislative History and Intent," www.lrl.state.tx.us/legis/legintent/legIntent.cfm

Southern Methodist University, Dedman School of Law, "Texas Legislative History," http://library.law.smu.edu/Research-Tools/Research-Guides/Texas-Law-%28300%29/302-Texas-Legislative-History

University of Texas School of Law, Tarlton Law Library, "Texas Legislative History Research," http://tarltonguides.law.utexas.edu/texas-legislative-history

University of Houston Law Center, O'Quinn Law Library, "Texas Legislative History Research," www.law.uh.edu/libraries/Publications/ResearchGuides/texasleghistory.htm

South Texas College of Law, Fred Parks Law Library, "Texas Legislative History Research," http://libguides.stcl.edu/TexasLegislativeHistory

Southern Methodist University, Dedman School of Law, "The Basics of Texas Superseded Statutory Research," http://library.law.smu.edu/Research-Tools/Research-Guides/Texas-Law-%28300%29/301-5-The-Basics-of-Texas-Superseded-Statutory-Res

Executive

Directory of State Departments/Agencies

Texas State Library and Archives Commission, "TRAIL List of Texas State Agencies," https://www.tsl.state.tx.us/apps/lrs/agencies/

State Rulemaking Process

USLegal, "Administrative Procedure Act—Texas," http://administrativelaw.uslegal.com/administrative-procedure-acts/texas/

Regulations

Research Guide

University of Texas School of Law, Tarlton Law Library, "Finding Texas Regulations," http://tarltonguides.law.utexas.edu/content.php?pid=89140&sid=663502

By Agency (Code)—Texas Administrative Code

[current]: Texas Secretary of State, "Texas Administrative Code," www.sos.state.tx.us/tac/
[1999–]: Texas Secretary of State, "Texas Administrative Code" [search], http://info.sos.state.tx.us/pls/pub/tacctx$.startup

In Chronological Order (Register)—Texas Register

[2000–]: Texas Secretary of State, "Texas Register Viewer" [search], http://info.sos.state.tx.us/pls/pub/regviewctx$.startup
[1976–]: Texas Secretary of State and University of North Texas Libraries, "Texas Register," http://texashistory.unt.edu/explore/collections/TR/

Local Laws

Directory of State Counties/Municipalities

State and Local Government on the Net, "Texas State and Local Government," www.statelocalgov.net/state-tx.cfm

Ordinances

Municode Code Corporation, "Texas," www.municode.com/library/TX

City of Dallas, "City of Dallas Codes," www.dallascityhall.com/html/codes.html

Practice Materials and Self-Help Resources

Research Guides

University of Texas School of Law, Tarlton Law Library, "Self-Help Materials," http://tarltonguides.law.utexas.edu/self-help
University of Texas School of Law, Tarlton Law Library, "Practice Guides and Form Books," http://tarltonguides.law.utexas.edu/content.php?pid=89282&sid=696934
South Texas College of Law, Fred Parks Law Library, "Bibliography of Electronic and Print Resources on Self Help Legal Materials," www.stcl.edu/library/SelfHelpLinks.html
Pro Bono Net, TexasLegalHelp.org, "Family Law," http://texaslawhelp.org/issues/family-law-and-domestic-violence
Pro Bono Net, TexasLegalHelp.org, "Probate Law," http://texaslawhelp.org/issues/wills-estates/probate-law

Court Rules

Texas Local Rules, www.texaslocalrules.com
Supreme Court of Texas, "Rules and Standards," www.supreme.courts.state.tx.us/rules/rules.asp

Forms

Texas Courts Online, "Publications, Forms and Online Information," www.courts.state.tx.us/pubs/pubs-home.asp

State Bar Association Consumer Brochures

State Bar of Texas, "For the Public: Free Legal Information," www.texasbar.com/AM/Template.cfm?Section=Free_Legal_Information
State Bar of Texas, Legal "Referral Directory for Low-Income Texans," www.texasbar.com/Content/NavigationMenu/ForThePublic/CantAffordaLawyer/

Court Brochures/Self-Help Centers

N/A

4

44

4444

Looking for an Attorney (for a fee or for free)

Legal Aid/Advocacy Groups/Pro Bono

University of Texas School of Law, Tarlton Law Library, "Attorney Referrals & Legal Aid," http://tarltonguides.law.utexas.edu/content.php?pid=118666&sid=1028061

Southern Methodist University, Dedman School of Law, "Legal Aid Societies," http://library.law.smu.edu/Research-Tools/Research-Guides/Legal-Directories/101-Legal-Aid-Societies

State Bar of Texas, "Can't Afford a Lawyer?" www.texasbar.com/AM/Template.cfm?Section=Can_t_Afford_a_Lawyer_

Houston Bar Association, "Resource & Referral Guide," www.hba.org/folder-services/pdfs/Resource-Referral-Guide.pdf

South Texas College of Law, "Library Guides Online: Pro Se Directory," www.stcl.edu/library/ProSeGuideOnline.html

Finding an Attorney/Lawyer Referrals

State Bar of Texas, "Do You Need a Lawyer?" www.texasbar.com/AM/Template.cfm?Section=Do_You_Need_a_Lawyer_

Miscellaneous

Southern Methodist University, Dedman School of Law, "Local Law Libraries," http://library.law.smu.edu/Research-Tools/Research-Guides/Legal-Directories/102-Local-Law-Libraries

University of Houston Law Center, People's Lawyer, "Legal Topics," www.peopleslawyer.net/legal-topics.html

Reference

Texas Legislative Council, Guide to Texas Legislative Information, "Glossary," www.tlc.state.tx.us/gtli/glossary/glossary.html

UTAH
Research Guides

AALL LISP, "Public Library Toolkit: Utah," www.aallnet.org/sections/lisp/Public-Library-Toolkit

Marsha C. Thomas and Jessica Van Buren, "Legal Research for Utah Public Libraries" (2007), http://pioneer.utah.gov/documents/libraryresearch.pdf

BYU, J. Reuben Clark Law School, Howard W. Hunter Law Library, "Utah Law," http://lawlibguides.byu.edu/utah

Utah State Courts, "Utah Legal Research," www.utcourts.gov/lawlibrary/research/utah.asp

Judicial

State Court Structure

Utah Department of Administrative Services, Division of Archives and Records Service, "Utah Court System," http://archives.utah.gov/research/guides/courts-system.htm

Court Statistics Project, "Utah" [diagram], www.courtstatistics.org/Other-Pages/State_Court_Structure_Charts/Utah.aspx

Directory of State Courts

Utah State Courts, "Utah State Court Directory," www.utcourts.gov/directory/

Opinions

Highest Court—Supreme Court

[1996–]: "Supreme Court Opinions," www.utcourts.gov/opinions/

Intermediate Appellate Court—Court of Appeals

[1997–]: "Court of Appeals Opinions," www.utcourts.gov/opinions/

Dockets/Court Records

Appellate Courts

Utah State Courts, "Appellate Docket Search," www.utcourts.gov/courts/appell/appellatesearch.htm

Trial Courts

Utah State Courts, "XChange Case Search: Repository of Court Records" [fee-based], www.utcourts.gov/xchange/

Legislative

State Legislative Process

Utah State Legislature, "How Ideas Become Bills, Then Law," http://le.utah.gov/documents/aboutthelegislature/billtolaw.htm

Statutes

By Subject (Code)—Utah Code

Utah State Legislature, "Utah Code," http://le.utah.gov/UtahCode/title.jsp

In Chronological Order (Session Laws)— Laws of Utah

[1998–]: Utah State Legislature, "Passed Bills," http://le.utah.gov/asp/passedbills/passedbills.asp?session=1998GS

Legislative History

Research Guides

Utah Department of Administrative Services, Division of Archives and Records Service, "Legislative Intent and Legislative History," http://archives.utah.gov/research/guides/legislative-history.htm

Utah State Law Library, "Utah Legislative History Resources," www.utcourts.gov/lawlibrary/docs/legislative_website.pdf

Utah State Bar, "Utah Legislative History Research Tips," http://webster.utahbar.org/barjournal/2008/11/utah_legislative_history_resea.html

Executive

Directory of State Departments/Agencies

Utah.gov, "State Agencies," www.utah.gov/government/agencylist.html

State Rulemaking Process

Utah Department of Administrative Services, Division of Administrative Rules, "Utah Administrative Rulemaking Process," www.rules.utah.gov/abtprocess.htm

Utah Division of Administrative Rules, "Utah Administrative Rulemaking Process" [diagram], www.rules.utah.gov/agencyresources/rulemakingprocess.pdf

Regulations

Research Guides

Utah Department of Administrative Services, Division of Archives and Records Service, "How to Research Administrative Rules," http://archives.utah.gov/research/guides/admin-rules.htm

Utah State Bar, "Researching Utah Administrative Law," http://webster.utahbar.org/barjournal/2009/03/researching_utah_administrative_law.html

By Agency (Code)—Utah Administrative Code

Utah Department of Administrative Services, Division of Administrative Rules, "Utah Administrative Code," www.rules.utah.gov/publicat/code.htm

In Chronological Order (Register)— Utah State Bulletin

[1996–]: Utah Department of Administrative Services, Division of Administrative Rules, "Utah State Bulletin," www.rules.utah.gov/publicat/bulletin.htm

Local Laws

Directory of State Counties/Municipalities

Utah.gov, "Utah City & County Government," www.utah.gov/government/citycounty.html

Utah.gov, Pioneer, "Utah Counties," http://pioneer.utah.gov/research/utah_counties/

Ordinances

University of Utah, S. J. Quinney College of Law, "Utah Law," www.law.utah.edu/library/utah-law/

Municipal Codes

BYU, J. Reuben Clark Law School, Howard W. Hunter Law Library, "Utah City Codes Online A–L," http://lawlibguides.byu.edu/content.php?pid=99171&sid=1286293

BYU, J. Reuben Clark Law School, Howard W. Hunter Law Library, "Utah City Codes Online M–Z," http://lawlibguides.byu.edu/content.php?pid=99171&sid=1286477

County Codes

BYU, J. Reuben Clark Law School, Howard W. Hunter Law Library, "Utah County Codes Online," http://lawlibguides.byu.edu/content.php?pid=99171&sid=1284058

Practice Materials and Self-Help Resources

Research Guides

Dixie State University Library, "Utah Legal Resources Online," http://libguides.dixie.edu/legal

University of Utah, S. J. Quinney College of Law, "Utah Law: Represent Yourself in Court," www.law.utah.edu/library/utah-law/

Court Rules

Utah State Courts, "Utah State Court Rules," www.utcourts.gov/resources/rules/

Forms

Utah State Courts, "Court Forms and Instructions," www.utcourts.gov/resources/forms/

State Bar Association Consumer Brochures

Utah State Bar, "Public Services," www.utahbar.org/public-services/

Court Brochures/Self-Help Centers

Utah State Courts, "Self-Help Resources / Self-Represented Parties," www.utcourts.govselfhelp/

Looking for an Attorney (for a fee or for free)

Legal Aid/Advocacy Groups/Pro Bono

Utah State Bar, "Find a Utah Lawyer," https://utahbar.org/LRS/Welcome.html

Utah State Courts, "Legal Clinics, Agencies & Organizations," www.utcourts.gov/howto/legalclinics/

University of Utah, S. J. Quinney College of Law, "Free Legal Clinics," www.law.utah.edu/probono/free-legal-clinics/

Finding an Attorney/Lawyer Referrals

Utah Bar, LegalMatch, http://utahbar.legalmatch.com

Miscellaneous

Utah.gov, "Utah Government Publications Online," http://publications.utah.gov/search/

Utah Department of Administrative Services, Division of Administrative Rules, "Utah State Digest" [1994–], www.rules.utah.gov/publicat/digest.htm

Reference

Utah State Legislature, "Glossary of Legislative Terms," http://le.utah.gov/documents/aboutthelegislature/glossary.htm

VERMONT

Research Guide

AALL LISP, "Public Library Toolkit: Vermont," www.aallnet.org/sections/lisp/Public-Library-Toolkit

Judicial

State Court Structure

Court Statistics Project, "Vermont" [diagram], www.courtstatistics.org/Other-Pages/State_Court_Structure_Charts/Vermont.aspx

Directory of State Courts

Vermont Judiciary, "Court Information," www.vermontjudiciary.org/GTC/

Opinions

Highest Court—Supreme Court

[1986–]: Vermont Department of Libraries, "Supreme Court Decisions," http://libraries.vermont.gov/law/supct

Intermediate Appellate Court—None

Dockets/Court Records

Trial Courts

VTCourtsOnline [fee-based], https://secure.vermont.gov/vtcdas/user

Legislative

State Legislative Process

Vermont State Legislature, "The Legislative Process," www.leg.state.vt.us/FieldTrip/TheLegislativeProcess.htm

Statutes

By Subject (Code)—Vermont Statutes

Vermont State Legislature, "Vermont Statutes Online," www.leg.state.vt.us/statutesMain.cfm

LexisNexis, "Vermont Statutes Unannotated and Vermont Court Rules," www.lexisnexis.com/hottopics/vtstatutesconstctrules/

In Chronological Order (Session Laws)— Public Acts

[1985–]: Vermont State House, "Legislative Research," www.leg.state.vt.us/researchmain.cfm

Legislative History

Research Guide

Paul Joseph Donovan, "Legislative History— Variations on a Theme," www.pauljdonovan.us/law/leghistvt.html

Executive

Directory of State Departments/Agencies

Vermont.gov, "State Government," www.vermont.gov/portal/government/atoz.php

State Rulemaking Process

Vermont Office of the Secretary of State, "Rule on Rulemaking," www.vermont-archives.org/aparules/rulemaking.htm

Regulations

By Agency (Code)—Code of Vermont Rules

LexisNexis, "Code of Vermont Rules," www.lexisnexis.com/hottopics/codeofvtrules/

In Chronological Order (Register)— Vermont Government Register

N/A

Local Laws

Directory of State Counties/Municipalities

Vermont Attorneys Title Corporation, "Town Clerk Directory," www.vermontattorneystitle.com/vermont-attorneys-title-corp/town-clerk-directory-choose-a-town/

Ordinances

Municode Code Corporation, "Vermont," www.municode.com/library/VT

General Code, "Vermont eCode360 Library," www.generalcode.com/ecode360/VT

Practice Materials and Self-Help Resources

Research Guide

Vermont Law Help, www.vtlawhelp.org

Court Rules

LexisNexis, "Vermont Statutes Unannotated and Vermont Court Rules," www.lexisnexis.com/hottopics/vtstatutesconstctrules/

Forms

Vermont Judiciary, "Court Forms," www.vermontjudiciary.org/MasterPages/Court-FormsIndex.aspx

State Bar Association Consumer Brochures

Vermont Bar Association, "For the Public: Self-Help Resources," https://www.vtbar.org

Court Brochures/Self-Help Centers

Vermont Judiciary, "Representing Yourself: Pro Se Education Program," http://vermontjudiciary.org/PE/prose.aspx

Vermont Judiciary, "Family Division: Information Pamphlets," www.vermontjudiciary.org/gtc/Family/Pamphlets.aspx

Looking for an Attorney (for a fee or for free)

Legal Aid/Advocacy Groups/Pro Bono

Law Line, Vermont Volunteer Lawyers Project, www.lawlinevt.org/vvlp

Finding an Attorney/Lawyer Referrals

Vermont Bar Association, "For the Public: Find a Lawyer," https://www.vtbar.org

Miscellaneous

University of Vermont, Vermont Legislative Research Service, www.uvm.edu/-vlrs/

References

Westlaw, "Glossary for Legal Research Basics," http://lawschool.westlaw.com/shared/marketinfodisplay.asp?code=RE&id=17&mainpage=23&rtid=116&rtcode=re

Cornell University Law School, Legal Information Institute, Wex [dictionary and encyclopedia], www.law.cornell.edu/wex/

VIRGINIA

Research Guides

AALL LISP, "Public Library Toolkit: Virginia," www.aallnet.org/sections/lisp/Public-Library-Toolkit

Georgetown University Law Library, "Virginia Research In-Depth," www.law.georgetown.edu/library/research/guides/virginia-in-depth.cfm

William and Mary Law School, "Legal Research in Virginia," http://law.wm.edu/library/research/researchguides/virginia/

University of Richmond School of Law, William Taylor Muse Law Library, "Research Guide:

Virginia Materials," http://law.richmond.edu/library/PDF/guidevamaterialsv2.pdf

Judicial

State Court Structure

Virginia's Judicial System, "Virginia Courts in Brief" [includes diagram], www.courts.state.va.us/courts/cib.pdf

Directory of State Courts

Virginia's Judicial System, "Map of Virginia's Judicial Circuits and Districts," www.courts.state.va.us/courts/maps/home.html

Opinions

Highest Court—Supreme Court

[1995–]: Virginia's Judicial System, "Supreme Court of Virginia Opinions," www.courts.state.va.us/scndex.htm

[1995–]: Virginia's Judicial System, "Opinions Search—Supreme Court of Virginia and Court of Appeals of Virginia," www.courts.state.va.us/search/textopinions.html

Intermediate Appellate Court—Court of Appeals

[1995–]: Virginia's Judicial System, "Opinions," www.courts.state.va.us/opinions/home.html

[1995–]: Virginia's Judicial System, "Opinions Search—Supreme Court of Virginia and Court of Appeals of Virginia," www.courts.state.va.us/search/textopinions.html

Dockets/Court Records

Supreme Court

Supreme Court of Virginia, Appellate Case Management System, "Supreme Court of Virginia Case Information," http://webdev.courts.state.va.us/acms-public/

Court of Appeals

Supreme Court of Virginia, Appellate Case Management System, "Court of Appeals of Virginia Case Information," http://webdev.courts.state.va.us/cav-public/

Circuit Courts

Virginia Courts Case Information, "Circuit Court Case Information," http://wasdmz2.courts.state .va.us/CJISWeb/circuit.html

General District Courts

General District Court Online Case Information System, http://epwsgdp1.courts.state.va.us/ gdcourts/caseSearch.do?welcomePage=welcome Page

Legislative

State Legislative Process

Virginia General Assembly, Capitol Classroom, "How a Bill Becomes a Law," http://capclass .virginiageneralassembly.gov/Middle/HowABill/ HowABill.html

University of Virginia, Office of State Governmental Relations, "How a Bill Becomes a Law: Virginia's Legislative Process" [diagram], www.virginia.edu/ governmentalrelations/leg_process.pdf

Statutes

By Subject (Code)—Code of Virginia

Virginia General Assembly, Legislative Information System, "Code of Virginia," http://lis.virginia.gov/000/src.htm

In Chronological Order (Session Laws)— Acts of Assembly

[1994–]: Virginia General Assembly, Legislative Information System, http://lis.virginia.gov/lis.htm

Legislative History

Research Guide

Virginia Division of Legislative Services, "Legislative History," http://dls.state.va.us/lrc/ leghist.htm

Executive

Directories of State Departments/Agencies

Virginia.gov, "Agencies," www.virginia.gov
Virginia.gov, "State Agency Search," www.agencydirectory.virginia.gov

State Rulemaking Process

Virginia Regulatory Town Hall, "Frequently Asked Questions about the Rulemaking Process," http://townhall.virginia.gov/um/ faqrulemaking.cfm

Regulations

By Agency (Code)—Virginia Administrative Code

Virginia General Assembly, Legislative Information System, "Virginia Administrative Code," http://lis.virginia.gov/000/reg/TOC.HTM

Virginia General Assembly, Legislative Information System, "Virginia Administrative Code" [search], http://lis.virginia.gov/cgi-bin/ legp604.exe?000+men+SRR

In Chronological Order (Register)— Virginia Register of Regulations

[1998–]: Virginia General Assembly, "Virginia Register of Regulations," http://register.dls.virginia.gov

Local Laws

Directory of State Counties/Municipalities

Virginia.gov, "Federal and Local: Local: Virginia Cities and Counties," www.virginia.gov/ government/federal-and-local

Ordinances

Municode Code Corporation, "Virginia," www.municode.com/library/VA

Practice Materials and Self-Help Resources

Research Guide

Appalachian School of Law Library, "Virginia Family Law: Starting Points," www.asl.edu/ Documents/Library/pubs/lrg_virfam.pdf

Court Rules

Virginia's Judicial System, "Rules of the Supreme Court of Virginia," www.courts.state .va.us/courts/scv/rules.html

Forms

Virginia's Judicial System, "Forms,"
www.courts.state.va.us/forms/

State Bar Association Consumer Brochures

Virginia State Bar, "Public Information
Pamphlets," www.vsb.org/site/publications/
public-information-pamphlets

Court Brochures/Self-Help Centers

Virginia's Judicial System, "Frequently Asked
Questions," www.courts.state.va.us/courtadmin/
aoc/legalresearch/faq.pdf

Looking for an Attorney
(for a fee or for free)

Legal Aid/Advocacy Groups/Pro Bono

Virginia State Bar, Conference of Local Bar
Associations, "Legally Informed,"
www.vsb.org/docs/LegallyInformed.pdf

Virginia State Bar Young Lawyers Conference
and the Legal Information Network for
Cancer, "Legal Handbook for Cancer
Survivors," www.vsb.org/docs/conferences/young
-lawyers/cancersurvivorshandbook.pdf

Finding an Attorney/Lawyer Referrals

William and Mary Law School, "How to Locate
an Attorney," http://law.wm.edu/library/research/
researchguides/howto/attorney/

Virginia State Bar, "Virginia Lawyer Referral
Service," www.vsb.org/site/public/lawyer-referral
-service/

Miscellaneous

Virginia General Assembly, "General Information:
Index to the Acts of the General Assembly"
[1996–], http://dela.state.va.us/Publications/
Publications.nsf/LegislativeResources?OpenView#

University of Richmond School of Law, William
Taylor Muse Law Library, "Virginia Supreme
Court Records & Briefs," http://law2.richmond
.edu/librarytech/varb/

Virginia Lawyer's Weekly, "Virginia Law Firms,"
http://valawyersweekly.com/virginia-law-firms/

Virginia's Judicial System, "Virginia Public Law
Libraries," www.courts.state.va.us/courtadmin/
library/virginia_public_lib.html

Virginia's Judicial System, "Legal Publications
Online," www.courts.state.va.us/courtadmin/
library/publications.html

Virginia State Bar, "Attorney Records Search,"
www.vsb.org/attorney/attSearch.asp

References

Westlaw, "Glossary for Legal Research
Basics," http://lawschool.westlaw.com/shared/
marketinfodisplay.asp?code=RE&id=17&mainpage
=23&rtid=116&rtcode=re

Cornell University Law School, Legal
Information Institute, *Wex* [dictionary and
encyclopedia], www.law.cornell.edu/wex/

WASHINGTON

Research Guides

General

AALL LISP, "Public Library Toolkit:
Washington," www.aallnet.org/sections/lisp/
Public-Library-Toolkit

University of Washington School of Law,
Gallagher Law Library, "Sources of Free Legal
Information on Washington State Law,"
http://lib.law.washington.edu/ref/legalinfo.html

Washington Courts, "Legal Research on the
Internet," www.courts.wa.gov/library/?fa=library
.display&fileID=netsrch

Topical

Public Law Library of King County, "Law Library
Research Guides," www.kcll.org/research-guides

University of Washington School of Law,
Gallagher Law Library, "Family Law Research
and Practice Guide," https://lib.law.washington
.edu/content/guides/familylaw

Judicial

State Court Structure

Washington Courts, "A Guide to Washington State Courts" [includes diagram], www.courts.wa.gov/newsinfo/resources/index.cfm?fa=newsinfo_jury.brochure_guide&altMenu=Citi

Directory of State Courts

Washington Courts, "Washington State Court Directories," www.courts.wa.gov/court_dir/

Opinions

Research Guide

Washington Courts, "Court Reports," www.courts.wa.gov/library/?fa=library.display&fileID=courtrpt

Highest Court—Supreme Court

[1854–]: Municipal Research and Services Center of Washington, "Washington State Supreme and Appellate Court Decisions" [*Washington Reports*], www.mrsc.org/wa/courts/index_dtSearch.html

Intermediate Appellate Court—Court of Appeals

[1969–]: Municipal Research and Services Center of Washington, "Washington State Supreme and Appellate Court Decisions" [*Washington Appellate Reports*], www.mrsc.org/wa/courts/index_dtSearch.html

Dockets/Court Records

Trial Courts

Washington Courts, "Search Case Records," http://dw.courts.wa.gov

Legislative

State Legislative Process

Washington State Legislature, "Overview of the Legislative Process," www.leg.wa.gov/legislature/Pages/Overview.aspx

Washington State Legislature, "How a Bill Becomes a Law" [diagram], www.leg.wa.gov/LIC/Documents/EducationAndInformation/How_A_Bill_Becomes_a_Law_Long%20Version.pdf

Statutes

Research Guides

Washington State Law Library, "Revised Code of Washington (RCW)," www.courts.wa.gov/library/?fa=library.display&fileID=rcw

Gonzaga University School of Law, Chastek Library, "Updating the *Revised Code of Washington Annotated* in Print," www.law.gonzaga.edu/files/UpdatingRCWAPrint.pdf

By Subject (Code)—
Revised Code of Washington (RCW)

Municipal Research and Services Center of Washington, "RCW/WAC," www.mrsc.org/rcwwac.aspx/index_dtsearch.html

In Chronological Order (Session Laws)—
Laws of Washington

[1854–]: Washington State Legislature, "Session Laws," www.leg.wa.gov/CodeReviser/Pages/session_laws.aspx

Legislative History

Research Guides

Public Law Library of King County, "Legislative History Guide," www.kcll.org/guides/legislative-history-guide

University of Washington School of Law, Gallagher Law Library, "Washington State Legislative History," https://lib.law.washington.edu/content/guides/washleghis

Washington Courts, "Washington Legislative History and Legislative Intent," www.courts.wa.gov/library/?fa=library.display&fileID=legis

Gonzaga University School of Law, Chastek Library, "Washington Legislative History," http://libguides.law.gonzaga.edu/waleghistory

Executive

Directory of State Departments/Agencies

Access Washington, "State Agencies, Boards and Commissions," http://access.wa.gov/agency

State Rulemaking Process

Washington State, Governor's Office of Regulatory Assistance, "Washington's Rulemaking Process," www.ora.wa.gov/regulatory/rulemaking.asp

Regulations

Research Guides

Washington Courts, "Washington Administrative Law," www.courts.wa.gov/library/?fa=library.display&fileID=wac

Gonzaga University School of Law, Chastek Library, "Updating *Washington Administrative Code* Regulations in Print," www.law.gonzaga.edu/files/UpdatingWACPrint.pdf

By Agency (Code)—
Washington Administrative Code

Washington State Legislature, "Washington Administrative Code (WAC)," http://apps.leg.wa.gov/wac/

Municipal Research and Services Center of Washington, "RCW/WAC," www.mrsc.org/wa/rcwwac/index_dtSearch.html

In Chronological Order (Register)—
Washington State Register

[1997–]: Washington State Register / State Law Committee, Office of the Code Reviser, "Washington State Register," http://search.leg.wa.gov

Local Laws

Research Guide

Gonzaga University School of Law, Chastek Library, "Municipal Law—Codes and Ordinances," www.law.gonzaga.edu/files/MunicipalLaw.pdf

Directories of State Counties/Municipalities

Municipal Research and Services Center of Washington, "Websites—Washington Counties," www.mrsc.org/byndmrsc/counties.aspx

Municipal Research and Services Center of Washington, "Websites—Washington Cities and Towns," www.mrsc.org/byndmrsc/cities.aspx

Ordinances

Municipal Research and Services Center of Washington, "City and County Codes," www.mrsc.org/codes.aspx

Practice Materials and Self-Help Resources

Research Guides

University of Washington School of Law, Gallagher Law Library, "Washington Practice Materials," https://lib.law.washington.edu/content/guides/waprac

Gonzaga University School of Law, Chastek Library, "Washington Business Law Materials," www.law.gonzaga.edu/files/WashingtonBusinessLaw.pdf

Gonzaga University School of Law, Chastek Library, "Washington Consumer Law Materials," www.law.gonzaga.edu/files/WAConsumerLaw.pdf

Court Rules

Washington Courts, "Washington State Court Rules," www.courts.wa.gov/court_rules/

Forms

Washington Courts, "Washington State Court Forms," www.courts.wa.gov/forms/

State Bar Association Consumer Brochures

Washington State Bar Association, "Consumer Information Pamphlets," www.wsba.org/News-and-Events/Publications-Newsletters-Brochures/Consumer-Information-Pamphlets

Court Brochures/Self-Help Centers

Washington Courts, eService Center, https://aoc.custhelp.com/app/answers/list

Washington Courts, "Resources, Publications, and Reports," www.courts.wa.gov/newsinfo/index.cfm?fa=newsinfo.displayContent&theFile=content/ResourcesPubsReports

Looking for an Attorney
(for a fee or for free)

Legal Aid/Advocacy Groups/Pro Bono

Pro Bono Net, WashingtonLawHelp.org,
www.washingtonlawhelp.org

Northwest Justice Project, "Get Legal Help,"
http://nwjustice.org/get-legal-help

Finding an Attorney/Lawyer Referrals

Washington State Bar Association, "Find Legal
Help," www.wsba.org/Resources-and-Services/
Find-Legal-Help

Miscellaneous

Washington State Legislature, "Legislative
Documents: Educational and Instructional
Material," www.leg.wa.gov/LIC/Pages/legislative
_documents.aspx#education

Washington Courts, "Citators for Case Law,"
www.courts.wa.gov/library/?fa=library.display&fileID
=citators

Westlaw, "Washington Pattern Jury
Instructions," http://government.westlaw.com/
linkedslice/default.asp?SP=WCCJI-1000

CastRoller, "KCLL Klues: Washington State
Legal Research," http://castroller.com/podcasts/
KCLLKlues

References

Washington State Legislature, "Glossary of
Legislative Terms," http://apps.leg.wa.gov/
billinfo/glossary.aspx

Washington Courts, "Legal Citations," www.courts
.wa.gov/library/?fa=library.display&fileID=cites

WEST VIRGINIA

Research Guides

West Virginia University College of Law, "West
Virginia Research Guides," http://law.wvu.edu/
library/research_guides/west_virginia_research
_guide

Judicial

State Court Structure

Westlaw, "West Virginia Court Structure"
[diagram], http://wlwatch.westlaw.com/aca/west/
statecrtorg.htm#WV

Directory of State Courts

West Virginia Judiciary, "Court Information by
County," www.courtswv.gov/public-resources/
court-information-by-county.html

Opinions

Highest Court—Supreme Court
of Appeals of West Virginia

[1991–]: West Virginia Judiciary, "Opinions of
the Supreme Court of Appeals,"
www.courtswv.gov/supreme-court/opinions.html

Intermediate Appellate Court—None

Dockets/Court Records

Supreme Court of Appeals

West Virginia Judiciary, "West Virginia
Supreme Court of Appeals Court Calendar
and Docket," www.courtswv.gov/supreme-court/
calendar-docket.html

Trial Courts

N/A

Legislative

State Legislative Process

West Virginia Legislature, "Citizen's Guide to the
Legislature," www.legis.state.wv.us/educational/
citizens/process.cfm

West Virginia Legislature, "How a Bill Becomes
Law" [diagram], www.legis.state.wv.us/
Educational/Bill_Becomes_Law/Bill_Becomes
_Law.cfm

Statutes

Research Guide

West Virginia University College of Law, "Statutes and Codes," http://law.wvu.edu/library/research_guides/west_virginia_research_guide/statutes_and_codes

By Subject (Code)—West Virginia Code

West Virginia Legislature, "West Virginia Code," www.legis.state.wv.us/WVCODE/Code.cfm

In Chronological Order (Session Laws)—Acts of the General Assembly

N/A

Legislative History

Research Guide

West Virginia University, George R. Farmer, Jr. Law Library, "Guide to West Virginia Legislative History Research," http://law.wvu.edu/r/download/8443

Executive

Directory of State Departments/Agencies

WV.gov, "West Virginia Agencies," www.wv.gov/Pages/agencies.aspx

State Rulemaking Process

West Virginia Secretary of State, "Summary of Regular Rule Making Steps," www.sos.wv.gov/administrative-law/rulemaking/Pages/stepsummary.aspx

Regulations

Research Guides

West Virginia University College of Law, "West Virginia Administrative Rules Guide," http://law.wvu.edu/library/research_guides/west_virginia_research_guide/west_virginia__administrative_rules_guide

West Virginia University College of Law, "How to Update the West Virginia Code of State Rules (CSR)," http://law.wvu.edu/library/research_guides/west_virginia_research_guide/how_to_update_the_csr

By Agency (Code)—West Virginia Code of State Rules

West Virginia Secretary of State, "Index to the West Virginia Code of State Rules," www.sos.wv.gov/administrative-law/index/Pages/default.aspx

West Virginia Secretary of State, "Administrative Law: Code of State Rules Search," http://apps.sos.wv.gov/adlaw/csr/

In Chronological Order (Register)—West Virginia State Register

[1983–]: West Virginia Secretary of State, "State Register," www.sos.wv.gov/administrative-law/register/Pages/default.aspx

Local Laws

Directory of State Counties/Municipalities

WV.gov, "West Virginia Counties" [includes list of cities for each county], www.wv.gov/local/Pages/default.aspx

Ordinances

Municode Code Corporation, "West Virginia," www.municode.com/library/WV

ConwayGreene Co., "Municipal Codes," www.conwaygreene.com/municipalCodes.htm

Practice Materials and Self-Help Resources

Research Guide

Legal Aid of West Virginia, "Library," www.lawv.net/library

Court Rules

West Virginia Judiciary, "Court Rules," www.courtswv.gov/legal-community/court-rules.html

Forms

West Virginia Judiciary, "Court Forms," www.courtswv.gov/legal-community/court-forms.html

State Bar Association Consumer Brochures

N/A

Court Brochures/Self-Help Centers

West Virginia Judiciary, "Domestic Violence,"
www.courtswv.gov/public-resources/domestic/
domestic-violence.html

Looking for an Attorney
(for a fee or for free)

Legal Aid/Advocacy Groups/Pro Bono

Legal Aid of West Virginia, www.lawv.net/Home/
PublicWeb

West Virginia University Clinical Law Program,
Legal Help for West Virginians,
www.wvlegalservices.org

Finding an Attorney/Lawyer Referrals

West Virginia State Bar Lawyer Referral Service,
"Find a Lawyer," www.wvlawyerreferral.org/
search/

References

Westlaw, "Glossary for Legal Research
Basics," http://lawschool.westlaw.com/shared/
marketinfodisplay.asp?code=RE&id=17&mainpage
=23&rtid=116&rtcode=re

Cornell University Law School, Legal
Information Institute, *Wex* [dictionary and
encyclopedia], www.law.cornell.edu/wex/

WISCONSIN

Research Guides

AALL LISP, "Public Library Toolkit: Wisconsin,"
www.aallnet.org/sections/lisp/Public-Library-Toolkit

Wisconsin State Law Library, "A–Z Topics,"
http://wilawlibrary.gov/topics/witopicindex.html

Judicial

State Court Structure

Wisconsin Court System, "Court System
Overview," www.wicourts.gov/courts/overview/
overview.htm

Wisconsin Court System, "Court System
Overview: How a Case Moves through the
Courts" [diagram], www.wicourts.gov/courts/
overview/moves.htm

Directories of State Courts

Wisconsin Court System, "Court of Appeals:
District Map," www.wicourts.gov/courts/appeals/
map.htm

Wisconsin Court System, "Circuit Courts: Court
Websites," www.wicourts.gov/contact/ccsites.htm

Opinions

Highest Court—Supreme Court

[1995–]: Wisconsin Court System, "Supreme
Court Opinions," www.wicourts.gov/opinions/
supreme.jsp

Intermediate Appellate Court—Court of Appeals

[1995–]: Wisconsin Court System, "Court of
Appeals Opinions," www.wicourts.gov/opinions/
appeals.jsp

Dockets/Court Records

Appellate Courts

Wisconsin Court System, "Access to the Public
Records of the Wisconsin Supreme Court and
Court of Appeals (WSCCA),"
http://wscca.wicourts.gov

Trial Courts

Wisconsin Court System, "Access to the Public
Records of the Wisconsin Circuit Courts
(WCCA)," http://wcca.wicourts.gov

Legislative

State Legislative Process

Wisconsin General Assembly, Assembly Chief
Clerk, "How a Bill Becomes a Law" [includes
diagram], http://legis.wisconsin.gov/assembly/acc/
pdf/habbl.pdf

Statutes

By Subject (Code)—Wisconsin Statutes

Wisconsin Legislative Reference Bureau, "The
Updated Wisconsin Statutes & Annotations,"
www.legis.state.wi.us/rsb/stats.html

In Chronological Order (Session Laws)—
Laws of Wisconsin (Acts)

[1957–]: Wisconsin Legislative Reference
  Bureau, "Wisconsin Acts," www.legis.state.wi.us/
  rsb/2acts.html

Legislative History

Research Guides

Marquette University Law School, "Wisconsin
  Legislative History Research Guide,"
  http://law.marquette.edu/law-library/research
  -guides-wisconsin-legislative-history
University of Wisconsin Law Library,
  "Researching the Legislative History
  of Wisconsin Laws: An Annotated
  Bibliography," http://library.law.wisc.edu/cgi-bin/
  wp2html?wilegislativehistory.wpd
Wisconsin Briefs from the Legislative Reference
  Bureau, "Guide to Researching Wisconsin
  Legislation," www.legis.state.wi.us/lrb/pubs/
  wb/98wb8.pdf

Executive

Directory of State Departments/Agencies

Wisconsin.gov, "List of State Agencies,"
  www.wisconsin.gov/state/core/agency_index.html

State Rulemaking Process

Wisconsin Legislative Reference Bureau and
  Legislative Council Staff, "Administrative
  Rules Procedures Manual" [includes
  diagram], www.legis.state.wi.us/lc/adminrules/
  files/admin_rules_manual.pdf

Regulations

By Agency (Code)—
Wisconsin Administrative Code

Wisconsin Legislative Reference Bureau,
  "Wisconsin Administrative Code,"
  https://docs.legis.wisconsin.gov/code/prefaces/toc

In Chronological Order (Register)—
Wisconsin Administrative Register

[1956–]: Wisconsin Legislative Reference
  Bureau, "Administrative Register,"
  http://docs.legis.wisconsin.gov/code/register

Local Laws

Directories of State Counties/Municipalities

Wisconsin.gov, "Wisconsin Counties,"
  www.wisconsin.gov/state/core/wisconsin_counties
  .html
Wisconsin.gov, "Wisconsin Cities, Towns
  and Villages," www.wisconsin.gov/state/core/
  wisconsin_cities_towns_and_villages.html

Ordinances

Wisconsin State Law Library, "WI Ordinances
  & Codes," http://wilawlibrary.gov/topics/
  ordinances.php

Practice Materials and Self-Help Resources

Research Guides

Wisconsin State Law Library, "Start Here:
  A Selective List of Resources on Estate
  Planning," http://wilawlibrary.gov/learn/starthere/
  estate.pdf
Wisconsin State Law Library, "Foreclosure,"
  http://wilawlibrary.gov/topics/foreclosure.php
Wisconsin State Law Library, "Start Here:
  A Selective List of Resources on Product
  Liability," http://wilawlibrary.gov/learn/starthere/
  products.pdf

Court Rules

State Bar of Wisconsin, "Wisconsin Circuit Court
  Rules," www.wisbar.org/directories/courtrules/
  pages/circuit-court-rules.aspx

Forms

Wisconsin State Law Library, "Legal Forms,"
  http://wilawlibrary.gov/topics/wiforms.php

State Bar Association Consumer Brochures

State Bar of Wisconsin, "Publications &
  Resources," http://wilawlibrary.gov/topics/
  wiforms.php

Court Brochures/Self-Help Centers

Wisconsin Court System, "Self-Help Law
  Center," www.wicourts.gov/services/public/
  selfhelp/

Looking for an Attorney
(for a fee or for free)

Legal Aid/Advocacy Groups/Pro Bono

Wisconsin State Law Library, "Legal Assistance,"
http://wilawlibrary.gov/topics/assist.php

LawMoose Legal Reference Library, "Wisconsin
Legal Aid & Pro Bono Lawyers," www.law
moose.com/index.cfm?Action=Library.&Topic=WI38

Finding an Attorney/Lawyer Referrals

State Bar of Wisconsin, "I Need a Lawyer,"
www.wisbar.org/forPublic/INeedaLawyer/Pages/
i-need-a-lawyer.aspx

Miscellaneous

Law Libraries Association of Wisconsin,
"Published Articles Written by LLAW
Members," www.aallnet.org/chapter/llaw/articles/

Law Librarians Association of Wisconsin, "WI
Law Libraries Open to the Public,"
www.aallnet.org/chapter/llaw/legallinks/wilawlib.pdf

Reference

Law Librarians Association of Wisconsin,
"Introduction to Legal Materials: A Manual
for Non-Law Librarians in Wisconsin,"
appendix A, "Glossary," www.aallnet.org/
chapter/llaw/paliguide/

WYOMING

Research Guide

AALL LISP, "Public Library Toolkit: Wyoming,"
www.aallnet.org/sections/lisp/Public-Library-Toolkit

Judicial

State Court Structure

Court Statistics Project, "Wyoming" [diagram],
www.courtstatistics.org/Other-Pages/State_Court
_Structure_Charts/Wyoming.aspx

Directories of State Courts

Wyoming Judicial Branch, "District Courts
Directory," www.courts.state.wy.us/DistrictCourt
Directory.aspx?MenuItemID=mnuDD

Wyoming Judicial Branch, "Circuit Courts
Directory," www.courts.state.wy.us/CircuitCourt
Directory.aspx?MenuItemID=mnuCC

Opinions

Highest Court—Supreme Court

[past three months]: Wyoming Judicial Branch,
"Supreme Court Decisions (Opinions),"
http://courts.state.wy.us/Opinions.aspx

[past three months]: Wyoming Judicial Branch,
"WSC Site Search," http://courts.state.wy.us/
Search.aspx

[1990–]: Wyoming State Law Library,
"Wyoming Supreme Court Cases,"
http://wyom.state.wy.us/applications/oscn/index
.asp?ftdb=STWY&level=1

Intermediate Appellate Court—None

Dockets/Court Records

Appellate Court

Wyoming Supreme Court, Clerk's Office,
"Wyoming Appellate Case Management
System," https://efiling.courts.state.wy.us/public/
caseSearch.do

Trial Courts

N/A

Legislative

State Legislative Process

Wyoming Legislature, "The Wyoming Legislative
Process," http://legisweb.state.wy.us/leginfo/
legprocess_files/v3_document.htm

Statutes

By Subject (Code)—Wyoming Statutes

Wyoming Legislature, "Wyoming State Statutes,"
http://legisweb.state.wy.us/LSOWeb/wyStatutes.
aspx

LexisNexis, "Wyoming Statutes Annotated," www.lexisnexis.com/hottopics/wystatutes/

In Chronological Order (Session Laws)—
Session Laws of Wyoming

[2001–]: Wyoming Legislature, "Session Archives," http://legisweb.state.wy.us/LSOWEB/SessionArchives.aspx

Legislative History

Research Guides

Wyoming Legislature, "Legislative History of Wyoming Laws," http://legisweb.state.wy.us/leginfo/hiswylaw.htm

University of Wyoming College of Law, George W. Hopper Law Library, "Compiling Wyoming Legislative Histories," www.uwyo.edu/LAWLIB/researchguides/wyohistory.html

Executive

Directory of State Departments/Agencies

Wyoming.gov, "Locate a State Government Agency," http://wyoming.gov/agencies.aspx

State Rulemaking Process

USLegal, "Administrative Procedure Act—Wyoming," http://administrativelaw.uslegal.com/administrative-procedure-acts/wyoming/

Regulations

By Agency (Code)—Code of Wyoming Rules

Wyoming Secretary of State, "Public Access to Rules," http://soswy.state.wy.us/Rules/

In Chronological Order (Register)—
Wyoming Administrative Register

N/A

Local Laws

Directory of State Counties/Municipalities

State and Local Government on the Net, "Wyoming State and Local Government," www.statelocalgov.net/state-wy.cfm

Ordinances

Wyoming Judicial Branch, "Legislative Branch: Municipal City Codes," www.courts.state.wy.us/LawLibrary/wyoleg.aspx

Municode Code Corporation, "Wyoming," www.municode.com/library/WY

Practice Materials and Self-Help Resources

Research Guide

Legal Aid of Wyoming Inc., www.lawyoming.org

Court Rules

Wyoming Judicial Branch, "Court Rules," www.courts.state.wy.us/CourtRules.aspx

Forms

Wyoming Judicial Branch, "Frequently Asked Questions," www.courts.state.wy.us/LawLibrary/faq.aspx

State Bar Association Consumer Brochures

N/A

Court Brochures/Self-Help Centers

Wyoming Judicial Branch, "Self Help Center," www.courts.state.wy.us/AltMenu.aspx?MenuItemID=mnuSHC

Looking for an Attorney (for a fee or for free)

Legal Aid/Advocacy Groups/Pro Bono

Wyoming State Bar, "Public Assistance Resources," www.wyomingbar.org/resources/category.html?search_term=Public%20Assistance

Finding an Attorney/Lawyer Referrals

Wyoming State Bar, "Need to Hire a Lawyer?" www.wyomingbar.org/directory/need_lawyer.html

Miscellaneous

Wyoming State Law Library, *Law Library Letter* [blog], http://wyolawlibrary.blogspot.com

Reference

Wyoming Legislature, "Glossary of Words and
    Terms," http://legisweb.state.wy.us/LSOWeb/
    glossary.aspx

INDEX

A

AALL (American Association of
Law Libraries)
collaboration with, 21–22
Ethical Principles, 17–18
LISP-SIS (Legal Information
Services to the Public Special Interest Section), 22
overview, 21–22
AALL Spectrum, 61
abstracts, 71
administrative codes, 79
administrative court rules, 80
administrative law, 34, 77–80
administrative rulings
federal government, 89
Hawaii, 116
Idaho, 118
Illinois, 120
Iowa, 125
New Jersey, 157
Oklahoma, 171
adversarial nature of the legal
system, 7
agencies. *See* governmental
administrative agencies

ALA (American Library
Association) Code of
Ethics, 17, 18
Alabama, online legal resources
for, 92–94
Alaska, online legal resources
for, 94–96
ALR *(American Law Reports),*
49–50
American Jurisprudence, 44
American Law Institute, 50,
64
American legal system, structure
of. *See* structure of the
American legal system
annotated (unofficial) codes
overview, 58, 60
pocket parts, 60, 61–62
supplements, 60
updating, 60
annotations (ALR), 50
appellate court decisions, 68–
69, 70
appellate process, court rules
for, 81
approval of regulations, 79

Arizona, online legal resources
for, 96–98
Arkansas, online legal resources
for, 98–100
attitude, maintaining a good,
23–24
attorney general opinions
(Iowa), 126
attorneys. *See also* finding an
attorney
distrust of attorneys as
motivation for self-
representation, 8
referring users to, 24
"The Authorized Practice of
Legal Reference Service"
(Law Library Journal), 27

B

backward citation analysis,
72–73
bankruptcy, 40
basic structure of American
legal system, 32–33
basis defined, 45
Begg, Robert T., 26

Bench and Bar, 10
bibliographic issues for case law, 69–72
bills, 56–57, 85, 88
binding (mandatory) precedent, 35
Black's Law Dictionary, 44, 45
Bloomberg Law, 52
The Bluebook: A Uniform System of Citation, 35
book citation, 37
boundaries, maintaining, 23
Brown, Yvette, 26
Brown v. Board of Education, 69

C
California
    online legal resources for, 101–103
    pro se representation, statistics on, 10
case citation, 35–36, 74–77
case law
    abstracts, 71
    bibliographic issues, 69–72
    citation analysis, 72–73
    digests, 71–72
    overview, 33–34, 65–66
    publication of, 70
    researching, 73–74
    unpublished decisions, 70
case reporters
    case citation, 36, 75
    official, 70–71
    overview, 69, 76
    unofficial, 70–71
Casemaker, 52
casual users. *See* lay users
"Chicken Little at the Reference Desk: The Myth of Librarian Liability" *(Law Library Journal),* 26
circuit courts of appeals, 67, 76, 88
Circuit Riders Outreach Program, 22
citation analysis, 72–73
civil law, 38–39

civil procedure, court rules for, 80–81
claims and defenses, questions on, 42
Code of Ethics of the American Library Association, 17, 18
Code of Federal Regulations (CFR), 80
codes. *See also* annotated codes; official codes
    administrative, 79
    characteristics of, 57–58
    finding aids for, 60
    overview, 57–58
    previous code language, 60–62
    print codes, working with, 60
    publication of, 59
    revision of, 58
    supplementary material, 58
    updating issues, 60
collaboration, 21–22
collections, debts, foreclosure, credit, 40
Colorado, online legal resources for, 103–105
Commerce Clearing House (CCH), 48
common law, 33, 68–69
competence as motivation for self-representation, 9
complexity of legal materials, 7
complexity of the legal system, 7
concepts, legal. *See* legal concepts
Condon, Charles J., 26
confidentiality, 18
conflict of interest, 18
Connecticut, online legal resources for, 106–108
consideration defined, 45
Constitution of the United States
    overview, 32–33, 53–54
    rights established by, 54
    same-sex marriage, constitutionality of, 54

constitutions, 32–33, 53. *See also* Constitution of the United States; state constitutions
contract issues, 40
contract law, 39, 68
Cornell's Legal Information Institute, 74
Corpus Juris Secundum, 44
court brochures/self-help centers
    Alaska, 95
    California, 103
    Colorado, 105
    Connecticut, 107
    Delaware, 109
    Florida, 112
    Georgia, 114
    Hawaii, 116
    Idaho, 118
    Illinois, 121
    Indiana, 123
    Iowa, 125
    Kansas, 128
    Maine, 134
    Maryland, 136
    Massachusetts, 139
    Michigan, 141
    Minnesota, 143–144
    Missouri, 147
    Montana, 149
    Nebraska, 151
    Nevada, 153
    New Hampshire, 155
    New Jersey, 157
    New Mexico, 159
    New York, 162
    North Carolina, 165
    North Dakota, 166
    Ohio, 169
    Oregon, 174
    Pennsylvania, 176
    Rhode Island, 178
    South Carolina, 180
    South Dakota, 182
    Tennessee, 184
    Utah, 189
    Vermont, 191
    Virginia, 193

Washington, 195
West Virginia, 198
Wisconsin, 199
Wyoming, 201
court records. *See* dockets/court
    records
court rules
    Alabama, 93
    Alaska, 95
    Arizona, 98
    Arkansas, 100
    California, 102
    Colorado, 105
    Connecticut, 107
    Delaware, 109
    federal government, 89
    Florida, 111–112
    Georgia, 114
    Hawaii, 116
    Idaho, 118
    Illinois, 121
    Indiana, 123
    Iowa, 125
    Kansas, 127
    Kentucky, 130
    Louisiana, 132
    Maine, 134
    Maryland, 136
    Massachusetts, 138–139
    Michigan, 141
    Minnesota, 143
    Mississippi, 145
    Missouri, 147
    Montana, 149
    Nebraska, 151
    Nevada, 153
    New Hampshire, 155
    New Jersey, 157
    New Mexico, 159
    New York, 162
    North Carolina, 164
    North Dakota, 166
    Ohio, 169
    Oklahoma, 171
    Oregon, 173–174
    overview, 80–81
    Pennsylvania, 176
    Rhode Island, 177

South Carolina, 180
South Dakota, 181
Tennessee, 183
Texas, 186
Utah, 189
Vermont, 190
Virginia, 192
Washington, 195
Washington, D.C., 91
West Virginia, 197
Wisconsin, 199
Wyoming, 201
court-specific rules, 81
court structure. *See also* state
        court structure
    federal government, 87
    Washington, D.C., 90
courthouses
    access to Westlaw or Lexis
        through, 51
    referring users to, avoiding,
        24
credit, debts, collections,
        foreclosure, 40
criminal charge, 40
criminal law, 38
criminal procedure, court rules
        for, 81
criminal prosecutions, 38
currency of statutes, 61
custody and divorce, 40

D
dates for case citation, 36, 75
debts, collections, foreclosure,
        credit, 40
Delaware, online legal resources
        for, 108–109
demographic data on self-
        represented litigants, 9
determining sources, 23
dictionaries, legal, 44
digests, 71–72
directories of federal courts, 87
directories of state counties/
        municipalities
    Alabama, 93
    Alaska, 95

Arizona, 97
Arkansas, 99
California, 102
Colorado, 105
Connecticut, 107
Delaware, 109
Florida, 111
Georgia, 113
Hawaii, 116
Idaho, 118
Illinois, 120
Indiana, 123
Iowa, 125
Kansas, 127
Kentucky, 129
Louisiana, 132
Maine, 133
Maryland, 136
Massachusetts, 138
Michigan, 141
Minnesota, 143
Mississippi, 145
Missouri, 147
Montana, 149
Nebraska, 151
Nevada, 153
New Hampshire, 155
New Jersey, 157
New Mexico, 159
New York, 162
North Carolina, 164
North Dakota, 166
Ohio, 168
Oklahoma, 171
Oregon, 173
Pennsylvania, 175
Rhode Island, 177
South Carolina, 179
South Dakota, 181
Tennessee, 183
Texas, 186
Utah, 188
Vermont, 190
Virginia, 192
Washington, 195
West Virginia, 197
Wisconsin, 199
Wyoming, 201

directories of state courts
  Alabama, 92
  Alaska, 94
  Arizona, 96
  Arkansas, 99
  California, 100
  Colorado, 103
  Connecticut, 106
  Delaware, 108
  Florida, 110
  Georgia, 112
  Hawaii, 114
  Idaho, 117
  Illinois, 119
  Indiana, 121
  Iowa, 124
  Kansas, 126
  Kentucky, 128
  Louisiana, 131
  Maine, 133
  Maryland, 134–135
  Massachusetts, 137
  Michigan, 140
  Minnesota, 142
  Mississippi, 144
  Missouri, 146
  Montana, 148
  Nebraska, 150
  Nevada, 152
  New Hampshire, 154
  New Jersey, 156
  New Mexico, 158
  New York, 160
  North Carolina, 163
  North Dakota, 165
  Ohio, 167
  Oklahoma, 170
  Oregon, 172
  Pennsylvania, 174
  Rhode Island, 176
  South Carolina, 178
  South Dakota, 180
  Tennessee, 182
  Texas, 185
  Utah, 187
  Vermont, 189
  Virginia, 191
  Washington, 194
  West Virginia, 196
  Wisconsin, 198
  Wyoming, 200
directories of state departments/
    agencies
  Alabama, 93
  Alaska, 95
  Arizona, 97
  Arkansas, 99
  California, 102
  Colorado, 104
  Connecticut, 107
  Delaware, 108
  Florida, 111
  Georgia, 113
  Hawaii, 115
  Idaho, 117
  Illinois, 120
  Indiana, 122
  Iowa, 124
  Kansas, 127
  Kentucky, 129
  Louisiana, 131
  Maine, 133
  Maryland, 135
  Massachusetts, 138
  Michigan, 140
  Minnesota, 143
  Mississippi, 145
  Missouri, 146
  Montana, 148
  Nebraska, 150
  Nevada, 152
  New Hampshire, 154
  New Jersey, 156
  New Mexico, 158
  New York, 161
  North Carolina, 164
  North Dakota, 166
  Ohio, 168
  Oklahoma, 171
  Oregon, 173
  Pennsylvania, 175
  Rhode Island, 177
  South Carolina, 179
  South Dakota, 181
  Tennessee, 183
  Texas, 186
  Utah, 188
  Vermont, 190
  Virginia, 192–193
  Washington, 194
  West Virginia, 197
  Wisconsin, 199
  Wyoming, 201
directory of D.C. courts, 90
directory of D.C. departments/
    agencies, 91
directory of federal agencies, 89
discussions, avoiding extended,
    23
"Dispensing Law at the Front
    Lines: Ethical Dilemmas
    in Law Librarianship"
    (*Library Trends*), 27
district courts, 66, 76
distrust of attorneys as
    motivation for self-
    representation, 8
divorce and custody, 40
dockets/court records
  Alabama, 92
  Alaska, 94
  Arizona, 96–97
  Arkansas, 99
  California, 101
  Colorado, 104
  Connecticut, 106
  Delaware, 108
  Florida, 110
  general legal research and
    most states, 84
  Georgia, 113
  Hawaii, 115
  Idaho, 117
  Illinois, 119
  Indiana, 122
  Iowa, 124
  Kansas, 126
  Kentucky, 129
  Louisiana, 131
  Maryland, 135
  Massachusetts, 137
  Michigan, 140
  Minnesota, 142
  Mississippi, 145

Missouri, 146
Montana, 148
Nebraska, 150
Nevada, 152
New Hampshire, 154
New Jersey, 156
New Mexico, 158
New York, 161
North Carolina, 163
North Dakota, 165
Ohio, 167–168
Oklahoma, 170
Oregon, 172
Pennsylvania, 175
Rhode Island, 177
South Carolina, 179
South Dakota, 181
Tennessee, 183
Texas, 185
Utah, 187–188
Vermont, 190
Virginia, 191–192
Washington, 194
Washington, D.C., 90
West Virginia, 196
Wisconsin, 198
Wyoming, 200
drafting regulations, 79

E
employment, 40
employment discrimination,
40
enabling legislation, 77, 78
encyclopedias, legal, 44
escheat defined, 45
ethical issues, 17–19
Ethical Principles of AALL
(American Association of
Law Libraries), 17–18
events, questions on, 42
executive branch of government
Alabama, 93
Alaska, 95
Arizona, 97
Arkansas, 99
California, 102
Colorado, 104

Connecticut, 107
Delaware, 108–109
federal government,
89–90
Florida, 111
general legal research and
most states, 85–86
Georgia, 113
Hawaii, 115–116
Idaho, 117–118
Illinois, 120
Indiana, 122–123
Iowa, 124–125
Kansas, 127
Kentucky, 129
Louisiana, 131
Maine, 133
Maryland, 135–136
Massachusetts, 138
Michigan, 140–141
Minnesota, 143
Mississippi, 145
Missouri, 146–147
Montana, 148–149
Nebraska, 150
Nevada, 152
New Hampshire, 154
New Jersey, 156–157
New Mexico, 158–159
New York, 161
North Carolina, 164
North Dakota, 166
Ohio, 168
Oklahoma, 171
Oregon, 173
overview, 32
Pennsylvania, 175
Rhode Island, 177
South Carolina, 179
South Dakota, 181
Tennessee, 183
Texas, 186
Utah, 188
Vermont, 190
Virginia, 192
Washington, 194–195
Washington, D.C., 91
West Virginia, 197

Wisconsin, 199
Wyoming, 201
expertise of librarian, 14–15

F
Faretta v. California, 6
Fastcase, 52
federal circuit courts of appeals,
67, 76
federal courts and statistics on
pro se representation, 10
federal crimes, 38
federal government, online legal
resources for, 87–90
Federal Judiciary Act, 6
Federal Register, 79–80, 80
federal regulations, 79–80
federal session law, 59
federal supremacy, 54
fifty-state surveys of laws, 85
finding aids for codes, 60
finding an attorney
Alabama, 94
Alaska, 96
Arizona, 98
Arkansas, 100
California, 103
Colorado, 105
Connecticut, 107
Delaware, 109
Florida, 112
general legal research and
most states, 86
Georgia, 114
Hawaii, 116
Idaho, 118
Illinois, 121
Indiana, 123
Iowa, 125
Kansas, 128
Kentucky, 130
Louisiana, 132
Maine, 134
Maryland, 136
Massachusetts, 139
Michigan, 141
Minnesota, 144
Mississippi, 145–146

finding an attorney (cont.)
  Missouri, 147
  Montana, 149
  Nebraska, 151
  Nevada, 153
  New Hampshire, 155
  New Jersey, 157
  New Mexico, 159
  New York, 162
  North Carolina, 165
  North Dakota, 166
  Ohio, 169
  Oklahoma, 172
  Oregon, 174
  Pennsylvania, 176
  Rhode Island, 178
  South Carolina, 180
  South Dakota, 182
  Tennessee, 184
  Texas, 187
  Utah, 189
  Vermont, 191
  Virginia, 193
  Washington, 196
  Washington, D.C., 91
  West Virginia, 198
  Wisconsin, 200
  Wyoming, 201
FindLaw, 52
Florida
  online legal resources for, 110–112
  pro se representation, statistics on, 10
foreclosure, debts, collections, credit, 40
forms
  Alabama, 93
  Alaska, 95
  Arizona, 98
  Arkansas, 100
  California, 103
  Colorado, 105
  Connecticut, 107
  Delaware, 109
  federal government, 89–90
  Florida, 112
  Georgia, 114

  Hawaii, 116
  Idaho, 118
  Illinois, 121
  Indiana, 123
  Iowa, 125
  Kansas, 127–128
  Kentucky, 130
  Louisiana, 132
  Maine, 134
  Maryland, 136
  Massachusetts, 139
  Michigan, 141
  Minnesota, 143
  Mississippi, 145
  Missouri, 147
  Montana, 149
  Nebraska, 151
  Nevada, 153
  New Hampshire, 155
  New Jersey, 157
  New Mexico, 159
  New York, 162
  North Carolina, 164
  North Dakota, 166
  Ohio, 169
  Oklahoma, 171
  Oregon, 174
  Pennsylvania, 176
  Rhode Island, 178
  South Carolina, 180
  South Dakota, 182
  Tennessee, 183
  Texas, 186
  Utah, 189
  Vermont, 190
  Virginia, 193
  Washington, 195
  West Virginia, 197
  Wisconsin, 199
  Wyoming, 201
forward citation analysis, 73
free legal clinics, referring users to, 24
"From the Reference Desk to the Jail House: Unauthorized Practice of Law and Librarians" (Law Reference Services Quarterly), 26

G
Garner, Bryan, 44
general legal research and most states, online legal resources for, 84–87
general research guides, 84, 86
Georgia, online legal resources for, 112–114
Google Scholar, 74
Government Printing Office, 80
government set up by state constitutions, 55
governmental administrative agencies, 34, 78–80
Graecen, John M., 26
guidelines
  for handling reference questions, 22–24
  for referrals, 24

H
handouts, 24
harm, 18–19
Hawaii, online legal resources for, 114–116
Healey, Paul D., 25, 26–27
Hellyer, Paul, 61
house of representatives, 33
housing, 40
"How to Avoid the Unauthorized Practice of Law at the Reference Desk" (Law Reference Services Quarterly), 26

I
Idaho, online legal resources for, 116–118
Illinois, online legal resources for, 119–121
"In Search of the Delicate Balance: Legal and Ethical Questions in Assisting the Pro Se Patron" (Law Library Journal), 26–27
Indiana, online legal resources for, 121–123
instruction on using sources, 23

intellectual property, 40
interests at stake in litigation, 7–8
intermediate court of appeals
    jurisdiction, 67
    opinions, 88
    overview, 66
Iowa
    online legal resources for, 124–126
    pro se representation, statistics on, 10

J

journal citation, 37–38
judicial branch of government
    Alabama, 92
    Alaska, 94
    Arizona, 96–97
    Arkansas, 98–99
    California, 100–101
    Colorado, 103–104
    Connecticut, 106
    Delaware, 108
    federal government, 87–88
    Florida, 110
    general legal research and most states, 84
    Georgia, 112–113
    Hawaii, 114–115
    Idaho, 116–117
    Illinois, 119
    Indiana, 121–122
    Iowa, 124
    Kansas, 126
    Kentucky, 128–129
    Louisiana, 130–131
    Maine, 132–133
    Maryland, 134–135
    Massachusetts, 137
    Michigan, 139–140
    Minnesota, 142
    Mississippi, 144–145
    Missouri, 146
    Montana, 148
    Nebraska, 150
    Nevada, 152
    New Hampshire, 154
    New Jersey, 155–156
    New Mexico, 158
    New York, 160–161
    North Carolina, 163
    North Dakota, 165
    Ohio, 167–168
    Oklahoma, 170
    Oregon, 172
    overview, 32
    Pennsylvania, 174–175
    Rhode Island, 176–177
    South Carolina, 178–179
    South Dakota, 180–181
    Tennessee, 182–183
    Texas, 184–185
    Utah, 187–188
    Vermont, 189–190
    Virginia, 191–192
    Washington, 194
    Washington, D.C., 90
    West Virginia, 196
    Wisconsin, 198
    Wyoming, 200
jurisdiction
    by level of court, 67
    overview, 34, 66–68
    by persons, 34, 68
    by subject matter, 34, 67–68
jurisdictional statement in case citation, 36, 75

K

Kansas, online legal resources for, 126–128
Kentucky, online legal resources for, 128–130
Key Number System (West), 71–72
KeyCite (West Publishing), 73

L

Lake v. Wal-Mart Stores, Inc., 49
landlord-tenant, 40
law libraries
    access to Westlaw or Lexis through, 51
    referring users to, 24
    for secondary legal information, 46
law reviews, 46
Laws of X (where X is name of state), 57
lawyers. *See* attorneys
lay users
    differentiating from other types of users, 6
    overview, 4
    pro se library users compared, 4
legal advice, 16, 19
legal advocacy and legal aid, 24, 86
legal citation
    book citation, 37
    case citation, 35–36
    journal citation, 37–38
    overview, 35
    statute citation, 36–37
legal citators, 73
legal concepts
    jurisdiction, 34
    precedent, 35
    primary legal information, 34
    private law, 35
    public law, 35
    secondary legal information, 34
legal dictionaries, 44
legal encyclopedias, 44
legal materials, complexity of, 7
legal periodicals, 46–47
legal professionals asking legal reference questions, 4
legal research process
    claims and defenses, questions on, 42
    events, questions on, 42
    legal theory, questions on, 42
    overview, 39–42
    parties and relationships, questions on, 42
    places and things, questions on, 42
    relief sought, questions on, 42

legal resource aggregators/
    portals, 84
legal terminology, 45
legal theory, questions on, 42
legal topics
    civil law, 38–39
    criminal law, 38
    list of, 40
    regulatory law, 39
legislation. *See also* codes
    bills, 56–57
    legislative history, 56–57
    model codes, 63–64
    overview, 33, 56
    publication of, 59
    session law, 57
    uniform laws, 62–63
legislative branch of government
    Alabama, 92–93
    Alaska, 94–95
    Arizona, 97
    Arkansas, 99
    California, 101
    Colorado, 104
    Connecticut, 106
    Delaware, 108
    federal government, 88
    Florida, 110–111
    general legal research and
        most states, 85
    Georgia, 113
    Hawaii, 115
    Idaho, 117
    Illinois, 119–120
    Indiana, 122
    Iowa, 124
    Kansas, 126–127
    Kentucky, 129
    Louisiana, 131
    Maine, 133
    Maryland, 135
    Massachusetts, 137–138
    Michigan, 140
    Minnesota, 142
    Mississippi, 145
    Missouri, 146
    Montana, 148
    Nebraska, 150

Nevada, 152
New Hampshire, 154
New Jersey, 156
New Mexico, 158
New York, 161
North Carolina, 163–164
North Dakota, 165–166
Ohio, 168
Oklahoma, 170–171
Oregon, 172–173
overview, 32
Pennsylvania, 175
Rhode Island, 177
South Carolina, 179
South Dakota, 181
Tennessee, 183
Texas, 185
Utah, 188
Vermont, 190
Virginia, 192
Washington, 194
Washington, D.C., 91
West Virginia, 196–197
Wisconsin, 198–199
Wyoming, 200–201
legislative history
    Alabama, 93
    Alaska, 95
    Arizona, 97
    Arkansas, 99
    California, 101
    Colorado, 104
    Connecticut, 106
    Delaware, 108
    federal government, 88
    Florida, 111
    general legal research and
        most states, 85
    Georgia, 113
    Hawaii, 115
    Idaho, 117
    Illinois, 119–120
    Indiana, 122
    Iowa, 124
    Kansas, 127
    Kentucky, 129
    Louisiana, 131
    Maine, 133

Maryland, 135
Massachusetts, 138
Michigan, 140
Minnesota, 142
Missouri, 146
Montana, 148
Nebraska, 150
Nevada, 152
New Hampshire, 154
New Jersey, 156
New York, 161
North Carolina, 164
Ohio, 168
Oklahoma, 171
Oregon, 173
overview, 56–57
Pennsylvania, 175
Rhode Island, 177
South Carolina, 179
South Dakota, 181
Tennessee, 183
Texas, 185
Utah, 188
Vermont, 190
Virginia, 192
Washington, 194
Washington, D.C., 91
West Virginia, 197
Wisconsin, 199
Wyoming, 201
legislatures, 33, 55
Leone, Gerome, 27
level of court, jurisdiction by, 67
LexisNexis, 50–52, 59, 71
LexisNexis Academic, 51–52
LexisNexis Communities Portal,
    52
LexisOne, 52
liability for librarians, 14–15
library policies toward pro se
    users, 19–20
The Library's Legal Answer Book
    (Minow and Lipinski), 25
Lipinski, Tomas A., 25
LISP-SIS (Legal Information
    Services to the Public
    Special Interest Section),
    22

LISP-SIS Public Library Toolkit,
    22
litigation, 7–8, 40
local court rules, 81
local laws
    Alabama, 93
    Alaska, 95
    Arizona, 97–98
    Arkansas, 99
    California, 102
    Colorado, 105
    Connecticut, 107
    Delaware, 109
    Florida, 111
    general legal research and
        most states, 86
    Georgia, 113
    Hawaii, 116
    Idaho, 118
    Illinois, 120
    Indiana, 123
    Iowa, 125
    Kansas, 127
    Kentucky, 129–130
    Louisiana, 132
    Maine, 133
    Maryland, 136
    Massachusetts, 138
    Michigan, 141
    Minnesota, 143
    Mississippi, 145
    Missouri, 147
    Montana, 149
    Nebraska, 151
    Nevada, 153
    New Hampshire, 155
    New Jersey, 157
    New Mexico, 159
    New York, 161–162
    North Carolina, 164
    North Dakota, 166
    Ohio, 168
    Oklahoma, 171
    Oregon, 173
    Pennsylvania, 175
    Rhode Island, 177
    South Carolina, 179
    South Dakota, 181

    Tennessee, 183
    Texas, 186
    Utah, 188–189
    Vermont, 190
    Virginia, 192
    Washington, 195
    West Virginia, 197
    Wisconsin, 199
    Wyoming, 201
LoislawConnect, 52
Louisiana, online legal resources
    for, 130–132

M
Maine, online legal resources
    for, 132–134
malpractice, 15, 40
"Malpractice Liability of a Law
    Librarian?" (Law Library
    Journal), 27
mandatory precedent, 35
Maryland, online legal resources
    for, 134–137
Massachusetts, online legal
    resources for, 137–139
mentally ill as self-represented
    litigants, 9
Michigan, online legal resources
    for, 139–141
military courts, 34
Mills, Robin K., 27
Minnesota, online legal
    resources for, 142–144
Minow, Mary, 25
Mississippi, online legal
    resources for,
    144–146
Missouri, online legal resources
    for, 146–147
model codes, 63–64
Model Penal Code, 64
money as motivation for self-
    representation, 8
Montana, online legal resources
    for, 148–149
Mosley, Madison, Jr., 27
motivations for self-
    representation, 8–9

N
National Center for State Courts
    (NCSC), 10, 25
National Conference of
    Commissioners on
    Uniform State Laws
    (NCCUSL), 62–63
Nebraska
    online legal resources for,
        149–151
    unicameral (single chamber)
        legislature, 33, 55
negligence, 14
neutrality of court, 7
Nevada, online legal resources
    for, 152–153
New Hampshire
    online legal resources for,
        154–155
    pro se representation,
        statistics on, 10
New Jersey, online legal
    resources for, 155–157
New Mexico, online legal
    resources for, 158–159
New York, online legal resources
    for, 160–163
"No Legal Advice from Court
    Personnel: What Does
    That Mean?" (The Judges
    Journal), 26
Nolo, 47
North Carolina, online legal
    resources for, 163–165
North Dakota, online legal
    resources for, 165–167

O
official case reporters, 70–71
official codes
    overview, 58, 60
    republishing of, 59, 61
Ohio, online legal resources for,
    167–170
Oklahoma, online legal
    resources for, 170–172
on-site self-help legal centers,
    47

online legal resources
  for Alabama, 92–94
  for Alaska, 94–96
  for Arizona, 96–98
  for Arkansas, 98–100
  for California, 100–103
  Code of Federal Regulations,
    80
  for Colorado, 103–105
  for Connecticut, 106–107
  for court rules, 81
  for Delaware, 108–109
  for federal government,
    87–90
  Federal Register, 80
  for Florida, 110–112
  for general legal research and
    most states, 84–87
  for Georgia, 112–114
  for Hawaii, 114–116
  for Idaho, 116–118
  for Illinois, 119–121
  for Indiana, 121–123
  for Iowa, 124–126
  for Kansas, 126–128
  for Kentucky, 128–130
  legal citators, 73
  for Louisiana, 130–132
  for Maine, 132–134
  for Maryland, 134–137
  for Massachusetts, 137–139
  for Michigan, 139–141
  for Minnesota, 142–144
  for Mississippi, 144–146
  for Missouri, 146–147
  for Montana, 147–149
  for Nebraska, 150–151
  for Nevada, 152–153
  for New Hampshire, 154–155
  for New Jersey, 155–157
  for New Mexico, 158–159
  for New York, 160–163
  for North Carolina, 163–165
  for North Dakota, 165–167
  for Ohio, 167–169
  for Oklahoma, 170–172
  for Oregon, 172–174
  for Pennsylvania, 174–176

  for Rhode Island, 176–178
  as secondary legal resources,
    46–48
  self-help legal centers, 47
  for South Carolina, 178–180
  for South Dakota, 180–182
  statutes, 61, 62
  for Tennessee, 182–184
  for Texas, 184–187
  for unpublished case law, 70
  for Utah, 187–189
  for Vermont, 189–191
  for Virginia, 191–193
  for Washington, 193–196
  for Washington, D.C., 90–92
  for West Virginia, 196–198
  for Wisconsin, 198–200
  for Wyoming, 200–202
opinions
  Alabama, 92
  Alaska, 94
  Arizona, 96
  Arkansas, 99
  California, 100–101
  Colorado, 103–104
  Connecticut, 106
  Delaware, 108
  federal government, 87–88
  Florida, 110
  general legal research and
    most states, 84
  Georgia, 112
  Hawaii, 115
  Idaho, 117
  Illinois, 119
  Indiana, 122
  Iowa, 124
  Kansas, 126
  Kentucky, 128
  Louisiana, 131
  Maine, 133
  Maryland, 135
  Massachusetts, 137
  Michigan, 140
  Minnesota, 142
  Mississippi, 144
  Missouri, 146
  Montana, 148

  Nebraska, 150
  Nevada, 152
  New Hampshire, 154
  New Jersey, 156
  New Mexico, 158
  New York, 160
  North Carolina, 163
  North Dakota, 165
  Ohio, 167
  Oklahoma, 170
  Oregon, 172
  Pennsylvania, 174–175
  Rhode Island, 176
  South Carolina, 178
  South Dakota, 180
  Tennessee, 182
  Texas, 185
  Utah, 187
  Vermont, 190
  Virginia, 191
  Washington, 194
  Washington, D.C., 90
  West Virginia, 196
  Wisconsin, 198
  Wyoming, 200
ordinances
  Alabama, 93
  Alaska, 95
  Arizona, 98
  Arkansas, 99
  California, 102
  Colorado, 105
  Connecticut, 107
  Delaware, 109
  Florida, 111
  general legal research and
    most states, 86
  Georgia, 113
  Hawaii, 116
  Idaho, 118
  Illinois, 120
  Indiana, 123
  Iowa, 125
  Kansas, 127
  Kentucky, 130
  Louisiana, 132
  Maine, 133
  Maryland, 136

Massachusetts, 138
Michigan, 141
Minnesota, 143
Mississippi, 145
Missouri, 147
Montana, 149
Nebraska, 151
Nevada, 153
New Hampshire, 155
New Jersey, 157
New Mexico, 159
New York, 162
North Carolina, 164
North Dakota, 166
Ohio, 168
Oklahoma, 171
Oregon, 173
Pennsylvania, 175
Rhode Island, 177
South Carolina, 179
South Dakota, 181
Tennessee, 183
Texas, 186
Utah, 188–189
Vermont, 190
Virginia, 192
Washington, 195
West Virginia, 197
Wisconsin, 199
Wyoming, 201
Oregon, online legal resources
    for, 172–174

P

parallel citations, 75
parties and relationships,
    questions on, 42
party names in case citation,
    36, 75
pathfinders, 24–25
Pennsylvania, online legal
    resources for, 174–176
perils of self-representation, 6–8
periodicals, legal, 46–47
personal jurisdiction, 34, 68
persuasive precedent, 35
phrases for librarians, list of
    useful, 23

pin citation, 75
places and things, questions
    on, 42
Plessy v. Ferguson, 69
pocket parts for annotated
    codes, 60, 61–62
policies of your library toward
    pro se users, 19–20
practice materials and self-help
    resources
    Alabama, 93–94
    Alaska, 95–96
    Arizona, 98
    Arkansas, 100
    California, 102–103
    Colorado, 105
    Connecticut, 107
    Delaware, 109
    federal government, 89
    Florida, 111–112
    general legal research and
        most states, 86
    Georgia, 114
    Hawaii, 116
    Idaho, 118
    Illinois, 120–121
    Indiana, 123
    Iowa, 125
    Kansas, 127–128
    Kentucky, 130
    Louisiana, 132
    Maine, 134
    Maryland, 136
    Massachusetts, 138–139
    Michigan, 141
    Minnesota, 143–144
    Mississippi, 145–146
    Missouri, 147
    Montana, 149
    Nebraska, 151
    Nevada, 153
    New Hampshire, 155
    New Jersey, 157
    New Mexico, 159
    New York, 162
    North Carolina, 164–165
    North Dakota, 166
    Ohio, 169

    Oklahoma, 171–172
    Oregon, 173–174
    Pennsylvania, 176
    Rhode Island, 177–178
    South Carolina, 180
    South Dakota, 181–182
    Tennessee, 183–184
    Texas, 186–187
    Utah, 189
    Vermont, 190–191
    Virginia, 192–193
    Washington, 195–196
    Washington, D.C., 91–92
    West Virginia, 197–198
    Wisconsin, 199–200
    Wyoming, 201
precedent
    and common law, 68–69
    overview, 35
    published case law as, 70
    subject access to, 71–72
previous code language, 60–62
primary legal information, 34
print codes, working with, 60
private law, 35, 38, 57, 68. *See
    also* common law
pro per defined, 5
pro se defined, 4–5
pro se library users. *See also* self-
    represented litigants
    differentiating from other
        types of users, 6
    lay users compared, 4
    overview, 4–5, 11
    self-represented litigants
        compared, 5
"Pro Se Users. Reference
    Liability and the
    Unauthorized Practice
    of Law: Twenty-Five
    Selected Readings" *(Law
    Library Journal),* 26
procedural law, 5
professional issues, 18–19
professional liability
    overview, 14–15
    unauthorized practice of law
        compared, 16

Professional Liability Issues for Librarians and Information Professionals (Healey), 14, 25
professional secondary resources (loose-leafs), 46
property law, 39, 68
Protti, Maria E., 27
proximate cause defined, 45
public laws (laws of general effect), 35, 58
public notices of library policies on legal reference questions, 25
publication
   of case law, 70
   of codes, 59
   of legislation, 59
   of regulations, 79
   of session law, 59
published case law as precedent, 70

R
ready-reference requests, 23
Reed Elsevier, 20, 50, 51, 52
reference questions, guidelines for handling, 22–24
"Reference Service *vs.* Legal Advice: Is It Possible to Draw the Line?" *(Law Library Journal),* 27
references
   Alabama, 94
   Alaska, 96
   Arizona, 98
   Arkansas, 100
   California, 103
   Colorado, 105
   Connecticut, 108
   Delaware, 109
   federal government, 90
   Florida, 112
   general legal research and most states, 87
   Georgia, 114
   Hawaii, 116
   Idaho, 118

   Illinois, 121
   Indiana, 123
   Iowa, 126
   Kansas, 128
   Kentucky, 130
   Louisiana, 132
   Maine, 134
   Maryland, 137
   Massachusetts, 139
   Michigan, 141
   Minnesota, 144
   Mississippi, 146
   Missouri, 147
   Montana, 149
   Nebraska, 151
   Nevada, 153
   New Hampshire, 155
   New Jersey, 158
   New Mexico, 160
   New York, 163
   North Carolina, 165
   North Dakota, 167
   Ohio, 169–170
   Oklahoma, 172
   Oregon, 174
   Pennsylvania, 176
   Rhode Island, 178
   South Carolina, 180
   South Dakota, 182
   Tennessee, 184
   Texas, 187
   Utah, 189
   Vermont, 191
   Virginia, 193
   Washington, 196
   Washington, D.C., 91
   West Virginia, 198
   Wisconsin, 200
   Wyoming, 202
"The Reference Librarian and the Pro Se Patron" *(Law Library Journal),* 26
referrals
   guidelines for, 24
   overview, 25
registers, 79
regulations

Alabama, 93
Alaska, 95
approval of, 79
Arizona, 97
Arkansas, 99
California, 102
Colorado, 104
Connecticut, 107
court rules, 80–81
Delaware, 109
drafting, 79
federal, 79–80
federal government, 89
Florida, 111
general legal research and most states, 86
Georgia, 113
Hawaii, 115
Idaho, 117–118
Illinois, 120
Indiana, 122–123
Iowa, 125
Kansas, 127
Kentucky, 129
Louisiana, 131
Maine, 134
Maryland, 135–136
Massachusetts, 138
Michigan, 140–141
Minnesota, 143
Missouri, 147
Montana, 148–149
Nebraska, 150
Nevada, 152
New Hampshire, 154
New Jersey, 156–157
New Mexico, 159
New York, 161
North Carolina, 164
North Dakota, 166
Ohio, 168
Oklahoma, 171
Oregon, 173
overview, 77–79
Pennsylvania, 175
publication of, 79
Rhode Island, 177
South Carolina, 179

South Dakota, 181
state, 80
Tennessee, 183
Texas, 186
Utah, 188
Vermont, 190
Virginia, 192
Washington, 195
Washington, D.C., 91
West Virginia, 197
Wisconsin, 199
Wyoming, 201
regulations.gov, 79
regulatory law, 39
reliance, 18–19
relief sought, questions on, 42
remainder defined, 45
reporters. *See* case reporters
republishing of official codes, 59, 61
res ipsa loquitur defined, 45
"Research at Your Own Risk" *(AALL Spectrum),* 61
research guides
  Alabama, 92
  Alaska, 94
  Arizona, 96, 98
  Arkansas, 98, 100
  California, 100, 102
  Colorado, 103
  Connecticut, 106, 107
  Delaware, 108, 109
  federal government, 87, 89
  Florida, 109–110, 111
  Georgia, 112, 114
  Hawaii, 114, 116
  Idaho, 116, 118
  Illinois, 119, 120–121
  Indiana, 121, 123
  Iowa, 124, 125
  Kansas, 126, 127
  Kentucky, 128, 130
  Louisiana, 130, 132
  Maine, 132, 134
  Maryland, 134, 136
  Massachusetts, 137, 138

Michigan, 139, 141
Minnesota, 142, 143
Mississippi, 144, 145
Missouri, 146, 147
Montana, 147–148, 149
Nebraska, 149, 151
Nevada, 151–152, 153
New Hampshire, 154, 155
New Jersey, 155, 157
New Mexico, 158, 159
New York, 160, 161–162
North Carolina, 163, 164
North Dakota, 165, 166
Ohio, 167, 168, 169
Oklahoma, 170, 171
Oregon, 172, 173
Pennsylvania, 174, 176
Rhode Island, 176, 177
South Carolina, 178, 180
South Dakota, 180, 181
Tennessee, 182, 183
Texas, 184, 186
Utah, 187, 189
Vermont, 189, 190
Virginia, 191, 192
Washington, 193, 195
Washington, D.C., 90, 91
West Virginia, 196, 197
Wisconsin, 198, 199
Wyoming, 200, 201
research process, legal. *See* legal research process
research requests, 23
researching case law, 73–74
restatements, 48–50
restriction on state constitutions, 55
reversal of appellate court decisions, 68–69
revision of codes, 58
Rhode Island, online legal resources for, 176–178
right to self-representation, 6
rights established by the Constitution of the United States, 54
rule against perpetuities defined, 45

S
same-sex marriage, constitutionality of, 54
Schanck, Peter C., 28
secondary legal resources
  ALR *(American Law Reports),* 49–50
  law libraries, 47
  legal dictionaries, 44
  legal encyclopedias, 44
  legal periodicals, 46–48
  LexisNexis, 50–52
  on-site self-help legal centers, 47
  online resources, 47, 48
  online self-help legal centers, 47
  overview, 34, 43–44
  professional secondary resources (loose-leafs), 46
  restatements, 48–50
  treatises, 44–45
  Westlaw, 50–52
self-help centers. *See* court brochures/self-help centers
self-help resources. *See* practice materials and self-help resources
Self-Representation Resource Guide, 25
Self-Representation State Links, 25
self-represented litigants
  demographic data on, 9
  differentiating from other types of users, 6
  interests at stake in litigation, 7–8
  judgment, relying on their own, 7
  mentally ill as, 9
  motivations for self-representation, 8–9
  overview, 5–6
  perils of self-representation, 6–8

self-represented litigants (cont.)
  pro se library users
    compared, 5
  right to self-representation, 6
  statistics on, 9–11
senate, 33
session law
  general legal research and
    most states, 85
  overview, 57
  publication of, 59
Shepard's Citations (LexisNexis),
  73
simple, belief that law is, 9
Sixth Amendment, 6
slip opinions, 70
South Carolina, online legal
  resources for, 178–180
South Dakota, online legal
  resources for, 180–182
specialized courts, court rules
  for, 81
staff training, 22–24
Standard Federal Tax Reporter,
  48
stare decisis, 68, 69
state bar association consumer
  brochures
  Alabama, 93
  Colorado, 105
  Delaware, 109
  Florida, 112
  Idaho, 118
  Illinois, 121
  Iowa, 125
  Kansas, 128
  Louisiana, 132
  Maine, 134
  Maryland, 136
  Massachusetts, 139
  Michigan, 141
  Minnesota, 143
  Mississippi, 145
  Missouri, 147
  Montana, 149
  Nebraska, 151
  Nevada, 153
  New Hampshire, 155

  New Jersey, 157
  New Mexico, 159
  New York, 162
  North Carolina, 164
  North Dakota, 166
  Ohio, 169
  Oklahoma, 171
  Oregon, 174
  Pennsylvania, 176
  Rhode Island, 178
  South Carolina, 180
  South Dakota, 182
  Tennessee, 184
  Texas, 186
  Utah, 189
  Vermont, 190
  Virginia, 193
  Washington, 195
  Washington, D.C., 91
  Wisconsin, 199
state constitutions
  government set up by, 55
  overview, 32–33, 54–55
  restriction on, 55
  same-sex marriage,
    constitutionality of, 54
state court structure
  Alabama, 92
  Alaska, 94
  Arizona, 96
  Arkansas, 98
  California, 100
  Colorado, 103
  Connecticut, 106
  Delaware, 108
  Florida, 110
  Georgia, 112
  Hawaii, 114
  Idaho, 116
  Illinois, 119
  Indiana, 121
  Iowa, 124
  Kansas, 126
  Kentucky, 128
  Louisiana, 130–131
  Maine, 132
  Maryland, 134
  Massachusetts, 137

  Michigan, 139
  Minnesota, 142
  Mississippi, 144
  Missouri, 146
  Montana, 148
  Nebraska, 150
  Nevada, 152
  New Hampshire, 154
  New Jersey, 155–156
  New Mexico, 158
  New York, 160
  North Carolina, 163
  North Dakota, 165
  Ohio, 167
  Oklahoma, 170
  Oregon, 172
  Pennsylvania, 174
  Rhode Island, 176
  South Carolina, 178
  South Dakota, 180
  Tennessee, 182
  Texas, 184
  Utah, 187
  Vermont, 189
  Virginia, 191
  Washington, 194
  West Virginia, 196
  Wisconsin, 198
  Wyoming, 200
state courts
  case reporters, 76
  pro se representation,
    statistics on, 10
state legislative process
  Alabama, 92–93
  Alaska, 94
  Arizona, 97
  Arkansas, 99
  California, 101
  Colorado, 104
  Connecticut, 106
  Delaware, 108
  Florida, 110
  Georgia, 113
  Hawaii, 115
  Idaho, 117
  Illinois, 119
  Indiana, 122

Iowa, 124
Kansas, 126
Kentucky, 129
Louisiana, 131
Maine, 133
Maryland, 135
Massachusetts, 137
Michigan, 140
Minnesota, 142
Mississippi, 145
Missouri, 146
Montana, 148
Nebraska, 150
Nevada, 152
New Hampshire, 154
New Jersey, 156
New Mexico, 158
New York, 161
North Carolina, 163
North Dakota, 165
Ohio, 168
Oklahoma, 170
Oregon, 172
Pennsylvania, 175
Rhode Island, 177
South Carolina, 179
South Dakota, 181
Tennessee, 183
Texas, 185
Utah, 188
Vermont, 190
Virginia, 192
Washington, 194
Washington, D.C., 91
West Virginia, 196
Wisconsin, 198
Wyoming, 200
state rulemaking process
    Alabama, 93
    Alaska, 95
    Arizona, 97
    Arkansas, 99
    California, 102
    Colorado, 104
    Connecticut, 107
    Delaware, 108
    Florida, 111
    Georgia, 113

Hawaii, 115
Idaho, 117
Illinois, 120
Indiana, 122
Iowa, 125
Kansas, 127
Kentucky, 129
Louisiana, 131
Maine, 133
Maryland, 135
Massachusetts, 138
Michigan, 140
Minnesota, 143
Mississippi, 145
Missouri, 147
Montana, 148
Nebraska, 150
Nevada, 152
New Hampshire, 154
New Jersey, 156
New Mexico, 158
New York, 161
North Carolina, 164
North Dakota, 166
Ohio, 168
Oklahoma, 171
Oregon, 173
Pennsylvania, 175
Rhode Island, 177
South Carolina, 179
South Dakota, 181
Tennessee, 183
Texas, 186
Utah, 188
Vermont, 190
Virginia, 192
Washington, 195
West Virginia, 197
Wisconsin, 199
Wyoming, 201
states. *See also* directories of
    state courts; directories
    of state departments/
    agencies; state
    constitutions; state court
    structure; state legislative
    process; state rulemaking
    process

courts
    case reporters, 76
    pro se representation,
        statistics on, 10
    general legal research and
        most states, online legal
        resources for, 84–87
    legislature, power of, 56
    regulations, 80
    session law, 59
statistics on self-represented
    litigants, 9–11
statutes
    Alabama, 93
    Alaska, 94–95
    Arizona, 97
    Arkansas, 99
    California, 101
    citation, 36–37
    Colorado, 104
    Connecticut, 106
    currency of, 61
    Delaware, 108
    federal government, 88
    Florida, 110–111
    general legal research and
        most states, 85
    Georgia, 113
    Hawaii, 115
    Idaho, 117
    Illinois, 119
    Indiana, 122
    Iowa, 124
    Kansas, 127
    Kentucky, 129
    Louisiana, 131
    Maine, 133
    Maryland, 135
    Massachusetts, 137–138
    Michigan, 140
    Minnesota, 142
    Mississippi, 145
    Missouri, 146
    Montana, 148
    Nebraska, 150
    Nevada, 152
    New Hampshire, 154
    New Jersey, 156

statutes (cont.)
    New Mexico, 158
    New York, 161
    North Carolina, 163
    North Dakota, 165–166
    Ohio, 168
    Oklahoma, 170
    online access, 61, 62
    Oregon, 172–173
    overview, 61, 62
    Pennsylvania, 175
    Rhode Island, 177
    South Carolina, 179
    South Dakota, 181
    Tennessee, 183
    Texas, 185
    Utah, 188
    Vermont, 190
    Virginia, 192
    Washington, 194
    Washington, D.C., 91
    West Virginia, 197
    Wisconsin, 198–199
    Wyoming, 200–201
Statutes at Large, 57, 59
structure of the American legal
        system
    administrative law, 34
    basic structure, 32–33
    case law, 33–34
    constitutions, 32–33
    executive branch, 32
    judicial branch, 32
    legislation, 33
    legislative branch, 32
    overview, 31–32
subject access to precedent,
        71–72
subject matter
    jurisdiction by, 34, 67–68
    librarian as expert, 14–15
substantive law, 5
supplements for codes, 58, 60
supreme courts
    jurisdiction, 67
    overview, 66

system will protect them, belief
        that, 8–9

T
Tennessee, online legal
        resources for, 182–184
terminology, legal, 45
territorial jurisdiction, 34
Texas, online legal resources for,
        184–187
theory, questions on legal, 42
"thinking like a lawyer," 7
Thomson Reuters, 20, 44, 50,
        52
topics, legal. *See* legal topics
tort law, 38–39, 40, 68
treatises, 44–45
trial courts
    jurisdiction, 67
    overview, 66

U
ultra vires, 77, 78
unauthorized practice of law,
        15–17
"Unauthorized Practice of Law
        and the Legal Reference
        Librarian" *(Law Library
        Journal),* 28
unicameral (single chamber)
        legislature, 33, 55
Uniform Child Custody
        Jurisdiction and
        Enforcement Act
        (UCCJEA), 63
Uniform Law Commission
        (ULC), 62–63
uniform laws, 62–63
*United States Code Annotated
        (USCA),* 59
*United States Code Service
        (USCS),* 59
United States Code (USC), 59
University of South Carolina
        School of Law, 22
unofficial case reporters, 70–71

unofficial codes. *See* annotated
        (unofficial) codes
unpublished case law, 70
unpublished decisions, 70
updating annotated codes, 60
U.S. Constitution. *See*
        Constitution of the United
        States
U.S. Supreme Court
    case reporters for, 76
    jurisdiction, 67
    opinions, 87–88
*USCCAN (United States Code
        Congressional and
        Administrative News),* 59
Utah
    online legal resources for,
        187–189
    pro se representation,
        statistics on, 10

V
Vermont, online legal resources
        for, 189–191
VersusLaw, 52
Virginia, online legal resources
        for, 191–193
voir dire defined, 45

W
Washington, D.C., online legal
        resources for, 90–92
Washington, online legal
        resources for, 193–196
West, John, 70
West Key Number System,
        71–72
West National Reporter System,
        71, 74
West Publishing Company, 44,
        59, 70–71
West Regional Reporter, 71
West Virginia, online legal
        resources for,
        196–198
Westlaw, 50–52, 73

who is asking legal reference
  questions, 3–4. *See also*
  lay users; pro se library
  users; self-represented
  litigants
wills, estate planning, probate,
  40
Wisconsin
  online legal resources for,
    198–200

pro se representation,
  statistics on, 10
Wyoming, online legal resources
  for, 200–201

Z
Zhang, Xiaolu (Renee), 83